D0498521

7

CRACK

A shattering account of the crack cocaine years from award-winning American historian David Farber, *Crack* tells the story of the young men who bet their lives on the rewards of selling "rock" cocaine, the people who gave themselves over to the crack pipe, and the often-merciless authorities who incarcerated legions of African Americans caught in the crack cocaine underworld. Based on interviews, archival research, judicial records, underground videos, and prison memoirs, *Crack* explains why, in a de-industrializing America in which market forces ruled and entrepreneurial risk-taking was celebrated, the crack industry was a lucrative enterprise for the "Horatio Alger boys" of their place and time. These young, predominately African American entrepreneurs were profit-sharing partners in a deviant, criminal form of economic globalization. Hip-hop artists often celebrated their exploits but overwhelmingly, Americans – across racial lines – did not. *Crack* takes a hard look at the dark side of late twentieth-century capitalism.

David Farber is Roy A. Roberts Distinguished Professor of History at the University of Kansas. He is the author of numerous books, including *Everybody Ought to be Rich* (2013), *The Rise and Fall of Modern American Conservatism* (2010), *Taken Hostage* (2004), *Sloan Rules* (2002), *The Age of Great Dreams* (1994), and *Chicago '68* (1988). He lived in New York City with his family at the height of the crack cocaine years and later lived across the street from a small-time crack distributorship in Philadelphia.

David Farber

CRACK

Rock
Cocaine,
Street
Capitalism,
and the
Decade
of Greed

CAMBRIDGE
UNIVERSITY PRESS

CAMBRIDGE
UNIVERSITY PRESS

University Printing House, Cambridge CB2 8BS, United Kingdom

One Liberty Plaza, 20th Floor, New York, NY 10006, USA

477 Williamstown Road, Port Melbourne, VIC 3207, Australia

314–321, 3rd Floor, Plot 3, Splendor Forum, Jasola District Centre, New Delhi – 110025, India

79 Anson Road, #06–04/06, Singapore 079906

Cambridge University Press is part of the University of Cambridge.

It furthers the University's mission by disseminating knowledge in the pursuit of education, learning, and research at the highest international levels of excellence.

www.cambridge.org
Information on this title: www.cambridge.org/9781108425278
DOI: 10.1017/9781108349055

© David Farber 2019

First published 2019

Printed in the United Kingdom by TJ International Ltd. Padstow Cornwall

A catalogue record for this publication is available from the British Library.

ISBN 978-1-108-42527-8 Hardback

"Up against Goliath, to bring butter home
I'm David on pavement, sling another stone"

Ka

Contents

Figures

Crack: A Playlist

Music to Read By
  Eric Clapton, "Cocaine" (1977)
  Lynyrd Skynyrd, "That Smell" (1977)
  Glenn Frey, "Smuggler's Blues" (1985)
  Immortal Technique, "Peruvian Cocaine" (2003)
  Grandmaster Flash and Melle Mel, "White Lines (Don't Do It)" (1983)
  N.W.A., "Dopeman" (1988)
  Public Enemy, "Night of the Living Baseheads" (1988)
  UGK, "Pocketful of Stones" (1992)
  Too Short, "The Ghetto" (1990)
  Shinehead, "Gimme No Crack" (1988)
  Notorious B.I.G., "Ten Crack Commandments" (1997)
  Bone Thugs and Harmony, "Foe the Love ol $" (1994)
  Nas, "Represent" (1994)
  Jay Z, "Rap Game / Crack Game" (1997)
  Ghostface Killah, "Columbus Exchange (Skit) / Crack Spot" (2006)
  Gucci Mane, "My Kitchen" (2007)
  The Clipse, "Virginia" (2002)
  Ka, "Up Against Goliath" (2012)
  Killer Mike, "Reagan" (2012)
  Pusha T, "Nosetalgia" (2013)
  Compiled by Max Bailey/Farber and David Farber

Figure 1 Crack cocaine. (United States Drug Enforcement Administration.)

Choosing Crack: An Introduction

BLACK MAN WHO HAD SERVED ALMOST A DECADE IN THE penitentiary came home to the South Side of Chicago in the mid-1980s. He watched young men – at first just a few – set up shop on the corners in his neighborhood. They were selling crack cocaine.

He was tempted – to buy, to sell – but he steered clear. Still, he understood the draw. From his own younger days and from his years in prison, he knew the men who organized the operations that moved the product from wholesale purchase to hand-to-hand sale. In his estimation, these were righteous men, men whose names he did not discuss, knowing full well what it would mean if he used their names with the wrong people. These were men that, he understood, "had to make their choices. And they made 'em." Improbably, given where they began, these men had made money, lots of money, and not just for themselves. They also made money for "the nation." That's how this ex-offender, who had found a new religion behind prison walls, thought of it.

Wrong or right, what the young ones did made cold, hard sense. The teenage boys who leaned against the walls of Chicago's high-rise public housing projects were caught in a situation he well understood. And in response to those who clucked their tongues at these young men's misdeeds, he just shook his head: "What do you expect, when you've got a whole subsection of unemployed people? When the mills is closing down? When General Motors and Ford is acting crazy? They got kids at home and here comes some white gold. What do you think they are going to do? Man, they are going to take it and they are going to sell it. And try to provide for their families and their kids."

1

This "old head" was not naïve. He knew there was more to it than that. He saw the "flossing," the mad desire to have and display. And he gently mocked: "'I want a gold chain, I want a Cadillac.'" "I know," he said, "about that greediness and showing off." But he insisted that before the avarice took hold and before the dog-eat-dog violence came it had all "started with the underprivileged and the poor people that couldn't pay their bills." This man had used his time in prison to read and educate himself. Crack dealers, as he saw it, were just the refuse of Reaganomics. Crack distribution, he believed, was a criminal industry tailor-made for poor black people by a merciless white America that left those who were locked out of its go-go post-industrial economy to fend for themselves.[1]

In 1984 Ronald Reagan, old pitchman that he was, hit his marks and told the American people that the United States was open for business: "It's Morning Again in America." Capital, lifeblood of the marketplace, was flowing. Financial deregulation and tax cuts had turned on the money spigot. As economists would say, people with the right "animal spirits" emerged; "creative destruction" ruled the day. Moneymen were reinventing whole sectors of the economy – the airlines industry, trucking, financial services – tearing apart old sclerotic corporations to salvage profits wherever they could. On occasion, these debt equity vultures, leverage buyout artists, and bare-knuckled speculators crossed what blurry financial lines remained; a few even went to jail. But most of the new breed of CEOs and financiers stayed within Reaganomics' buccaneer rules, and a broad array of Americans cheered the uptick in GDP, productivity, and overall job creation. In November 1984, nearly 60 percent voted for Ronald Reagan, celebrating the end of Big Government and the glory of free markets.

For people who lived in the "other" America – the poorer, inner-city America never pictured in Reagan's pastel-colored campaign advertisements – capital did not flow. Investment did not come. Instead, President Reagan oversaw governmental disinvestment in their corners of the nation. Jobs continued to move outward from city centers to newly capitalized suburban office parks, exurban freight depots, and anti-labor Sunbelt states. Ever more sophisticated global supply chains and international logistical networks allowed for offshored manufacturing and assembly plants. The working-class jobs that had brought poor people, especially poor African Americans, from the south to the north-east, midwest, and California in the 1940s and 1950s dried up under the fierce rationalization that savvy capitalists brought to the transitioning economy of the 1980s.

Still, opportunities in the old big cities and dying industrial towns did exist. They just were not always legal ones. The "animal spirits" that led people to take risks and bet their lives on untested market opportunities ran up and down the economic ladder. And just like some of the new sectors that were invigorating the national economy, these extra-legal opportunities similarly depended on international economic interde-pendence, global supply chains, and cross-cultural business relations. Best yet, they offered a chance for the undercapitalized little guy who was willing to do what it took to prosper.

It was in 1984, at the dawn of Reagan's "Morning," that crack cocaine first became widely available in the United States. Crack depended on global supply chains: The cocaine from which crack was made came from South America. Colombians dominated the coca production and inter-national distribution end of the business. A host of Latin American and Caribbean people managed the trans-shipment, with much of the cocaine in the mid 1980s coming to the United States through the Bahamas, the Dominican Republic, Mexico, and various corrupt entre-pots in Central America. US-based kinsmen and countrymen of these initial distributors and smugglers then sold off the bulk cocaine. But the men who turned that powder cocaine into crack and sold "rocks" at the local level were, disproportionately, low-income African Americans. Deviant globalization had arrived in America's economic wastelands.

To become a crack dealer at the local level took very little upfront capital. A relatively small supply of powder cocaine could be made into a tidy amount of "rock," which could be quickly turned over, allowing for a rapid cash flow – a fast nickel, in other words, beat a slow dime. Crack cocaine was a business tailor-made for ambitious young people willing to operate outside the law in return for a high rate of return on a limited investment.

Crack was nothing more than cocaine mixed with baking powder, then cooked down to a hard pellet – a "rock" – that could be sold for as little as $2.50. As a commodity, crack was the perfect drug for people who lived dollar to dollar but were desperate to escape, as often as possible, from the drudgery, pain, boredom, or sadness of their lives. Lots of drug users smoked crack; a majority were white. But crack's core customers were disproportionately low-income African Americans who were already disconnected from the labor market.

A potentially explosive demand existed, and servicing this need became a major market opportunity for young black men in inner-city neighborhoods. These were young men with initiative who had not found their main chance in Reagan's America; the official unemployment rate of black teenagers in 1984 hovered at around 40 percent. In the crack business, these young men saw unprecedented and easily accessible opportunity to gain economic security and even riches, the consequences for their communities and even for their own long-term futures be damned.

In the United States, in the late 1980s and the early 1990s, crack cocaine shattered lives – and disproportionately, black lives. Crack poisoned bodies, ravaged minds, ripped apart families, and tore jagged holes in communities. Politicians on both the left and right offered no solace for those whose lives, families, and communities had been torn asunder; instead they poured gasoline on the fires of despair and anomie that had sparked the crack outbreak. They did not treat crack use as a public health crisis – as a later generation of politicians would treat an opiate epidemic of the twenty-first century that primarily affected white communities. Instead, policymakers condemned users. And they slammed the prison door shut on the legions of young black men who had, in search of steady income and with dreams of wealth, distributed crack cocaine. Public figures legitimated this fierce punishment regime with tales of doomed "crack babies" and uncontrollably violent "crackheads"; almost all of these accounts later proved exaggerated or even flat-out wrong. The ways that powerful Americans responded to the rise of crack use in poor communities, especially poor black neighborhoods, turned the ravages of the crack epidemic into a national tragedy of racial injustice and cruelty.

It is critically important to recognize the punishment-begetting hysteria and sometimes-racist charges that characterized the public's responses to crack use in poor black communities. But at the same time, it is also critical to recognize that there *was* an inner-city crack crisis, and that it produced tragic outcomes in poor black neighborhoods during the 1980s and early 1990s. Between 1984 and 1994 the homicide rate of young black teenagers doubled. The number of black children in foster care also doubled. Other markers of despair and destruction directly linked to crack use, such as fetal death rates, or to crack sales, such as weapons arrests, soared. White neighborhoods felt none of these changes.

The explosion of crack users and the proliferation of distributors gave the lie to so much that so many Americans wanted to believe. Two decades after the Civil Rights Act of 1964, white Americans wanted to believe that racial injustice was on the wane and that equal opportunity was real and that America was no longer divided into two Americas, one white and one black. In the midst of the Reagan "recovery" and then the economic boom of the Clinton years, many Americans wanted to believe that the American dream was alive and well, accessible to anyone who wanted it.

This historical context helps to explain why so many contemporary Americans, black and white, responded so angrily and punitively to those caught up in crack use and distribution. Americans then, along with scholars today, ask: Why were so many habitual crack users black in a period of economic prosperity and racial progress? Why did so many street corners in inner-city black neighborhoods become war zones with rival crews killing one another in the fight for the right to sell cheap rocks to their desperate neighbors? Why, then, did so many people in America's inner cities turn to the crack pipe, exchanging a short rush of euphoria for almost certain personal devastation? What had brought so many so low, and what was it about crack, in particular, that met the specific need of so many people at that time and in that place? What was it about Reagan's "morning in America" that fueled the fury of crack?

To an extent, *Crack* is a history of what some social scientists and journalists at the time called the "underclass," inner-city residents who did not and could not escape the ravages of racism that structured their lives and who did not have the means to – or chose not to – adapt to a mainstream world in which their skills, their codes of conduct, and their ambitions were either unrewarded or disdained. Members of the underclass, according to the sociologist William Julius Wilson, were not simply individuals who had lost their way. During the 1970s and early 1980s, he observes, the number of black households with incomes over $25,000 increased dramatically, but so did the number of black households with incomes under $5,000. A rapid decline of manufacturing jobs during those years, work that had provided decent incomes for relatively unschooled men and women, says Wilson, played a major role in the large and growing number of black Americans who lost their foothold in America's economy, pushing them into what he dubbed "the under-class." While the term is deeply problematic – and will be discussed and critiqued – it helps to explain the large market of poor people, dispro-portionately African American, who would find crack a balm for their troubled, insecure, and often desperate lives.[2]

While Wilson stresses the structural forces that knocked people out of the labor force and into troubled lives, Philippe Bourgois's masterful ethnography of crack users and crack sellers adds another dimension to this story.[3] Uneducated men of color in particular, Bourgois argues, struggled to adapt to the service-driven, social and cultural capital-intensive demands of the "new" economy that was producing so many of the jobs in financial and legal services, healthcare, and sales in the 1980s and 1990s. Left out of, or refusing to abide by, the codes of middle-class demeanor and civility these sorts of jobs demanded, they chose instead to embrace the rough life of the streets. Street culture reveled in intoxication, violent sexual behavior, and general lawless-ness; it offered a way of life that too often put no stock in the promise of a meaningful future. Buying, using, and selling drugs was integral to this present-tense way of life. Crack, with its fifteen minutes of wildly intense, euphoric and sexually exciting high, fit these anomic souls' basest needs and grandest expectations.

The crack crisis is the dark side of the Reagan–Bush–Clinton years. An accounting of it necessarily foregrounds the lives of desperate people, both the most habituated users who believed they had to smoke crack to find pleasure and release from their dire circumstances and the har-dened distributors who saw in the destruction of their neighbors and their community the quickest route to their own desires.

But the story of crack is also a history of neo-liberalism and its cousin, economic globalization, from the ground up. In a de-industrializing

America in which market forces ruled, service industries abounded, and entrepreneurial risk-taking was celebrated, the crack industry was a lucrative enterprise for the self-made men – the "Horatio Alger boys" of their place and time – who were willing to do whatever it took to improve their lot in life. These crack distributors took a South American commodity, often trans-shipped through Mexico, Central America or the Caribbean, added value to it through a low-tech manufacturing process, and then deployed a networked, community-based sales force to create a remarkably innovative and lucrative enterprise. These young, predominately male African American entrepreneurs were profit-sharing partners in a deviant, criminal form of economic globalization. From their perspective, distributing crack was a smart play in a bad hand.

While many condemned these "ghetto" globalizers, others offered praise. Hip-hop artists of the era, some of whom were direct participants in the crack business, often – though not always – celebrated the gangster entrepreneurs and street merchants of the crack trade. In hip-hop circles, these men often served as underground heroes in a racist society that left too many black men with too little dignity and too few opportunities for exuberant economic success. That some of the men who made money in the crack trade went on to invest – even if only to launder their ill-gotten gains – in a variety of black-owned businesses, including night-clubs, recording studios, music labels, hair and nail salons, clothing boutiques, video stores, gaming galleries, and other black owned, black employing, black-neighborhood enterprises, gilded the hip-hop lily. This entrepreneurial, capital-accumulating, creativity-celebrating, black bolstering hip-hop culture is part of the story of crack, too.

Along with sellers, users, and celebrators, this history of crack focuses, too, on the people who fought to stop the sale and use of crack cocaine. Most politicians and public officials who observed the ravages of crack use and the violence bred by crack distribution reacted sharply to the devastation. Their first response was to demand that people caught up in the embrace of crack be punished, removed from their communities, and swept into America's burgeoning carceral state.

Such impulses led to the Anti-Drug Abuse Act of 1986, which mandated that anyone found guilty of distributing five grams of crack receive a five-year prison sentence – even as it took five *hundred* grams of powdered cocaine to earn those five years. The fact that most small-time crack cocaine dealers were African Americans and most large-scale dealers of powdered cocaine were white or Hispanic was baked into this particularly draconian and objectively racist law. Given how American politicians and the law-enforcement community have responded to the purveyors and distributors of opioids – who are overwhelmingly white – that racism appears even more obvious. Given, as well, the extraordinary license government officials have granted big pharmaceutical companies, "pain" doctors, medical clinic operators, and pharmacy owners to distribute their addictive and deadly wares to the public, it is obvious that the wealthy and the credentialed have escaped accountability in a way that poor, inner-city drug operators never have – and this despite the brutal fact that opioids have killed and damaged far more people than crack cocaine ever did. Racism and classism are integral to the story of crack cocaine.

But racism does not explain the motives of all those who fought the ravages of crack. Many African American leaders believed that only fierce measures could stop the street-corner violence and familial destruction crack had brought to their communities. Many of these leaders soon came to believe that the supposed cure – mass incarceration – was worse than the underlying problem. By the early 1990s some of these community leaders sought, and found, alternative solutions that did not simply drive more black men and women into the embrace of the carceral state, even as black clergy, local politicians, and community activists continued to recoil in anger and fear from the damage done to their neighbors, families, and friends by the epidemic of crack.

Crack's hold on poor communities, especially in black inner-city neighborhoods, began to wane in the mid 1990s. Community leaders' implementation of drug-diversion programs, support groups, and public health-oriented approaches to the crack epidemic played a role. So, too, did the imprisonment of so many people caught up in the selling and buying of crack. Nonetheless, many social scientists argue that the primary reason crack use declined was neither incarceration nor social-service programming of one kind or another. Crack use declined because people, most especially young people, looked at what ten years of intense crack abuse had done to their communities – to their loved ones – and chose not to use. They weren't "scared straight." They took up other illegal drugs, like "lean" or "purple drank," a codeine and promethazine prescription cough syrup mixed with soda. But crack users, they observed, paid too high a price for their rush. Crack did not, by any means, disappear. It is still easy to buy. Many still fall prey to abuse. But the intense use, arguably epidemic in poor African American communities, had burned itself out.

The history of the crack crisis is a dark tale. We prefer stories of national uplift and progress, of heroes who challenged long odds to make our country a better place. The story of crack in America offers no such uplift. It provides no such heroes – though there were men and women who struggled to bring hope and reform. The history of the crack era turns the American dream upside down.

Sometimes, we need to stare at the drear reaches of our national soul to understand who we are and who we wish to be. This brief, grim history of crack use, crack distribution, crack culture, and crack public policy aims to keep us from forgetting the many Americans left behind in our economically merciless times. It is one more chapter in the story of the racial injustice that has long structured life in the United States.

A history of crack also illustrates the central economic, political, social, and cultural role illegal drugs have long played in American life – illegal drug regimes directly affect the life course of the American people in ways that rarely enter conventional histories. The *Intoxicated State* has been and probably always will be with us. How we treat those who fall prey to drug addiction and how we reconcile ourselves to the commonplace desire to get high is one measure of who we are as a people. During the crack years, we came up short and hundreds of thousands of people suffered for our collective inability to treat each other with decency and mercy.

CHAPTER 1

First Comes Cocaine, Then Comes Crack:
Origin Stories

W ITHOUT A STEADY SUPPLY OF COCAINE THERE IS NO crack. Without the global war on cocaine, the crack trade would be neither so profitable nor so punishing. Thus to understand crack, it helps to first understand cocaine, how that drug went from widely available pharmaceutical marvel to illicit and glamorous narcotic. First comes cocaine, then comes crack.[1]

Not that long ago, cocaine was just another thing a person could buy. It was legal in the United States and pretty much everywhere else. It was cheap. It was made by a small group of major pharmaceutical houses. And while cocaine was sold in powder form it also was a critical ingredient in medicinal syrups, patent medicine elixirs, and, to use an anachronistic term, energy drinks. Procurement of powder cocaine or a cocaine-infused consumer product took no more than a walk to a corner store.

Cocaine was made illegal in increments. In the United States, that process began at the local and state level in the late nineteenth century.[2] Cocaine drew federal attention in 1906, when legislators who were concerned about the promiscuous and habit-forming use of cocaine, opium, and morphine in a bevy of popular elixirs, patent medicines, and even children's cough suppressants, passed the Pure Food and Drug Act. This act mandated that such substances and others, including alcohol, be clearly labeled as ingredients if they were included in products. Such packaging did not always lead directly to reduced consumption. Only in 1914, by which time all forty-eight states had legislated some form of regulatory or punitive cocaine regime, did the federal government directly take on the open sale of cocaine. At this point the Treasury Department, by virtue of the Harrison Narcotic Tax Act, began to enforce

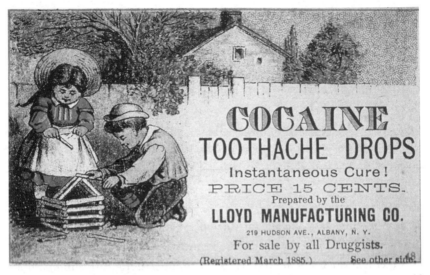

Figure 2 Cocaine toothache drops: In the late nineteenth century, consumers could purchase cocaine remedies for all sorts of needs. This charming print ad appeared in the 1890s. (NLM/Science Source via Getty Images.)

Figure 3 Bricks of cocaine: In the 1980s, Mexican cartels began smuggling massive loads of cocaine into the United States. Some of the cartels branded their kilos with attention-grabbing logos. (United States Drug Enforcement Administration.)

regulations that made it increasingly difficult to purchase cocaine legally. And in 1922, the Narcotic Drug Import and Export Act put the weight of the federal government behind the drive to criminalize most everyone connected to the sale, distribution, and use of cocaine.

This full-court press by every level of government in the United States did not end the sale and use of cocaine; instead, it inspired an illegal, international cocaine supply line. By the early 1980s, that international supply line would enable the production and distribution of crack cocaine in the United States.

* * *

Before cocaine became illegal throughout the United States, a lot of people had fallen in love with it. Scientists marveled at its properties and medical doctors cheered its use as an anesthetic. Consumers, both famous and infamous, relished its effects. Sigmund Freud, whose international reputation as the father of psychoanalysis was still on the horizon, championed its stimulative and curative power in his 1884 article "Über Coca" and, for a time, doled out the powder to his patients and to himself with a liberal hand. Writing around the same time, Arthur Conan Doyle had his indomitable consulting detective, Sherlock Holmes, inject a "seven percent solution" of cocaine to fight ennui and boredom between cases. Doyle, a frequent user, knew of what he wrote. In 1885, former President Ulysses S. Grant, dying painfully from throat cancer and desperate to finish writing his memoirs, which would, when published, assure his family's financial security, relied on a steady flow of a cocaine elixir (and later a more potent doctor-prescribed cocaine solution) to get through his work day – a fact the elixir's manufacturer advertised to good effect.[3] By the end of the nineteenth century, consumers in the United States, Germany, France, Great Britain, and a great many other nations throughout the globe embraced cocaine, across class and racial lines, as a pick-me-up, a health tonic, a recreational uplift, and a general cure-all. Taming that enthusiasm took a good deal of effort on the part of the reformers who feared that cocaine was too much of a good thing.

For centuries, Europeans had been aware of the coca leaf chewing habits of the indigenous peoples of the South American Andean realm.

These outsiders were quite impressed by the stamina and general good health these coca chewers enjoyed. The Bishop of Cuzco in Peru, in a cheery sixteenth-century note to the King of Spain, reported, "There is a leaf of a small tree ... the Indians always have in their mouths when walking, and they say it sustains and refreshes them ... in this country it is worth like gold."[4] By the mid nineteenth century, scientists curious about the chemical properties of the leaves of the coca bush had begun to experiment, seeking the properties that produced its effects. In 1860, German chemists had isolated the alkaloid that gave coca its kick and named it cocaine. (To the question of nomenclature: "Ine" is the scientific indicator of an alkaloid. Alkaloids, of which scientists have isolated some 3,000, are "a class of nitrogenous organic compounds of plant origin that have pronounced physiological actions on humans." They include morphine, nicotine, caffeine, and mescaline, as well as other substances with a host of uses, from the medicinal to the recreational.)[5]

As scientists investigated the properties and potential uses of cocaine, more entrepreneurial sorts rushed in. A Frenchman of Corsican roots, Angelo Mariani, had followed the very early research on coca's stimulatory effects. In 1863 he concocted a tonic, Vin Mariani, that combined red wine and coca leaves, which he marketed to consumers looking for a pick-me-up. By mixing the coca directly into the wine, Mariani had actually come up with a simple, if crude, way of extracting the alkaloid in the leaves. The ethanol in the wine acted as a solvent on the coca leaves, which resulted in ... cocaine wine.

People in Europe and the United States thrilled to Mariani's heavily advertised drink. His cocaine wine was among the first celebrity-advertised consumer products; Pope Leo XIII was one of the product's many famous endorsers. Covering all bases, Mariani also reached out to the medical community. By 1902 he had received letters of praise for his tonic from some 8,000 doctors. Once the drink became popular in the United States – the inventor Thomas Edison raved about it and formally endorsed its use – it inspired many imitators. Among them was the "French Coca Wine" formulated in 1884 by Atlanta pharmacist John Pemberton. In 1885, when Atlanta became one of the first cities in the United States to ban the purchase of alcoholic beverages, Pemberton removed the alcohol from his version of coca-leaf infused wine. He added more sugar, along with caffeine from the cola nut, then constituted his beverage with a bit of pure cocaine – thus was born Coca-Cola.

By the 1890s, coca and its alkaloid, cocaine, had become international products. The Peruvian government supported the development of the coca leaf and national production of raw cocaine, both of which made their way to the United States and to Europe, where they were used in a slew of consumer-oriented products.[6] Among those products were an abundance of patent medicines, many of which, reasonably enough, targeted inflammation of the nasal mucus membranes; e.g., symptoms of the common cold, as well as seasonal allergies. In the early twentieth-century United States, one of the most popular was the cleverly titled "Ryno's Hay Fever-n-Catarrh Remedy." It was 99.5 percent pure cocaine and definitely left users feeling better.[7] And no history of cocaine's early days is complete without reference to an 1885 product sold across the counter in pharmacies throughout the United States. "Cocaine Toothache Drops" was charmingly advertised with a color illustration of a young boy and girl playing enthusiastically, apparently after a successful dosing of the drops.

The links between Andean producers of the raw material and recreational consumers elsewhere had been forged. Increasingly key to that connection were the major pharmaceutical companies that manufactured and marketed highly refined cocaine. In the United States, those included Merck and Parke-Davis (now a subsidiary of Big Pharma standard-bearer Pfizer). Peruvian entrepreneurs, including those of Croatian, Chinese, and German background, played a major role in the supply chain. With government support, and sometimes in concert with European partners, such Peruvian entrepreneurs sold not only coca leaf but also refined the leaves into a crude cocaine that would be further refined by their European or North American associates.

By 1900, Peru was exporting around two million pounds of coca – most of it to the United States – and more than 22,000 pounds of crude cocaine, mostly to Germany.[8] Americans preferred importing coca leaves and not crude cocaine for a good reason: coca leaves, as a raw product, could be imported to the United States duty-free and then processed; crude cocaine, like most manufactured goods in protectionist-dominated America, faced heavy import tariffs.[9] US demands helped shape

14

the industry. Even as, at the turn of the century, cocaine was a big, international business with markets all over the world, the United States – even then – was the biggest of those markets. By 1900, cocaine historian Paul Gootenberg states, "Americans were the world's largest, most avid consumers and boosters" of coca and cocaine.[10]

* * *

Coca and cocaine, like opium and the newly crafted super opiate, heroin, were still almost completely unregulated and licit in the late nineteenth century. In the United States, all that began to change rapidly in the first years of the twentieth century. Americans, as would be true over the course of the twentieth century, took global leadership in efforts to end the legal, widespread use of "narcotics," including cocaine. Within the United States, this emerging anti-cocaine coalition was an unlikely-appearing alliance of concerned medical and health professionals, white supremacists, and prohibitionists. Incredibly, from the perspective of the multitudes who, in the "Gay '90s," found their kick in the pleasures of a snort or dram of cocaine, by 1922 coke had become a heavily regulated, often illegal substance. Except under increasingly circum-scribed conditions, sale of coke had become a criminal offense enforced by a bevy of local, state, and federal authorities. Under this punitive regime, the production, distribution, and sale of cocaine became, step by step, a criminal enterprise that depended on an underground supply line.

Doctors, both in Europe and the United States, were among the first to reconsider the popular and professional enthusiasm for cocaine. Some people, these medical professionals observed, had become for all practical purposes addicted to the narcotic. (Unlike opiates, which pro-duces agonizing physical symptoms in withdrawal, cocaine withdrawal mostly is characterized by a hard-to-resist, fierce craving for the drug.) By the late 1880s, these "cocaine fiends" had begun to appear, in relatively small numbers, across the United States.

Charles A. Bunting, the head administrator of the New York City Christian Home for Intemperate Men, saw such "fiends" at their lowest ebb. He was shocked by the effects of cocaine use on the men who came to him for help, many of whom had started using cocaine under a doctor's supervision. Mr. Bunting was accustomed to caring for long-term alcoholics and they were, by and large, a sorry lot. But they did not compare, in his mind, to those who had fallen prey to what he called "THE COCAINE HABIT." In 1888, he wrote:

> This cocaine habit seems to be the very acme of pernicious appetite, and reduces its slave to the lowest depths … a very caricature of manhood, with a look like a hunted beast, the shrunken frame trembling, the will-power utterly wrecked, every lingering sense of personal honor and cleanliness destroyed, and but one madding desire – to use the awful drug at all cost, at any peril.[11]

Cocaine, some had begun to realize, was not necessarily a risk-free solution to life's travails or a harmless form of stimulatory recreation.

In the early years of the twentieth century, scientists, as well as other health professionals, increasingly spoke out against intemperate – and often inadvertent – use of cocaine. At a 1910 meeting of the American Association for the Advancement of Science, the state chemist of Oklahoma reported that eighty-four of the eighty-seven "soft drinks" he had tested contained cocaine. He insisted, "The cocaine is used in order to make people form a habit for the particular drink." The *Cincinnati Enquirer* headlined its story on the report: "Deadly Dope."[12] That same day, a small-town newspaper in Pennsylvania warned its readers about popular cold medicines; "Beware of Cocaine in Catarrh Remedies" cautioned that "Thousands of Drug Fiends have been started on their downward course through Catarrh snuffs containing this habit forming drug."[13] Such claims were gross exaggerations of the danger of cocaine; few people who snagged an occasional cocaine beverage or took a cold remedy became dissolute fiends. But *some* did, and that risk scared people.

Those concerned about cocaine's habit-forming qualities were not alone in reconsidering the open and easy availability of the coca alkaloid. Particularly in the American south, white supremacists took to arguing that cocaine made African Americans particularly crazy, dangerous, and lustful. "[M]any of the horrible crimes committed in the Southern States by the colored people can be traced directly to the cocaine habit," reported a Georgia-based correspondent for the *New York Tribune.*

White racists in the North agreed: "Most attacks upon the white women of the South are the direct result of a coke-crazed brain," the director of the Pharmacy Board of Pennsylvania, Dr. Christopher Koch, testified before Congress in 1914 during hearings to determine the legal fate of cocaine. That Dr. Koch offered no proof of his claim seemed to matter little to members of Congress or to the newspapers that reported on his testimony.[14]

In the first years of the twentieth century, African Americans did, evidence suggests, use cocaine disproportionately as compared to whites. Some limited evidence demonstrates that black southerners, at least, were twice as likely as white southerners to use cocaine.[15] Writing about such evidence, the eminent drug historian David Courtwright reminds us that scholars have to account for the toxins of racism that poison the Jim Crow-era evidentiary record. Still, he finds it likely that African Americans in the Deep South used cocaine more than their white counterparts for reasons that were both practical and recreational.[16]

African Americans probably first used cocaine for the same reason that Sigmund Freud took it up and for the same reason the coca-chewers of the Andean realm found coca leaves useful: it gave them a boost of energy. Late nineteenth-century observers noted that black stevedores and roustabouts in New Orleans snorted cocaine to push through their grueling labors unloading steamboats; these men sometimes worked seventy straight hours in fulfilling their duties. Cocaine was a lifesaver. Other black manual laborers, those stuck with the most physically demanding, grueling work, soon began using coke on the job.[17] And while African Americans may first have used cocaine to increase stamina for backbreaking work, soon enough some began to indulge for another reason: cocaine made a person feel good.

A second reason African Americans in the early twentieth century were more likely to use cocaine than were whites is because drug usage, like most of life in the United States at that time, was racially inflected. White Americans used proportionately less cocaine than did black Americans, but they used quite a lot of opiates. That is in large part because whites, overall, had greater access to medical professionals than did African Americans. And it was doctors, in the late nineteenth century and early twentieth century, who directed – pushed? – people, especially women of the middle and upper classes, to use opiates to mitigate ailments of almost every mental and physical sort. Opiates, doctors assured their patients, were a scientifically authorized, medically indicated sort of drug, appropriate for respectable white people.

Ironically, then, white racism and the black poverty it produced made it *less* likely that African Americans would be in a position to consult with those medical professionals who peddled opiates. African Americans, as a result, were less likely to be addicted to heroin or other opiates than were whites. That doesn't mean that they eschewed all forms of easily available alkaloids (heroin is derived from the opiate alkaloid morphine) and the varyingly desirable effects they produced. But rather than fall prey to the "white"-linked opiates, more chose to get their kick from cocaine.

White authorities in the south noted, with great unease, black men's enthusiasm for cocaine. Cocaine, they argued, made black men aggressive. Cocaine, they reported, made black men crazy. Cocaine, they insisted, unleashed blacks' innate criminality and depraved hypersexuality.

Historians have rightly pointed out the long history of overt racism that motivated such claims. The claims whites made are fully embedded in ideas of racial hierarchy; these white critics were distraught, above all, about black men's use of cocaine because, they believed, it led black men to challenge white authority. Nonetheless, in pointing out these racist assumptions, historians have downplayed the effects of the drug itself.

Cocaine stimulates the release of dopamine; it increases noradrenaline and serotonin. These changes in brain chemistry make a person feel good, more confident, more capable, and more energetic. They can also impair judgment and increase the likelihood of impulsive, risky behavior. Cocaine induces most people to move more extravagantly across the social stage. Such self-confident – often overly self-confident – behavior can cause individuals to reject or ignore the social conventions that govern everyday life. For African Americans in the Jim Crow south of the early twentieth century, men and women who were forced to appear subservient before whites under threat of violent reprisals, cocaine was a dangerous drug. Cocaine made it more difficult to wear the public mask of subservience. Like other alkaloids, it made people less amenable to the social conventions and social hierarchies that regulate everyday life.

Black people on cocaine – at least some of them – did challenge the racial hierarchy. Whites who pointed out that fact were racist, but they were not wrong.

White authorities, in decrying African Americans' use of cocaine, argued that the drug did more than increase blacks' propensity to act "uppity." Cocaine, they insisted, unleashed black criminality. Here, in all likelihood, the authorities had the matter mostly backwards. By the early twentieth century, it was not so much that cocaine made people, African American or otherwise, criminals. It was more that criminals of many races and ethnicities in the United States, increasingly, were using cocaine.

Even as doctors and other health professionals were warning "respectable" people away from indiscriminate use of cocaine, the alkaloid was increasingly used by a melange of people considered by the mainstream to be of the lower orders. The demi-monde and the criminal underworld were taking up cocaine with a vengeance. By 1900, cocaine was ubiquitous in New Orleans's Storyville, America's most notorious red-light district. At New Orleans dance halls – the Hot Cat, the Honky Tonk, and the Pig Ankle – black patrons, as well as the occasional white visitor, slammed back potent cocaine wine that sold for ten cents a glass (whiskey was cheaper, at five cents a shot). New Orleans prostitutes, black, white, and creole, estimated to number well over 2,000, were voracious users. According to the New Orleans *Daily States*, cocaine had become a necessary anodyne, "a merciful friend," for the city's poor and disreputable men and women, for it "spread[s] a golden cloud over a wretched past and hopeless future and evoke[s] visions of wealth, contentment and happiness."[18] Cocaine then, as would be true later of crack, appealed to those who needed its particular kick to veil their difficult circumstances and to embolden their claims on a society that disdained them.

Police and other authorities claimed that white prostitutes in cities around the country, as well as other white "lowlifes" and criminals, picked up the cocaine habit from their black counterparts. Evidence exists to support this claim, but cocaine was also becoming popular in bohemian and underworld circles that had little or no contact with African Americans. Hollywood's brand new silent film industry abounded with cocaine. Most notoriously, the Keystone studio, home of such risqué stars as Mabel Normand and Fatty Arbuckle (both cocaine users), had its own in-resident dealer, "the Count."[19] In San Francisco's underworld, white criminals gathered in dope houses to inject cocaine. As reported by Fred Williams in *The Hop-Heads*: "The men in the party were young and well, if not expensively, dressed. I knew them to be yeggs [burglars and safe-crackers] ... The women, on the other hand, were sisters in crime – 'boosters' [shoplifters] and 'dips' [pickpockets] as well as prostitutes in times of emergency."[20] For men and women, using cocaine – and opiates – was part of the underworld life in San Francisco.

Likewise, in New York City, a number of the Jewish gangsters who, according to NYC police commissioner Theodore A. Bingham, made up 50 percent of the city's underworld, used cocaine.[21] Notoriously, Jewish hit men "Lefty" Louie Rosenberg and Harry "Gyp the Blood" Horowitz were "coked to the gills" at 4 a.m. July 12, 1912 when they gunned down fellow Jew, gambler-turned-stool-pigeon Harry Rosenthal.[22] The criminologist Alan A. Block states that Jewish gangsters used cocaine, sold cocaine, and made cocaine an integral part of New York City nightlife. He goes so far as to say that the Jewish-run cocaine racket brought together New York's multi-ethnic underworld.[23] Cocaine had become a drug of choice for those who had slipped the bounds of propriety.

Main Street Americans observed cocaine's fall from grace with fear and disgust. What had once been seen as a healthy pick-me-up and general curative was now broadly perceived as a dangerous, addictive drug evermore associated with the undesirable lower orders of American society. In little more than twenty years, respectable Americans had turned against cocaine. Their increasing disdain for cocaine was not occurring in a cultural vacuum. The anti-cocaine groundswell was a piece of a much bigger prohibitionist movement.

American prohibitionists had been battling their pleasure-seeking neighbors for a long time. Pietistic Christians – mostly Baptists, Methodists, and Presbyterians who believe in individual holiness, moral purity, and aggressively ridding the world of sin – led the fight. Their battle against intoxication took root in 1825 with the organization of the American Temperance Society. By the mid 1830s the Society had well over a million members. Their "Dry Crusade" ebbed and flowed over the next several decades, gaining political traction in the post-Civil War era with the founding of the Woman's Christian Temperance Union in 1873. In 1881, Kansas became the first state to ban the sale of alcoholic beverages. This religiously inspired anti-alcohol crusade gained power in the late nineteenth century when it joined forces with more secular-oriented, so-called progressive reformers, who feared the unruly and unassimilated behaviors of the millions of Catholic and Jewish immigrants who were pouring into American cities. By the early twentieth century, this broad-based coalition had the political might to work its will on the nation, expanding its temperance crusade to include not just alcohol but most every other form of intoxication.

By 1922, cocaine, opiates, marijuana, and alcoholic beverages were all broadly and legally forbidden at both the state and federal level in the United States. The Prohibitionists, working in tandem with medical and scientific authorities, white supremacists, and progressive social-control advocates had won their war against the most visible and potent forms of altered consciousness.

To ban alcohol nationwide, the Prohibitionists successfully engineered passage of the Eighteenth Amendment to the Constitution in 1919. Congress passed the Volstead Act later that same year, and so provided federal funds to enforce the new law. Beginning in January 1920, the manufacture, sale, and distribution of alcoholic beverages was outlawed.[24] Cocaine, marijuana, and opiates were phased out through normal statutory means at the local, state, and national level. In 1922, the Narcotic Drugs Import and Export Act was the final legal nail in the coffin for opiates, cocaine, and even coca leaves. The act made it "unlawful to import any narcotic drug into the United States or any territory under its control or jurisdiction." There was a loophole for "medical and legitimate uses" – think Coca-Cola, which still used coca leaves – but the law was strict and it was punitive:

> That if any person fraudulently or knowingly imports or brings any narcotic drug into the United States ... or receives, conceals, buys, sells, or in any manner facilitates the transportation, concealment, or sale of any such narcotic drug ... [he] shall upon conviction be fined not more than $5000 and imprisoned for not more than ten years.[25]

The Harrison Act of 1914 had already charged the Treasury Department with regulating the legal importation and sale of narcotic drugs. The 1922 Act strengthened the hand of the Treasury Department by giving its agents full authority, under a newly created Federal Narcotics Control Board, to administer all aspects of the law. In practice, the Treasury Department would focus on stopping narcotics at the nation's borders. State and local authorities, working under their own laws, which also called for fines and imprisonment, would police the sale and use of cocaine within the United States. By 1922, cocaine was illegal everywhere in the United States and people who imported it or sold it or used it could be arrested and jailed by local police, state authorities, or federal officials, depending on the exact nature of their relationship to the cocaine to which law enforcement connected them.

The criminalization of cocaine made the once thriving and legal cocaine distribution and sales business a very different kind of operation. Between 1900 and 1920 or so, thousands of low-level purveyors kept cocaine supply lines open for those who wanted the drug. Most of the cocaine that found its way to criminals, thrill-seekers, actors and other members of the demi-monde came by way of legal production that was subverted and diverted for illegal use. During this period thousands and thousands of newspaper stories appeared in local papers reporting on the bust of local cocaine sales rings.

During the first twenty years of the new, punitive cocaine regime, most cocaine that found its way into users' hands (and then noses or veins) was diverted from supplies still legally possessed by pharmacies and doctors, creating what Joseph Spillane, historian of the early cocaine market in the United States, calls the "shadow market."[26] During these years, cocaine was still legally prescribed by doctors and, thus, was widely stocked by pharmacists. But some pharmacists, overwhelmingly located in the most disreputable parts of town, sold cocaine with little eye toward confirming the legitimacy of their patients' health needs or of a doctor's note. This business model would be replicated in the opioid trade roughly a hundred years later. In New York City, in 1909, police investigators reported that they had found sixty-three drugstores that sold suspiciously large quantities of cocaine despite supposedly strict rules limiting its usage. A muckraking reporter observed that "empty boxes" of cocaine remedies bought from local pharmacies could be seen "littering the gutters of Broadway any Saturday night."[27]

These disreputable, avaricious drugstore owners, found in small towns as well as big cities in the first decades of the twentieth century, often dodged narcotic laws and the men enforcing them. But that wayward path was becoming more difficult in the 1910s. Progressive reformers, muckraking journalists, and honest law-enforcement authorities were cracking down on these gray market entrepreneurs, pushing cocaine sales and the commodity chain that supplied such sales further underground.

Increasingly, after the 1914 Harrison Act and the crackdown on illegal drugstore sales by local officials, cocaine users had to depend evermore on smuggled cocaine supplied to them by underworld sources. Cocaine was smuggled into the United States at numerous ports, including in New York City and New Orleans, but also up and down the Pacific coast. In the 1910s and early 1920s, these smugglers appear to have been overwhelmingly small-time operators, mostly ship's crew, who bought a pound or two of cocaine legally in Europe or Latin America with hopes of making some side money off-loading it in the United States. For example, in November 1920, a sailor brought in about $10,000 worth of cocaine, as well as other narcotics, to San Francisco where he attempted to sell his small load to a local pool hall operator. In this case the pool hall operator, with the assistance of two corrupt San Francisco police detectives, ripped off the smuggler, who was so angry that he brazenly reported the affair to the authorities.[28]

A few days after that incident, one Adolph Candis, captain of the steamer-ship the *Cuzco* (smuggling cocaine on a ship named after a major Peruvian city is probably a bad idea), was arrested in New York City after attempting to bring in seventy-three bottles of cocaine, valued at $7,500.[29] In Portland, authorities claimed that it was "Orientals" who were "smuggling cocaine and morphine into this country on almost every boat that lands at any port on the Pacific coast." The task force, however, was only able to arrest four white "boys," who worked for a messenger service that was distributing drugs throughout the city. They were caught red-handed supplying "cocaine parties, where cocaine is 'served' instead of liquor ... [The] boys are said to have purchased their wholesale supply in a North End Chinese den." No mention is made of where the "Orientals" got their supply of cocaine.[30]

That same year, a tragic smuggling tale was reported from New York. There, Manuel Garcia Cayon, a fireman on the steamer the *Atlantic Son*, lost his nerve just before docking after a trip from Rotterdam. He killed himself after telling his crewmates that he was afraid of being caught on his second smuggling voyage. Under his bunk 240 bottles of cocaine were found, most likely purchased legally in the Netherlands or in Germany.[31]

It is hard to know how many relatively amateur smugglers were bringing cocaine into the United States during the late 1910s and early 1920s. What is known is that cocaine sales and arrests were, during this time, very much in the news. In 1920 alone at least 4,648 newspaper stories about cocaine appeared throughout the nation, almost all of them involving arrests or reports on illegal sales.[32] Given the low priority local law officials and the Treasury Department gave cocaine arrests during this first year of alcohol prohibition, such numbers indicate that the cocaine business remained extensive, if small-scale. The American market for cocaine had, of course, fallen precipitously since its legal heyday in the 1890s and the first years of the twentieth century, in the days when powder cocaine was sold as a pick-me-up and cocaine-laced patent medicines and beverages were available in pharmacies and groceries. By 1920, so-called respectable people were rarely, if ever, buying cocaine. But the demand for coke by less reputable folk remained, and deviant entrepreneurs who participated in a rinky-dink, global supply chain were happy to meet it.

Cocaine demand, soon enough, caught the attention of the kind of people who specialized in organizing businesses that existed outside the law. The first illegal organized effort to meet the demand for cocaine emerged in the New York-based Jewish underworld.[33] Jewish gangsters, as was noted earlier, were drawn to cocaine. In part, cocaine was a natural ally for men who made their living illegally at night, gambling, running rackets, hanging out at clubs, managing speakeasies, and prowling city streets. Perhaps, too, Jewish gangsters enjoyed the bravado and fearlessness cocaine gave them as they hustled their way through a straight world that was largely controlled by anti-Semites.

Jewish gangsters, however, were particularly well positioned for the cocaine trade. They tended to have international connections based on the ethnic and religious ties that made for trustworthy business relationships; these ties extended especially but not only to Europe, where cocaine was still mostly legal and relatively easy to buy. Jewish control of underworld casinos, shadowy nightclubs, and an array of other illegal operations, meant that they already had a network perfect for selling illegal commodities of various sorts. For them, smuggling and selling illegal cocaine was just another way to make money. Most of the heavy Jewish gangsters involved in the cocaine business in the late 1910s and 1920s were involved in any number of rackets and sold other narcotics, as well as cocaine. Heroin, in fact, was their number one commodity.[34]

Sometime in the 1920s, the Jewish-run drug business became more organized and better capitalized. The loads came in large shipments from Europe. Until 1925 cocaine, heroin, and the other drugs remained legal and easily purchased there; after 1925, when most of Europe followed the American lead and adopted anti-drug laws, purchase was less easy but far from impossible.[35] Helping to finance and organize this drug smuggling and distribution trade, until his murder in 1928, was the notorious underworld kingpin Arnold Rothstein. (Rothstein was most infamous for his never-proven but almost certain role in fixing the 1919 World Series.)

Rothstein was known in New York City during this era, and ever after, as a big-time gambler, which he was.[36] He was also involved in most every other form of organized crime in New York City. Sometime in the mid 1920s, though possibly earlier, Rothstein became the head of a massive drug-smuggling ring. Rothstein used connections he had made smuggling alcohol from Europe into the United States to set up his drug-smuggling enterprise; he used the same network within the United States to distribute loads of cocaine and heroin from France, Germany, and the Netherlands.[37] Rothstein brought the drugs in on freighters.

Rothstein was protected by New York City's political establishment, especially after James J. Walker, a *bon vivant* speakeasy regular, became mayor in 1925. Rothstein also hired the dissolute and only son of Harry M. Dougherty, the Attorney General of the United States, to "work" in one of his front businesses; the son and the son-in-law of the Chief of the

Treasury Department's Narcotics Division, as well as the top New York City federal narcotics agent, worked for him as well. Rothstein was a generous man; he "lent" tens of thousands of dollars to many well-placed New York politicians.[38]

Despite Rothstein's corrupt political connections, he was not immune to law enforcement, at least not at the federal level. In 1926, a 1220-pound shipload of heroin, morphine, and cocaine – listed on the freight manifest as bowling balls and pins – from Germany was busted by custom agents in New York City. Rothstein brazenly posted cash bail of $25,000 (that is about $350,000 in 2018 dollars) for each of his arrested associates. Federal agents, who believed that the Rothstein ring had brought over some 3000 more pounds of narcotics in the months prior to the bust, deduced that they had a smuggling problem. They tightened their customs inspections as a federally-led task force, composed of agents from the FBI and Treasury Department along with investigators from the office of the District Attorney for the Southern District of New York, began to close in on Rothstein's narcotics ring.[39]

On November 4, 1928 – before authorities could arrest Rothstein – New York's gangster mastermind was mysteriously gunned down. In investigating the murder, government agents quickly began to realize how much cocaine and heroin they had missed, even after their supposed crackdown. Authorities discovered Rothstein's meticulously maintained business ledgers, spelling out a host of ongoing drug deals. Those federal authorities, despite being warned directly by telephone by gangsters that "you want to lay off or you won't stay healthy," made bust after bust.[40] They grabbed $2 million worth of heroin, opium and cocaine on a train baggage car that had left New York for Chicago. They seized $500,000 in narcotics in the hotel stash room of a former "actress" on the north side of Chicago. They seized $4 million in narcotics, including at least 1,000 ounces of cocaine, on the docks in Jersey City where cargo was being unloaded from the French ocean liner *Rochambeau*. According to Charles Tuttle, the United States district attorney leading the Rothstein task force, "This seizure and the one made the other day shows the existence of a big international drug ring with headquarters in France or Switzerland."[41] Not surprisingly, given the numerous relatives and associates of important government officials on Rothstein's payroll, most of

Rothstein's scrupulously kept business records somehow disappeared, and only one major member of the narcotics ring ended up going to jail.

* * *

The investigation into Rothstein's drug ring fizzled out, but the drug enterprise continued. Associates of Rothstein, most importantly "Lucky" Luciano, took over leadership. Luciano focused on heroin. So did the other gangsters, mostly Jews and Italians. Heroin had a nice steady market of hard-core addicts and it was relatively easy to buy, first in France, and then after the US government began pressuring the French, in Turkey. And as heroin became a growth industry in the United States, cocaine began to lose its customer base during the 1930s and 1940s.

No one can say for sure why cocaine seemed to lose its allure in the 1930s. Heroin was more easily available and with the repeal of Prohibition in 1933, alcohol – Americans' traditional party drug – was once again legal. Even more relevant, perhaps, was the new legal alternative to cocaine, one that provided some of the same kicks.

In 1933, pharmaceutical giant Smith, Kline, and French introduced amphetamines to the American public. Their over-the-counter Benzedrine inhalers, supposedly intended to reduce "congestion," contained 325 mg of amphetamine base. They were cheap, legal, and readily purchased at any neighborhood pharmacy. While the high was not identical to cocaine, amphetamines gave users a similar, though longer lasting, burst of energy, sense of confidence, and general feeling of well-being. Amphetamines were, then, generally regarded as safe, and they were prescribed by doctors for reasons including weight loss and depression, and for a general pick me up. During World War II, amphetamines were regularly provided to servicemen in combat zones to keep them alert. Over half a million Americans were regular consumers by 1945. In 1962, Americans legally purchased enough amphetamines to supply every American man, woman, and child with forty-three standard doses a year. Illegal cocaine had a hard time competing with legal, easy-to-access amphetamines.[42]

Cocaine was not only illegal in the United States, it was also increasingly difficult to get. During the 1930s, authorities in France, Germany, and the Netherlands clamped down on the gray market, making it increasingly difficult to divert supplies to illicit markets. To a small extent, European sources were replaced by cocaine smuggled in from Japan. The Japanese had their own coca plantations in one of their colonies, Taiwan, and had constructed major cocaine production facilities. In 1935, custom agents in Long Beach arrested a ring of Japanese and Chinese drug traffickers after finding nearly 12 pounds of cocaine, as well as 200 pounds of opium, on a ship from Japan.[43]

The head of the Federal Bureau of Narcotics, Harry Anslinger, warned then that cocaine "has been regularly smuggled from Japan to the Pacific coast for some time past."[44] Anslinger, known to posterity for his hysterical claims about the evils of marijuana, was always looking to increase his agency's budget; he was prone to exaggeration. It is hard to judge his claim, especially since just two years earlier he had claimed that cocaine smuggling had become just "a rivulet compared to the river which was emptying into the country for a long period of time."[45] Anslinger's claims aside, in July 1940 custom agents seized another 17 pounds of cocaine in Oakland that had been brought in on a Japanese freighter. A Japanese crewman was arrested; newspapers blared that he was part of "one of the Coast's biggest narcotics smuggling plots."[46] Little has been discovered about the Japanese cocaine-smuggling rings; the targets of these busts may have been anomalies, or their hauls may represent just a small amount of the cocaine smuggled into the West Coast of the United States before the outbreak of World War II.

During World War II, the amount of illegal narcotics smuggled into the United States declined greatly. Cocaine imports declined along with the others. Japanese and German sources, obviously, were out of the picture, as were any sort of goods from the rest of Nazi-occupied Europe. Both Atlantic and Pacific Ocean shipping lanes were war zones, which put a premium on cargo space on every freighter; to prevent enemy sabotage, American ports were rigorously scrutinized and guarded. Notorious gangster "Lucky" Luciano, whose cronies played a major corrupting role on New York's waterfront docks, helped US authorities with port security during the war, and his efforts were seemingly honest. But illegal narcotics still crossed US borders. Smugglers brought loads in from Mexico. Cuba, too, became an important trans-shipment point for illegal drugs, mostly heroin but including cocaine.

After the war, and for the next couple of decades, the illegal cocaine business staged a slow but steady comeback. In part, the cocaine business could grow because the Federal Bureau of Narcotics was focused on the heroin trade. In the post–World War II years, in response to public outcries and Cold War concerns, FBN agents went after heroin manufacturers and distributors in Europe and the Middle East, as well as the ethnic Italian and Jewish gangsters who controlled the American heroin market. Cocaine was largely off their radar.

Thus during the 1940s and 1950s, with drug enforcement efforts directed elsewhere, Latin American smugglers worked steadily to bring cocaine back into the United States market. With European and Asian pharmaceutical cocaine producers largely out of the business, Latin America filled the gap. Pure cocaine was being brought up from the Andean countries of South America, as well as from Chile and Cuba. Demand for the drug was not large but in the 1950s it was growing. The modern cocaine business, in which cocaine from South America is smuggled into the United States by organized rings of drug dealers, had begun.

Judging by the busts made in the immediate post–World War II years, the amount of cocaine smuggled into the United States was still relatively small. Demand was still limited to the demi-monde and criminal set that had kept cocaine sales up in the 1920s. Jazz musicians indulged, sometimes taking speedballs of heroin mixed with coke.[47] Gangsters, black and white, snorted coke, as did prostitutes. Malcolm X – still Malcolm Little and a smalltime hoodlum in the 1940s – snorted regularly before he was jailed in 1946. An outré crew of wealthy white socialites and Hollywood celebrities were still aficionados of the drug. But cocaine was not the drug of choice for most Americans looking to get high. In the 1950s, heroin use had exploded. Suburban housewives abused "downers." Middle-class whites and a racially mixed assortment of bohemians took "speed." Millions of Americans indulged daily in a drink or two. Cocaine users, between the end of World War II and the advent of the 1960s, were a fairly small niche market.

Sometime in the mid 1960s, however, that niche market began to grow. Custom agents were among the first to see the change. In 1964, agents at New York City's newly renamed Kennedy Airport picked up on a suspicious pattern. They began to notice "fast"-looking, single white women, carrying large suitcases, passing through customs after quick trips to Chile.

In December 1964, an agent took an interest in one Juanita Bradbie. When he opened her suitcase, it appeared that her clothes were too "shallow." He worked out that her suitcases had false compartments. Bradbie, who had been arrested previously on prostitution charges, was carrying 10 kilos of coke. A few days later, Sybil Horowitz, with a big black bouffant hair-do and heavily mascaraed eyes, was caught with 10 kilos of pure cocaine in three false-bottomed suitcases. Miss Horowitz was a traveling con artist, or "grifter," who had been in and out of jail since she was in her early twenties. Though Horowitz and Bradbie were terrified of the people who had hired them, they told the custom agents everything they could, naming names, in hopes of reduced sentences.[48]

Horowitz said she had been paid $5,000 – the contemporary equivalent of around $40,000 – plus another $2,000 for expenses to smuggle the coke from Santiago, Chile. According to authorities, she was one of several white women who muled the coke for a major international drug-smuggling ring, which they identified as one of the biggest distributors of cocaine operating in the United States.

The US ringleader was a career criminal named Raphael Santana; associates knew him as "Red Nova." (Santana would serve time for this cocaine bust but, after his release, went back to the drug trade in a major way and eventually served a life term for conspiracy to import 1,000 kilos of heroin into the United States.) The Federal Bureau of Narcotics was able to trace the coke back to its source in Chile. With the cooperation of Chilean authorities, they arrested four people, including a senior member of one of the major narco-trafficking families in South America who had roots in the Middle East and long-standing connections to growers in Bolivia. According to the United States Attorney's office in Brooklyn, which handled the case, the ring had brought in around $25 million in cocaine – the contemporary equivalent of some $200 million – before the arrests were made.[49]

These busts were made in December 1964, well before cocaine, let alone crack, had become an object of mass desire in the United States. According to a government agent asked to comment on the case – probably a member of the Federal Bureau of Narcotics – cocaine had a limited market in the United States. Cocaine, he said, was most popular "in the fur and jewelry set." It was, he said, "a society narcotic ... If you want to set a party really swinging, you sniff the stuff." He did not, however, mean to endorse its use. "[C]oke is the hook," he warned readers. "Once you start sniffing, you belong to the junkies."[50] While the agent was convinced of cocaine's dangers, an increasing number of Americans were beginning to think differently about cocaine, specifically, and illegal drugs, more generally.

No one has offered an easy or definitive answer as to why the use of illegal drugs exploded among white, middle-class youths during the late 1960s and, even more so, in the early 1970s. Elsewhere, I have argued that "at the most conventional level, drug use was handed down from parents to children."[51] In 1965, those middle-class parents were the primary beneficiaries of 123 million prescriptions for tranquilizers and sedatives and 24 million prescriptions for amphetamines. They boozed it up and a majority smoked. The white, middle-class "Baby Boomers," however, did not stick to alcohol, nicotine, and doctor-prescribed uppers and downers. They went on the prowl for their own, generation-specific highs.

This open-minded search for alternative, illegal highs was surely stoked by rebellion against those cultural and political authorities who had both championed the failed Vietnam War and maintained a racist, sexist society. Combine those factors with broad national prosperity and an unprecedented consumer cornucopia and many young Americans saw the opportunity to reinvent both the medicine chest and the liquor cabinet. While some discovered brand new drugs, most famously LSD, others turned to the traditional highs of the underground and the bohemian set. As marijuana became the biggest-selling illegal high, it created a massive market that was first served by imported product from Mexico, and then, increasingly, from Colombia. This marijuana trade – both in terms of demand and supply – did not end in the 1970s. Indeed, the market exploded, working its way down to younger and younger teenagers and across race, ethnic, and class lines.[52] But despite the promise of LSD and the growing use of marijuana, for drug cognoscenti in the 1970s, cocaine was becoming the drug of choice. At least for those who could afford it.

In 1977, rock guitar icon Eric Clapton released the song, "Cocaine." Though not a simple celebration of the drug, its driving beat drove home the song's lyrical message: cocaine kept you riding high; cocaine drove away the "blues"; cocaine kept the night alive. Such promise was a long way from the Beatles' whimsical acid masterpiece, "Lucy in the Sky with Diamonds," or the Jefferson Airplane's homage to tripping, "White Rabbit." In the 1970s, white youth's cultural arbiters, rock musicians, were advocating for a different kind of high.

The managing editor of *Rolling Stone* magazine, Charles Perry, saw broader implications. He mournfully recalled, "There was no longer the feeling during the psychedelic days of the rapport of seeing Janis [Joplin] on the street or of sharing a joint with Jerry Garcia ... Rock and roll was becoming a big business. It was the time of big recording contracts and international tours."[53] In that music industry, cocaine was a tool not of introspection or mind expansion, as marijuana and LSD had been. Cocaine was a confidence-building energy driver. It was a drug made for professionals who put in long nights and then wanted to let loose with some hard partying. Cocaine was fun and sexy, perfect for touring musicians whose down-time often began well after midnight.

Some 1960s veterans mourned this changing drug culture. Music producer David Rothchild believed that cocaine, unlike marijuana and acid, drove people apart. Within the rock community, he believed, cocaine fed people's competitive and selfish desires, exacerbating the music industry's money-driven ethos. "One consciousness," the one stimulated by marijuana and LSD, he insisted, "brought about sharing, the other," stimulated by cocaine, "brought about greed."[54] While Rothchild can be accused of overly romanticizing the drug culture – and the music industry – of the 1960s, many others shared his view.[55]

Rock musicians were by no means the only ones adapting their taste in drugs to their changing circumstances. To quote David Rothchild once again: "I knew all was lost when I saw what used to be the artists' world of drugs and creative exchange in the hands of lawyers and accountants, and when I saw the lawyers doing blow, I knew that an era had truly ended."[56] Cocaine was fast becoming America's new party drug, a perfect stimulant for both the eroticized 1970s and the risk-taking, entrepreneurial fever of the early 1980s. Cocaine drove its growing ranks of users to do everything harder and faster.

Media mavens and trendsetters hyped the cocaine rush. In 1974, slightly ahead of the curve, the editors of the *New York Times Magazine* ran a long story: "Cocaine: The Champagne of Drugs." While recounting some of the risks associated with regular use of coke, the writer claimed that its enthusiasts encompassed "all social and economic categories, but are particularly concentrated among what one specialist calls 'the glitter people': a Who's Who of Hollywood and Hollywood-on-the-Hudson that includes actors, models, athletes, artists, jazz musicians, designers and ad men."[57] Three years later, *Newsweek* described "The Cocaine Scene." According to the newsweekly, "pinstriped Wall Street lawyers take it from a 14-karat gold spoon at elegant parties."[58] Cocaine, which had spent decades in relative obscurity as the drug of the criminal underworld and the demi-monde, was back in the mainstream. Not since the late nineteenth century had cocaine received such a positive press.

By 1979, almost 20 percent of Americans between the age of eighteen and twenty-five claimed that they had used cocaine at least once in the previous year. Over 9 percent of all Americans over the age of twenty-six reported the same.[59] By 1980, cocaine was the fuel of a significant segment of America's hard-charging young urban professionals – Yuppies.

Cocaine's fast-rising popularity, especially among more affluent whites, created powerful demand. By 1979, a kilo of cocaine sold for $51,000, up about 50 percent from just a year earlier. And that was in Miami, where wholesale prices were at their lowest.[60] To meet that lucrative demand, a range of international drug-trafficking organizations, led by Colombians, rose to the fore.

The Colombians had not, at first, dominated the modern cocaine business. In the immediate post–World War II decades, Chileans had developed cocaine as a "cottage industry." They bought raw materials from Peru and Bolivia and refined it in their own laboratories. They did use Colombians, often, to do the actual smuggling into the United States.

Many of those Colombians were headquartered in Medellin, which had a long, if not distinguished, history as a smuggling center.[61]

In 1973, the rules of the cocaine industry changed. General Augusto Pinochet led a coup that overthrew the democratically elected, if not always effective, government of Chile. As part of his brutal law-and-order campaign, he smashed Chile's relatively small cocaine industry. The Chilean coke merchants tried to set up shop in Colombia but their Colombian smuggler partners saw their chance and they took it. They forced out – violently – the Chileans. They took control of the industry. The Colombian government, unlike the brutal Pinochet regime, lacked the authority, legitimacy, or the will to stop the cocaine industry. The Colombian entrepreneurs' timing could not have been better. The market, most especially in the United States, was taking off.

Many of the people invested in the new cocaine industry had a distinct advantage over their Chilean predecessors. They were professional smugglers. Some were deeply involved in flying huge quantities of high grade Colombian marijuana to the United States. They had a business model ready for easy adaptation to their new, far more lucrative commodity.

Prior to 1974, cocaine chroniclers Guy Gugliotta and Jeff Leen explain, coke smuggling was done a few kilos at a time. Like the women who were caught in the mid 1960s at Kennedy Airport, "mules" generally brought in small bags of coke hidden in their suitcases or taped to their bodies. In the 1960s, such simple methods were sufficient to meet the limited demand. Not so, even by the early 1970s. The solution was obvious. The same small planes that had been smuggling bales of "Colombian Red," "Colombian Gold," and other high grade types of weed could be used, instead, to fly in kilos of coke. Pound for pound, cocaine was much more profitable than marijuana.

Two men imprisoned together at the federal penitentiary at Danbury, Connecticut on marijuana charges, Colombian smuggler Carlos Lehder and American wholesaler George Jung, plotted out the new aviation-based business model. Lehder, who had the Colombian connections, explained to Jung that they could buy a kilo of coke in Colombia for $2,000 and sell it for more than $50,000 in the United States. Once out of prison, they began to implement the plan.

Lehder and Jung knew that flying big loads of cocaine would be risky; American interdiction efforts aimed at the marijuana trade meant that pilots would be caught and loads would be lost. But the profits were so insanely good that the risks were worth it. Air Cocaine was in business. The Bahamas served as a stopping-off spot, both for refueling and to confuse interdiction efforts. Lehder set up a smuggler's paradise, complete with a private airstrip, a couple of dozen or so Doberman Pinschers, and armed German guards in Norman Key in the Bahamas. By 1977, instead of one or two kilos smuggled in by one person at a time, air cargo loads of 250 kilos moved from Colombia to the Bahamas to rural, often makeshift air strips in southern Florida and other parts of the US south, and then, generally, on to Miami for distribution. Demand was so strong and growing so fast that prices remained high, despite the ever-increasing loads coming into the United States. Inside the United States, a new breed of networked drug dealers emerged to move the coke. Colombian émigrés in the United States, especially in the New York City metropolitan area, played major roles in the distribution end.[62]

The money involved in moving so much cocaine bred risk, mostly from rivals, and with risk came violence. In their account of the cocaine trade, Gugliotta and Leen quote the era's conventional wisdom: "A marijuana deal is done with a handshake and a cocaine deal is done with a gun."[63] In Colombia, fierce gangsters such as Pablo Escobar murdered their way to the top of the food chain. In Miami, wars broke out between Cuban gangsters and competing groups of Colombians over control of the trade. As the battles escalated, Miami's murder rate soared from an already high figure of 349 in 1979 to a catastrophic 621 in 1981. The rat-a-tat of Mac-10 machine guns became the soundtrack to Miami's cocaine wars.

The 1983 film *Scarface* brought home the violence to a national audience in a remake of the 1932 classic. The original had paid homage to the 1920s prohibition gangster Al Capone. The new film featured a fictional character, Miami-based Cuban refugee cocaine baron Tony Montana. At the film's end, Montana fearlessly takes on an army of assassins, screaming, "Say hello to my little friend" – a fully automatic, converted AR-15 with a grenade launcher. The move to fiction, near enough, matched the city's reality. Cocaine wars had turned early 1980s Miami into 1920s gangland Chicago.

Thanks to Colombian cartels, by the early 1980s America was awash in cocaine. The Drug Enforcement Agency estimated that about 65 tons were smuggled into the United States in 1983.[64] And supply was difficult to interrupt. When the Reagan administration began to throw money and resources at the Caribbean-based smuggling trade, setting up the South Florida Task Force under the able direction of Vice President George H. W. Bush, the Colombians simply redrew their supply routes. Mexican drug smugglers soon offered their service to the Colombian cartels. They had long experience bringing illegal drugs – primarily heroin and marijuana – across the border. These Mexican drug-trafficking organizations took on the lion's share of the cocaine brought into the United States, dominating the smuggling trade by the mid 1980s. They demanded and received a sizeable cut of the price for their diligent work. Mexican-delivered coke poured into Houston, El Paso, Phoenix, and Los Angeles. And while the wholesale price of coke oscillated, driven up by the occasional major bust and down by heavy supply, retail costs in the United States generally remained high – though lower than they had been in the late 1970s.[65]

The cocaine business was lucrative. But the consumer marketplace for the drug did have a limit. Coke, back then, generally cost about $100 (about $250 in today's dollars) a gram retail. To get reasonably high and stay that way took a fair amount of powder – a gram did not last long in the hands of "cokeheads." Moreover, lots of people did not have that kind of cash just lying around. Coke, as a result, was an upmarket drug; it inspired DEA agents and Hollywood celebrities to share the same joke: "Cocaine is God's way of telling you that you have too much money."[66] And if coke was expensive to purchase, it took even more money to get into the cocaine dealership game. An ounce of high-quality cocaine, pretty much the least a dealer needed to get started and keep his customers happy, could go for as much as $1,000.

For the entrepreneurial cocaine dealer, the questions were clear: Could the coke market be expanded? Was there a way to deliver a cocaine high to a broader base of customers, those who could not afford the $100 entry level price or who felt that the high they got from snorting expensive powder cocaine was not worth the cost? In other words, could cocaine, somehow, be sold at a cheaper price even as it generated a stronger high? Likewise, young hustlers began to wonder, might there be a way to buy into the cocaine wholesale market at a lower start-up cost? Could a mere gram of coke, say, be somehow processed into small but highly potent doses that could be sold at low cost, offering a high rate of return on a small capital investment?

Enter crack cocaine.

CHAPTER 2

Crack the Market: Commodification and Commercialization

I N 1972, A DRUG AFICIONADO COULD STOP BY HIS LOCAL "HEAD shop" and pick up a copy of *The Gourmet Cokebook: A Complete Guide to Cocaine*, published anonymously by the aptly named White Mountain Press. In it, he could find a simple recipe for cooking up a batch of crack. It was easy: Mix equal parts of powder cocaine and baking soda in a pot, add water, boil, let cool, and then break the hardened, desiccated mass into small pieces – rocks – suitable for smoking. Smoked cocaine, the cokehead learned, produced a more intense, if shorter-lived, high than snorted cocaine. Smoked cocaine goes straight into the lungs, where it is rapidly absorbed into the bloodstream, from whence it zooms into the smoker's brain; physiologically speaking, this is a much more efficient and effective process than snorting cocaine. Nasal membranes just cannot compete with the lungs for getting the drug to where it counts.

The information on how to make crack was there to be had in the 1970s. And it was not just in the underground *Gourmet Cokebook*. Druggies in the Bay area, including some well-educated Berkeley students, were smoking homemade crack as early as 1970. Los Angeles drug kingpin "Tootie" Reese discovered crack in the Bay area in 1976 and in a small-time way introduced it to some of his LA customers soon thereafter.[1] By 1978, a few scattered residents of Nickerson Gardens in the Watts section of Los Angeles, the largest public housing project west of the Mississippi, could be seen smoking crack cocaine.[2] That same year, The Twentieth Century Alchemist published *Pleasures of Cocaine*. It contained a simple and effective crack recipe. In the 1970s in the United States, people had begun cooking and smoking crack cocaine.

Figure 4 Kenneth "Supreme" McGriff: Mr. McGriff ran the "Supreme Team," one of the most successful crack cocaine operations in Queens, New York City. McGriff, in and out of jail in the 1980s and 1990s, was convicted of murder-for-hire in 2007 and is currently serving a life sentence. (NY Daily News Archive via Getty Images.)

But no one was whipping up a big mess of crack for commercial distribution. Crack cocaine was kind of like that other 1970s innovation, personal computers – it would take more than the basic technology knocked out by super-early adopters to bring the innovation successfully to market. Black market entrepreneurs would be needed to find the demand, distribute the product to consumers, and manage the new business's risks.

Figure 5 Almighty Black P. Stone Nation: This Chicago street gang was founded in the 1950s and by the late 1960s, when this photo was taken, was easily one of the most powerful gangs in Chicago. Beginning in the late 1980s, the Stones, along with the Gangster Disciples, became dominant players in the Chicago crack cocaine trade. (Chicago History Museum, ICHI-051724; Declan Haun, photographer.)

* * *

Before crack became widely available, a couple of smokeable cocaine options did exist in the marketplace.[3] In Latin America in the early 1970s – and after – people smoked *basuco*. It was relatively easy to make: cheap coca leaves were thoroughly mashed and then mixed with a solvent, commonly ether or even gasoline, producing a crudely processed, intermediate form of cocaine that could be smoked. Smoking *basuco* was not for everyone; it tasted foul and it was often full of dangerous adulterants. Still, it was a big hit, generally among the poor, in several South American countries.

Alternatively, in the United States, among the well-to-do cocaine cognoscenti, freebasing took off in the mid-to-late 1970s. Freebasing involved processing powder cocaine with ether. The result was a crystalline substance that could be fired up with a high-intensity butane or acetylene torch and smoked, usually through a water pipe. In the late

1970s the magazine *High Times* advertised freebase kits that provided a user with all the information and tools he or she needed to make and smoke "base." Cocaine chroniclers claim that as many as 400,000 Americans had tried freebasing by 1980.[4]

Still, even with instructional material and handy DIY kits, freebasing took some doing and could produce adverse results. The unfortunate poster-child for catastrophic freebasing mishaps was the celebrity cocaine enthusiast Richard Pryor. In June 1980, while on a freebasing binge, the comedian and film star caught on fire – exactly how remains controversial, though a quantity of 151-proof rum which Pryor poured on himself while smoking played a critical part. Poor Mr. Pryor ended up running naked down a Los Angeles street ablaze. Bad publicity for freebasing ensued. "Richard Pryor's Tragic Accident Spotlights a Dangerous Drug Craze: Freebasing," reported the inimitable *People* magazine.[5] Freebasing was clearly a risky challenge, not least because it called for a portion of high-grade expensive powder cocaine and good fire-management skills.

Some, however, have argued that even the bad publicity surrounding Pryor's debacle turned people's attention to the lure of smokeable cocaine. In a retrospective on the rise of crack, the *LA Times* reported: "[P]olice, professors and pushers all recall it [Pryor's freebasing debacle] as a pivotal moment. The publicity not only highlighted the dangers, but heightened awareness that cocaine could be smoked. The search was on for less volatile ingredients."[6] So, at the cusp of the 1970s and 1980s, people in the cocaine business, as well as a number of cocaine users, did already understand the attractions of smokeable cocaine. Taking that knowledge and turning into a profitable, mass business, however, was something else.

The exact origins of the commercial crack trade in the United States remain murky and complex. They involve an international cast of characters operating in a tangled web of uncertain circumstances and unintended consequences. In telling that history, people of good will and honest intent disagree about almost everything. One dedicated investigative journalist, Peter Katel, writing in the aftermath of the spectacular claims made by Gary Webb of the *San Jose Mercury* in 1996 that crack cocaine's rise in America's inner cities was the direct result of a CIA conspiracy, threw up his hands. After chasing the story of crack's origins down many a rabbit hole, he insisted: "The true origins of crack turns up not one conspiracy but hundreds of smaller ones."[7]

Michael Massing, writing for the *New York Times Magazine* in 1989, is much more specific. In the kind of New York City-centric piece that regularly are published in the *Times*, he deduces that the crack trade started in New York's ethnic cauldron. With some caveats, he argues, "Though crack's origins remain obscure – no one really knows who invented it – the Dominicans [in New York's Washington Heights] are generally credited with having first developed it [crack cocaine] for a mass market."[8] New York-based Dominican drug dealers had dabbled in the smokeable cocaine market early on; they had been offered *basuco* by their Colombian cocaine connections around 1980 and were told to try giving it away to see if a market for it could be established. But they had few takers. Instead, in the early 1980s, Dominican merchandisers came up with their own, more refined smokeable product. Instead of marketing *basuco*, the raw cocaine paste and ether admixture, they used a proprietary mix of powder cocaine, Arm & Hammer baking soda, and a relatively cheap additive they called "comeback," which Massing says was a variant of the prescription drug lidocaine, to cook up safe, easy to use, and inexpensive "crack" or "rock" cocaine. Operating out of corner stores and a variety of other fronts, the Dominicans had customers of all races and ethnicities coming from near and far, lining up for their product.

No doubt the Dominican dealers in New York played a significant role in establishing the crack trade as a big business. But their intervention was not unique or, in all likelihood, original. We can move further back into the supply chain and product-development phase. Earlier efforts in the Caribbean probably explain where these Dominican entrepreneurs got their recipe – though it is perfectly possible they came up with it themselves in a parallel development.

Crack genealogists argue that what we call "crack" took off around the Caribbean around 1979 and 1980, most importantly in the Bahamas. The argument goes that a massive glut of cocaine in the Bahamas at the end of the 1970s put a premium on local dealers' marketing skills. The glut was caused by Colombian exporters' decision to use the Bahamas' many small islands and remote cays as trans-shipment spots for massive loads of coke destined for the United States. Enough of that coke stayed in the

Bahamas to represent a competitive challenge for the dealers working the local market. With powder coke plentiful they took on the low-end *basuco* smokers' market and challenged the higher-end powder coke snorters' market by offering a better product: smokeable "rock" made from a boiled-down mix of powder cocaine and baking soda which they sold in small, cheap doses. Crack's fierce and nearly instant high was a huge hit with coke users of all kinds, especially poorer folk who could not afford the price of a gram of powder cocaine but could buy a cheap hit of the highly potent "rock." By 1983 crack had conquered the illegal drug market in the Bahamas. A wise local crack habitué in the Bahamas informed two drug researchers that "the pusher man switched to pushing only rock ... The pushers knew that crack addicts keep coming back for more and more."[9] Crack was a seller's dream: steady repeat customers who could hustle their way to purchasing one or two cheap hits at a time. The lucrative American market loomed ahead.

Caribbean immigrants had brought a form of *basuco* (mixed with baking soda and cooked down with water and rum to produce a smokeable product) to Miami no later than 1980. Sometime soon thereafter, either those same immigrants or possibly a different group of Caribbean immigrant cocaine dealers started selling proper crack made not from crude *basuco* but from powder cocaine. Crack had hit the streets of Miami. By 1981, the DEA reported that crack was also readily for sale in poor neighborhoods in Los Angeles, San Diego, and Houston. Everyone, from law-enforcement officials to scholars to industry leaders, agrees on one thing: the crack cocaine trade blew up in the 1980s, but in different cities at different times.[10]

Unlike a lot of the entrepreneurial innovations of the 1980s, crack demanded little technical knowledge and had a very low buy-in. Most anyone who had even a hundred dollars or so, who had access to a local cocaine dealer, and who was willing to take on the requisite risks could start up a crack dealership. While building a crack start-up was easy, keeping the business going would demand different skills and a different temperament. Willingness to deploy violence to protect and expand business almost always became a practical necessity.

Crack dealers, because they operated outside the law, could not depend on normal methods of capitalization, supply-chain development, employee recruitment, or conflict resolution. Nobody had a legally enforceable contract. Operators had to handle security in-house, though illicit relationships with the local police were not out of the question. Successful crack dealers, while occasionally mentored by veteran hustlers and gangsters, had to take almost all matters of management into their own heavy hands.

Crack kingpins had to be ready to use violence against competitors, against deadbeat customers, against unsatisfactory employees, against arrested compatriots who threatened to turn against them, against unguarded suppliers, against thieves and robbers, against community members who challenged their business, and even – though rarely – against law-enforcement personnel who got in their way. Because major crack crews depended on fear to maintain the security of their business, even minor displays of disrespect by anyone with whom they came into contact could challenge not only their sense of control but their sense of equilibrium as well, and so demanded violent reprisal. In 1988, as crack crews small and large fought to defend and expand their businesses, the head of the Manhattan District Attorney's Homicide Investigation Unit stated: "They have decided they cannot run drug businesses without killing … There have always been killings in the drug business, but these gangs believe that if they can intimidate everybody, they can operate openly and flourish." A member of a Harlem crack crew put it more simply: "We sell drugs, and we kill."[11] The crack trade, almost always, was murder.

* * *

Corey Pegues never became a big-time crack dealer. He started small and ended up a disgruntled, anxious employee for a notorious, murderous crack crew. Like many young men who found their way into the crack trade, he got out soon after he got in. He was lucky. He never got shot, he never shot anyone, and he never got arrested. Unlike too many, he went on to do just fine.

Corey Pegues grew up in St. Albans, Queens. As late as the 1960s, St. Albans had been a multi-racial neighborhood and many well-to-do black families had settled there. By the early 1980s, it was an all-black neighborhood with increasingly large pockets of impoverished residents. Corey's mother had moved to Queens from a small town in North Carolina with her four daughters. She met a man in Queens and had two more children, sons. Corey was the older of the two boys. Corey's father, who did not live full-time with the family, drank heavily. He was gone by the time Corey was in third grade. The Pegues were on welfare. Their electricity would get turned off. Sometimes they had no running water.[12]

Everybody called Corey Boo or Boobie. He was a good athlete and played basketball with older kids. The park where he played basketball was also where the hustlers sold drugs. One thing led to another and in 1982, at thirteen, he and a fifteen-year-old friend started selling loose joints. They'd get 100 joints, sell them for a dollar each, kick back $80 to the supplier, and split the $20 leftover. Soon, he and his partner, "Smooth," were buying 500 joints at a time, paying $380 and making $120 per package. At the end of a week, the boys had upwards of $400 that was theirs.

As Corey saw it, he needed the money: "I had the mom on welfare and the absent father." But the thing is, Smooth didn't need the money. He came from a middle-class, two-parent family. He went to a private school. As Corey tells it, "He made the choice. It was the culture, the environment we grew up in. It was seductive. The hustlers working the park, they were the baddest guys around ... Those were the guys we wanted to be like." Smooth used his money to buy things his parents wouldn't, the latest Pumas and whatever else the hustlers were styling.

Corey Pegues, looking back at the very young man he had been, made the obvious claim: "You're young, you're black, you don't see any prospects. Then you see these dealers, and they're living the American Dream ... It was impossible to hang around people selling drugs and making money and not get caught up in it."[13] Three thousand miles away, T. Rodgers, a founding member of the Bloods, put his own spin on the same story, with a specific focus on the turn toward crack: "It was like, 'I don't need no education, I don't got to kiss nobody's ass, I'm the boss, this is my enterprise – and I'm only 16.' ... Any kid old enough to hold a rock could become king for a day."[14] For many young men growing up in poor or declining urban neighborhoods in the 1980s and 1990s, selling illegal drugs seemed like an economic lifeline, an improbable but readily available ticket to the good life. Crack, as compared, say, to marijuana or heroin or cocaine, was simply the best financial bet.

Selling illegal drugs, crack, in particular, was more than about the money – though the money was always at the core. For many young men, especially young poorly educated black men living in inner cities during the 1980s and 1990s, when urban-based decently paid factory work or unskilled and semi-skilled construction jobs became rarities, selling crack was not just a way out financially. It was also work that demanded no compromises to their sense of manhood, to their dignity. A low-level Dominican crack dealer in East Harlem told ethnographer Philippe Bourgois that he had tried legal work: "I had a few jobs like where you got to take a lot of shit from fat, ugly bitches, and be a wimp ... a punk." It was a terrible way to live, he said. Bourgois argues, "Their macho-proletarian dream of working an eight-hour shift plus overtime throughout their adult lives at a rugged slot in a unionized shop had been replaced by a nightmare of poorly paid, highly feminized, office support work ... [T]hey find themselves propelled headlong into an explosive confrontation between their sense of cultural dignity versus the humiliating interpersonal subordination of service work."[15] Selling crack was not a good long-term plan and for low-level hand-to-hand sellers it did not even pay that well, but many of those who worked a corner or found other gainful employment in the crack trade preferred it, economically and culturally, to the readily available options.

Within a year, Corey Pegues, now known by his street name, "Life," and his partner Smooth were buying bulk marijuana from a corner store run by West Indians and selling nickel and dime bags. They also bought small quantities of mescaline and cocaine from a local dealer they knew from the park. Nobody bothered them, not the police and not local gangs. Pegues explains: "For a gang to take over an area, they need public housing towers to control. They need corners to occupy ... St. Albans is mostly a suburban, family type of environment ... Most of the corners in our neighborhood were people's yards. You can't sell drugs in people's yards."[16]

When Corey was fifteen, his local cocaine connection turned up with a surprise: a package full of crack vials: "Yo, I want y'all to start selling this now." It was fall 1984. According to Corey, they were the first in their neighborhood to sell crack: "The shit took off. I mean, like a rocket ship."[17] Selling marijuana had netted him, at best, around $100 a day. With crack, he and Smooth made $500, sometimes $1,000 a day.

As their business expanded, they connected directly with Harlem-based Colombian suppliers. The Colombians controlled an entire block around 131st Street. Armed men, in full public view, guarded the operation. To get resupplied, buyers moved past the armed gauntlet, stepped down a short flight of stairs, and walked through makeshift tunnels that connected the basements of a row of brownstones. The Colombians spoke little English. They didn't need it. People came to them with bundles of cash and they gave them crack vials. Corey and his small crew were selling as much as a thousand vials of crack a week. After an armed rip-off, Corey hired a bodyguard. He began carrying a gun. He was becoming something he had never imagined, a gangster. Because crack dealing demanded little upfront capital, a lot of small-time crack operations began as independent distributorships, like Corey's. Often, however, larger and more violent crews would move in on such operations.

In the summer of 1985, three older guys jumped Corey while he was playing basketball. Furious, he sought out his older sister's boyfriend, Spank, who had already served hard time for a shooting. He and Spank returned to the park and Spank, without hesitation, stabbed all three men. Spank was caught by the police and ended up in prison. Corey ran away, not from the police but from the friends of the men who had been stabbed. Corey Pegues, who had been happily running his own small-time crack business, fled to his aunt's house on the South Side of Jamaica, Queens, near Baisley Pond Park.

The Baisley Park Housing Projects was the headquarters of the Supreme Team, one of the larger and more notorious crack distribution rings in New York City. Corey, the one-time boss of his own small but lucrative operation, became an employee. "Working for the Supreme Team," he wrote, "was like going to work for a Fortune 500 company. There was a hierarchy and strict channels of communication ... You'd get your package, work your package, turn in the money, and get paid once a week, on Friday." In one fundamental regard, working for the Supreme Team, he adds, was different from working for a Fortune 500 company: "the Supreme Team was infamous for killing and beating people – its own people ... That's how they kept everyone in line. They ruled with fear. You cross us, you're gonna die."[18] Corey didn't have to worry about being ripped off, anymore. He worked for the Supreme Team for two years, never moving into the higher ranks of the organization.

(Coda: Corey Pegues now exits this story. At eighteen, he was done. He had had enough of selling drugs to his neighbors. He did not want to get shot and he decided he did not want to shoot anybody. Despite years in the drug game, he had no felony convictions – the NYPD had not yet started targeting crack dealers – and despite spending most of his high school years on the street, Corey had somehow managed to get his degree. He escaped into the US Army, an exit ramp unavailable to most young men from rough backgrounds; contrary to conventional wisdom, the all-volunteer military is and was quite selective. Among other criteria, in the late 1980s it required a high school diploma and a felony-free record. Pegues embraced army life. After four years he was honorably discharged. In a twist of fate, he then joined the New York police department. He went on to become a decorated deputy inspector before retiring.)

Corey Pegues had been a small cog in the Supreme Team's operation. He was not missed. The Supreme Team had hundreds of young men like Corey working for the organization. It was big-time.[19] Like most heavy street distribution rings, the Supreme Team controlled a housing project; in their case, the five, relatively small, red brick, eight-story buildings that made up Baisley Park Housing Projects in South Queens. The Baisley Park buildings and grounds provided them with a defensible space that made it hard for either rival gangs or the police to get up on them while they were operating. Low-level members, generally kids, were stationed on the project rooftops with walkie-talkies, keeping their eyes out on who was coming and going. "Soldiers," armed and ready, stopped and searched anyone who showed up at Supreme Team's headquarters at the projects looking to meet up with the leadership.[20]

The Supreme Team also controlled large swathes of the neighborhood surrounding the projects and had dealers on corners all over the area. They had nearby stash houses, too, to store their wares and cook up crack, as well as crack houses, where buyers could binge and have sex if they felt like it. Baisley Pond Park, nearby to the projects, with its basketball courts, baseball diamonds, fieldhouse, barbeque area, and big pond in the middle, had been for generations a neighborhood-gathering place. The Supreme Team took it over and used it as a major dealing ground.

All over the South Side of Jamaica, they ran three shifts a day, every day. There was no shirking. Corey Pegues remembers a time when one of his fellow workers, selling in Baisley Pond Park, took a little time off during a quiet phase of his midnight-to-eight shift. He thought no one would notice. He was wrong. At shift's end, his supervisor, Peter "Knowledge" Jimenez, called him over. Without warning, Knowledge punched him in the face and then gave him a vicious beat down: "You stand out here, motherfucker. All night long. You stay out here all motherfucking night. If I fucking find out that you left this fucking park, I'll fucking kill you."[21] In the late 1980s, at its height, the Supreme Team was selling up to $200,000 worth of crack, around the clock, every day.

Because of the nature of the business, crack sellers had to be ready to sell their vials at all hours. Their retail business model was quite different from that of the powder cocaine salesmen. Powder coke was generally sold in amounts no smaller than a gram for $100 or more (though in poor neighborhoods $20 bags were available). Their customers did not need constant access to a dealer. They bought their coke, took it home, snorted it, got high for a while, went about their business, and then, maybe, took some more. If they were hard-core users they might need to buy more cocaine in a few days or even sooner. But they were not looking to buy one or two hits, get intensely high for fifteen minutes, find a way to hustle for a five or ten dollar – twenty for a "jumbo" – vial, buy more drugs, get intensely high, and repeat as often as they could.

Not all crack buyers followed this pattern. As observers of the crack scene noted, plenty of people – whites, in particular – drove up to the drug corners, made their buys, often of multiple vials, and drove away and went home to get intensely high. But the steadiest crack customers were those who bought their vials in ones and twos and turned up throughout the day and night with their money in hand. Crack was a fast nickel kind of business as compared to powder cocaine, which was more of a slow dime kind of thing. To make big money in crack a successful operation had to be run 24/7 and it had to be easy to find. And given the short-term effect of the high, and habituated users' desire or need to smoke their rock as soon as possible after purchase, crack sellers knew that their business worked best in a territory that allowed for nearby use – in an alley or doorway where no one would or could complain – or close to the kind of desolate, unpoliced domiciles that could be turned into a binge-ready "crackhouse." Crack sellers, as a result, tended to work in poor neighborhoods in which underground economies were a part of everyday life – resulting in many residents' indifference, complicity, or wearied acceptance of the drug trade – and in which, for a variety of reasons, which very much included law enforcement's long history of racist practices, the police were generally not welcome or appreciated.[22]

Like many major crack-distribution rings, the Supreme Team was black-run and the young men who did the actual hand-to-hand crack sales were black, as well. But like a number of other major crews, the Supreme Team had Latino members. The Supreme Team, specifically, had Puerto Rican members who spoke Spanish and eased relations with the Colombian and Dominican traffickers who were their cocaine "connects."

The early members of the Supreme Team, like most of the young men who built the heavy side of the crack trade in the mid 1980s, were already seasoned gangsters. A core member, David "Bing" Robinson, explains that before taking up crack distribution and sales, "The team did banks and shit … We always had our hustles before we started dealing drugs and we were gangbanging."[23] With the capital they made from robbing and stealing, they got into the drug business. Before selling crack, they had already dealt marijuana, cocaine, and heroin. Early on, they got their narcotics from a local kingpin, Lorenzo "Fat Cat" Nichols, who ran a murderous drug gang, the Bebos. When crack came on in New York, Fat Cat and his ring first supplied the Supreme team. As demand increased, the Supreme Team's leadership saw the opportunity to build their own thing.

Kenneth "Supreme" McGriff was the criminal mastermind behind the Supreme Team. He had created the team in early 1983 with a strong crew of young men with whom he had been engaged in criminal activities of various kinds for several years. Despite a solid and comfortable two-parent, working-class background in Jamaica, Queens, McGriff had been on track from an early age to defy conventional expectations.

As a precocious ten-year-old, McGriff became fascinated by the teachings of the Five Percent Nation, also known later as the Nation of Gods and Earths. The Five Percent Nation was an all-black movement founded in Harlem in the early 1960s by "Allah the Father," who had been a member of the Nation of Islam before breaking away to form his own faith community. Five Percenters stood on street corners and rapped about their teachings. Young McGriff liked what he heard and he took on the Five Percenter derived name "Supreme" when he was just eleven. According to a prison friend of McGriff's, becoming a Five Percenter changed Supreme's life course, turning him away from the straight and narrow and cementing his distrust and disregard for the rules of white-controlled society.[24] While there is nothing at all inherently criminal or crime-inducing about the teachings of the Five Percent Nation, the knowledge they revere does make a strong case for the right of a black man – a divine being, a god, according to the teachings – to live a life of his own choosing. (Black women are not gods but earths – the gender teachings are more in the Southern Baptist complementarian tradition.) Supreme took that portion of the teachings of the Five Percent Nation seriously and used what he learned to help guide his path to criminal mastery. Likewise, he would use those teachings to unify the Supreme Team he was building, especially in its early years.

Five Percenters, whose early membership was disproportionately drawn from the ranks of convicts and ex-convicts, believe that most of humanity lives in ignorance. A small group of knowledgeable people – 10 percent – controls the benighted many, but only 5 percent of people both know the truth and care enough to save the rest from their ignorance and servitude. These are the "Five Percenters." Like the Nation of Islam, Five Percenters believe that whites are literally devils. But unlike the Nation of Islam, they also believe that black men are divine, i.e., gods. Five Percenters refer to themselves as gods and often take on deity-like names, such as Supreme. Major early figures in the Supreme Team included God B, Black Justice, Lightskin Knowledge, and Puerto Rican Righteous.

The truth about the world, according to this system, is contained in "Supreme Mathematics" (a numerological system) and the "Supreme Alphabet" (a system for deciphering texts), both of which were generated by "Allah the Father" and which acolytes must study. Many of the Supreme Team, even while dealing, carried around a notebook of these teachings and studied hard. Besides providing spiritual and life lessons that gave the organization's members a common set of under-standings, the Supreme Mathematics and the Supreme Alphabet were valuable tools for speaking in a kind of coded language that made it difficult for eavesdropping outsiders, especially law-enforcement offi-cials, to understand the ins and outs of the Supreme Team's illicit activities. Such ciphers made it possible for Supreme, after he was impri-soned, to continue to issue directives to his people.[25]

With the exception of the A-Team, in Brooklyn's then desperately poor East New York, no other major ring followed the precepts of the Five Percent Nation. However, many leading inner-city crack organizations had their own set of principles or a formal doctrine, often devised or adapted by an intellectually oriented leader, which shaped operations, structured management decisions, and unified its members. In Chicago, Larry Hoover issued a series of formal dictums for the Black Gangster Disciples (later known simply as the Gangster Disciples), a massive street gang that became a major player in Chicago's crack trade, and Jeff Fort introduced his South Side Chicago gang, the Almighty Black P. Stone Nation – the other extremely powerful Chicago street gang that would also, eventually, became a major crack distribution network – to a custo-mized set of Islamic beliefs and renamed his organization the El Rukns (not all Stones accepted the Islamic turn). While some of these gang or crew doctrines were grand in scope, others were much more pragmatic and business-like. The Notorious B.I.G. in "The Ten Crack Commandments" rapped the most elegant and stripped-down code of crack-dealing conduct. He informed his listeners, dark humor inten-tional, that after years in the trade he had written a manual of best practices. Among other things, he advised crack purveyors, in language more poetic, to never use their own product; provide no credit; avoid entangling family and business; and to keep their finances private and their moves quiet.[26]

Supreme was imprisoned just two years after he started the Supreme Team, just as the crack trade was truly taking off. Despite that setback, Supreme continued to play a role in overseeing his creation. He used

52

coded language to deliver messages from jail to his team. He also developed an intimate relationship with a woman prison guard; in exchange for Supreme's affections, as well as a brand new BMW, she acted as an intermediary, meeting regularly with Team members to pass on his instructions.[27] Such prison-based gang leadership is not uncommon; Chicago gangster mastermind Larry Hoover ran the Gangster Disciples from his cell for decades, as did his Chicago gang rival, Jeff Fort, leader of the Black P. Stone Nation/El Rukns. Supreme was incarcerated on state narcotics charges in 1985. He was released in 1987 on an appeal bond, but after being free for less than three months he pled guilty to federal "kingpin" charges – operating a continuing criminal enterprise. He rolled on no one, pled guilty in the face of overwhelming evidence, and received a twelve-year sentence.

Supreme did not waste time during his brief spell of freedom in the late summer and early fall of 1987. Right after he was released on the state charges, he called a formal meeting of his top twenty-five men and, according to his biographer, he laid out his plans for the crew. In addition, he met new members and received a detailed accounting of the team's connects, capital, weapons, and drug-dealing locations. He asked for a comprehensive rundown on security matters. In closing, "He instructed them to lock shit down."[28] When he entered the federal penitentiary in November 1987, he had an excellent command of both the Team's situation and the loyalty of his key men. So, even as he was incarcerated, Supreme continued to issue commands and was treated, if not in an everyday sort of way, as the Team's boss. The cry, "Word to Preme," could be heard on the lips of his men, punctuating their respect for their imprisoned leader.

Supreme's arrest did put a damper on the team. Gerald "Prince" Miller, Supreme's nephew and most trusted man, was also put behind bars, as were several other key figures. But the Team, if no longer firing on all cylinders, rolled on. The Supreme Team, like many major crack rings, was managed more like General Motors, in its heyday, than Ford. That's to say it was a decentralized operation in which semi-autonomous managers ran their own divisions. Those divisions, however, answered to the boss, Supreme, who set the ground rules and even in prison made some of the organization's strategic decisions. Not to press the analogy too far, the Supreme Team had its own version of Buick, Pontiac, Chevrolet, and Cadillac. Four different crews, authorized by McGriff, each with their own leader and their own hierarchy, each with their own company culture, which often included clothing styles, sold vials of crack marketed under separate color-coded caps. Unlike GM, though, all Supreme Team products sold for the same price – that was company policy. All divisions even shared the same purchasing plan, which was chanted by the hand-to-hand men to their lined-up customers: "No singles, no shorts." Given the scale of their operations, single dollar bills were just too much trouble – cumbersome and hard to "launder" – so customers had to find fives, tens, and twenties to pay for their vials. And "no shorts" simply meant that no matter how regular a customer, no credit would be given – crack was strictly a cash and carry business.[29]

The leaders of the Supreme Team's four divisions each became legendary figures, at least in Southland Queens. There was James "Bimmy" Antney who led the crew that sold green-capped vials (he says they were green – most others state they were blue – street lore is a contested arena). Troy "Babywise" Jones' crew dealt the red caps. Colbert "Black Justice" Johnson had the orange caps. And, most feared and most ambitious, first among equals, was Supreme's nephew, Gerald "Prince" Miller, whose crew sold crack in yellow-capped vials.[30]

Two of these leaders are particularly noteworthy for their differences. James "Bimmy" Antney had about one hundred young men working for him. They controlled much of Baisley Pond Park, as well as other spots around the neighborhood. Bimmy was a neighborhood kid and had entered the drug game early. When he was twelve, he worked after school at the local pharmacy where he caught the attention of Pop Freeman, the Black Godfather of southeast Queens. Pop was connected to the Gambino crime family; the Gambinos supplied Freeman with his heroin and cocaine. Bimmy was a likeable, quick-witted, and loquacious kid. He quickly stepped up from running errands for Freeman to selling his drugs. According to some, he also took part in a variety of armed robberies. Still a teenager, he met Supreme through his girlfriend. Bimmy, an extroverted, genuinely friendly sort, was world-class at meeting and ingratiating himself with the people he needed to move forward. He had a gift for accruing social capital. He was not an original "seed," as the men who started out with Supreme were called. He didn't embrace the Five-Percenter ideology. But Bimmy rose up fast into the first ranks. He was well regarded for his acumen and commanded a broad network of friends and allies, including several young men – such as Russell Simmons and LL Cool J – who would make it big in hip hop. In 1986, Bimmy was on stage, dancing, with Run-DMC on *Saturday Night Live*. Thanks to his deep background in the drug business, he always had his own stable cocaine connections. He saw himself as a businessman. Still, he understood that "if you're weak your block got taken." He surrounded himself with strong-armed lieutenants. Bimmy would serve time but never took a long bid; he would survive and even prosper, successfully transitioning into the world of hip hop.[31]

Gerald "Prince" Miller was a different sort of man. When Supreme first went to prison in 1985, he bestowed on Prince prime drug-selling territory and told the rest of the crew that his nephew was the street boss. Prince was just two years younger than his uncle. The two men had unbreakable bonds of both family and affection. Prince, though, lacked his uncle's personal magnetism and charm. He instead used violence to keep team members in line. In and out of jail during the late 1980s, Prince maintained his primacy through fear backed up by the open and copious use of violence. He had his own team within the team of hard-knuckled gunmen, which included several Puerto Ricans with fearsome reputations. One of the Team's stalwarts, David "Bing" Robinson, summarized: "Prince was about that gun smoke."[32]

Exactly how many men Prince killed or had killed to protect what he had and to expand his business is unknown, but the number is not small. The federal government claimed that, based on wiretaps and other evidence, they could directly tie Prince to eight murders in 1987 alone.[33] Using information supplied to him by two corrupt New York State Parole Division employees – besides paying them thousands of dollars for information, Prince's top enforcer had a sexual relationship with one of the women and Prince had an intimate relationship with the other – Prince regularly had police informants and potential witnesses killed.

Two stories give a sense for Prince's proclivities. Shortly after Supreme first went to prison in 1985, Prince also went inside for a short bid. Before departing, he turned his crew's drug spots and control of the Team's growing capital over to a trusted lieutenant, Bryan "Fat Pete" Rich. When Prince returned to Baisley Park projects a few months later, he and Fat Pete got into a beef about the status of the Team's money. Fat Pete, immediately thereafter, turned up dead. A government wiretap made at the time of the murder records Prince gleefully announcing to one of his subordinates: "Power. Equality. Truth. Equality." In coded Five Percent speech, Price was calling out the demise of P.E.T.E.[34]

Prince was behind an even more infamous quadruple murder in the summer of 1989. Back in prison for a short bid, he ordered his men to take off and kill a clutch of Colombian wholesalers who had been supplying the Team with duffle bags full of cocaine. At Baisley Park, according to law-enforcement officials, the Colombians were "handcuffed, gagged, strangled, and then they [Prince's men] bashed their skulls [with hammers]."[35] Prince was ticked off when his men told him that the dealers only had 5 kilos on them when they were taken down: "You didn't get ten," he yelled at his main muscle, Ernesto "Puerto Rican Righteous" Piniella.[36]

Pleased about the success of that operation, they repeated it a month later. They lured two more Colombian suppliers to the Baisley Park project. They took off their cocaine and this time affixed plastic bags to the Colombians' heads and, even as they were asphyxiating, a crew member smashed in their skulls with a baseball bat.[37] Worrying about loose ends, Prince's crew then killed one of their own, a Colombian named Gus Rivera, who thought he had ingratiated himself to the Team by introducing them to his fellow Colombians. Prince embraced the murderous violence that pervaded the business of crack cocaine.

During the last years of the 1980s and the early 1990s, Prince was the man most identified with the Supreme Team's great success and its fearsome brutality. Supreme, locked up during the Team's biggest and baddest years, was more street myth than lived presence. Still, both men became the stuff of hip-hop legend. In an often quoted lyric rapper 50 Cent, who grew up in South Queens, explained their reputations: "See, niggas feared Prince and respected Preme ... Preme was the business man and Prince was the killer."[38] Law-enforcement personnel, on the other hand, saw less difference between Prince and Supreme. New York

City prosecutor Carolyn Pokorney, hoping to put Supreme away for life for a series of murders, summed up the state's view of Kenneth "Supreme" McGriff: "That man sitting in the courtroom is one of the most dangerous, feared, ruthless gangsters in all of Queens ... And when Supreme gets in a fight with somebody ... he doesn't go to the cops. He doesn't hire a lawyer. He hires a hit team to assassinate them, to blow them away, so that their moms can barely recognize them when they go down to the morgue."[39]

One of Prince's men insisted that the Supreme Team were not merciless killers of innocent people, that they were more like the old-time gangsters of the 1920s who only took on other underworld figures: "We didn't hold people hostage or terrorize anyone. If a drug dealer got terrorized, that is part of the game. We weren't monsters."[40] The New York City police who patrolled South Queens disagreed. They noted that on just one Sunday night in July 1987, rival crack crews beefing over territory got into a shoot out – "It was like the OK Corral" – and nine local residents uninvolved in the drug business were hit by gunfire. A seventeen-year-old boy, a bystander, was killed protecting his girlfriend. One drug dealer, the actual target, was killed, as well. Prince's crew, the police suspected but could never prove, had set off the gunplay.[41] In 1990, at the height of the crack wars, when crews' need to defend and desire to expand their territory seemed boundless, murders in New York City peaked at 2,245 (in 2017 there were 290). At least a third of those homicides were directly linked to the crack trade.[42] Prince certainly believed that murderous violence was the price of doing business in a trade that had so few other barriers to vastly profitable market participation.

The Supreme Team, under Prince's violence-prone leadership, did not last long. Some of his men, breaking the edict handed down by Biggie, took to smoking crack. They became even more erratic and murderous, drawing more heat from law enforcement. Team loyalists argue that if Supreme had been on the streets this sort of behavior would not have been countenanced, that his leadership would have kept his lieutenants in line, loyal, and less prone to needless, ostentatious violence. The fact that Kenneth "Supreme" McGriff, after being released from prison in 1994, became entangled in multiple murders makes that a hard claim to verify.

The beginning of the end for the Supreme Team came on February 26, 1988. Their direct actions had nothing to do with what ensued. On that day Howard "Pappy" Mason had a police officer assassinated who had been guarding a witness against his drug organization. Four of Pappy's men shot the twenty-two-year-old officer five times in the head. Pappy, along with Fat Cat Nichols, headed the Bebos, Supreme's original drug connect and men with whom the Supreme Team had an ongoing criminal relationship. Pappy was, at the time, imprisoned and he was furious about what he perceived to be police "disrespect." He believed that killing officer Edward Byrne would send the police a strong message to lay off him and his people. The NYPD did not take the message the way Pappy had intended.[43]

Enraged, the NYPD decided instead to wage total war on the city's drug crews, starting in South Jamaica, Queens. The police organized a dedicated unit, the Tactical Narcotics Team or TNT, to flood the area with undercover officers and investigators. They began a massive buy-and-bust operation, aiming to round up the hand-to-hand salesmen and then turn them against their supervisors and on and on until entire drug crews, from top to bottom, were wiped out. Just from March 1988 through September 1988, police arrested 3,772 people involved in the distribution of illegal narcotics, almost all of them crack dealers.[44]

The NYPD, working with the FBI and the DEA, began to dismantle the Supreme Team, arresting multiple low-ranking members. The case against the leaders of the Team, based in part on more than a hundred wiretapped phone conversations made from September 1989 to March 1990, as well as testimony from previously arrested members seeking leniency, was overwhelming. The wiretaps, and other evidence, revealed just how the Supreme Team maintained its hold on the streets. In March 1990, New York state officials arrested Prince and several other high-ranking members of the Supreme Team. Prince hired the best criminal defense attorneys money could buy and beat the charges, including several counts of murder, on procedural grounds. New York City law-enforcement personnel were furious but not finished.

The Supreme Teams' celebration was short-lived. New York state officials turned over their trove of evidence to the Justice Department. The Feds had a better tool to take down the Team. They used the same weapon against the Team that they had used just a few years earlier, for the first time, to destroy the five families of the New York City Mafia: the Racketeer Influenced and Corrupt Organizations Act, aka RICO. Crew leaders were charged federally with "Conducting the affairs of the Supreme Team through a pattern of racketeering." Prince was also specifically charged, as Supreme had been earlier, with "engaging in a continuing criminal enterprise" and a slew of related offenses. Prince, as well as several of the men closest to him, spent a fortune in legal fees, challenging everything imaginable: that the jury was not fairly selected; that the wiretaps used against them were illegal; that the testimony against them was improperly gained; and on and on. This time, none of it worked.

Gerald "Prince" Miller was sentenced to seven concurrent life terms, plus twenty years to be served concurrently. Several of Prince's enforcers also received multiple life sentences. Others fared somewhat better, getting terms in the federal penitentiary of between thirteen years and thirty years. While a number of the Team's major figures escaped the punishing prosecutions of the early 1990s, and continued on as gangsters, selling drugs and wreaking havoc, the Supreme Team, as an organization, was finished.[45]

At the cusp of the 1980s and 1990s, with drug-driven homicides in New York exploding, the NYPD and the FBI did what they could to crush the crack crews. But it was slow work. Even as the NYPD and the FBI concentrated on taking down Prince and the Supreme Team in Queens, other crews took root all over New York. On the Upper West Side of Manhattan, around Amsterdam and 105th (two blocks from where I then lived with my wife and young son) and Columbus and 107th, rival, primarily Puerto Rican gangs, the YTC (Yellow Top Crew), the RTC (Red Top Crew), and the PTC (Purple Top Crew) rose up in murderous competition. The YTC, the dominant crew, sold as many as 10,000 crack vials a day in the early 1990s. Chango, the co-leader of YTC, told an interviewer, "We did what we had to do ... to survive ... In our case, it took killing to survive ... We were good at making difficult decisions. It was better to be dead wrong than just dead."[46] In 1994, forty-eight members of the YTC were indicted and charged with eight murders and thirteen attempted murders. The leaders of the YTC all served lengthy prison sentences.[47]

In Brooklyn, a bunch of rival Jamaican crack posses, including the deadly Gulleymen and the notorious outfit run by Delroy "Uzi" Edwards, dominated the borough; they spread their tentacles as far as Dallas, Philadelphia, and Washington, DC, as well as operating in a slew of smaller towns and suburbs. The Jamaican posses were infamous for their willingness to kill anyone in their way.[48] Other crews, such as Sex Money Murder, born in the South Bronx's Soundview Houses project and led by "Pistol" Pete Rollock, took over street corners all over the Bronx. S.M.M. had boys as young as eleven carrying out shootings against their rivals. Rollock would eventually plead guilty to six murders.[49] Dozens of other crews took corners for weeks, months, or even years before getting wiped out, taken down by the authorities, or, in some cases, adapting and developing to meet their changing circumstances. In NYC, no one gang or even small number of gangs controlled the massive marketplace; it was cut-throat capitalism, all the way.

* * *

The crack trade in New York, while not unique in all regards – violence was a common denominator in almost all major crack scenes – did not represent the way the crack industry developed in many other major markets. Like so many innovative business operations, whether legal or illegal, the crack trade developed locally in accord with specific existing economic circumstances and conditions, the will and wiles of the entrepreneurs who risked entering the industry, and a host of other market-affecting factors. Every big city crack operation had a history all its own, though over time national networks and influences would come to play an ever-larger role in how crack cocaine made its way from supplier to wholesaler to retailer to customer.

In its early years, the crack business in Chicago did not look like the crack business in New York. Critically, major crack distribution came to Chicago several years after it had begun in New York and crack would be distributed not so much by start-up operations like the Supreme Team or smaller crews such as the YTCs but by Chicago's well-established network of huge, if decentralized, street gangs.

In the summer of 1989, Chicago's elite political and law-enforcement circles were still bragging that their city had escaped the murderous violence and community-ravaging effects of crack cocaine. They were generally but not completely correct. Crack was available in Chicago earlier than the authorities claimed: it was being sold in a few South Side neighborhoods by the mid 1980s and crack dealers first began to operate in Robert Taylor Homes, Chicago's biggest public housing complex, in 1985 or early 1986. So crack came to Chicago as a commercial product at roughly the same time that crack was taking off in New York and after it had become a fact of life in Miami, Houston, Los Angeles, and several other cities. But no big-time crews were operating in Chicago during those years, and use was still, comparatively, limited.[50] Chicago's escape from massive crack distribution, however, was short-lived. Even before the Chicago police recognized – or admitted – that crack had come to Chicago in force, the city's venerable African American newspaper, the *Chicago Defender*, had issued a series of warnings. In January 1989 the paper warned, for the first time, of increased use in the city. By February, the *Defender* was covering efforts by community leaders to "halt the growing crack cocaine epidemic plague ravaging poor blacks."[51] The way the crack trade grew in Chicago demonstrated how little role either the police or the politicians had played in staying its course. In fact, during the mid 1980s law enforcement's successful efforts to curtail the more traditional drug trade perversely helped to enable crack's take-off. Crack was just too lucrative a business to stay sidelined in such a big marketplace.

Although crack sales in Chicago were small-scale in the mid 1980s, that did not mean that Chicago was not already awash in illegal drugs. Chicago's illegal drug market, in fact, was so big and so well-established that, for a while, market conditions limited the crack trade.

Until the late 1980s, powerful economic interests had kept crack on the illegal drug market's sidelines. Chicago's illegal drug players were already making big money running a stable, lucrative business. Like leaders of any quasi-monopolistic industry, they resisted market innovation. They understood the risk crack portended for their business model. Crack was a low-tech, low-capitalization product. Thus it was also potentially market-disrupting.

If enough people could connect with out-of-town crack suppliers or source enough cocaine locally to cook up their own crack, Chicago's well-organized illegal drug industry would become wide open to newcomers. Old, hierarchically organized drug-selling networks and alliances would then come under threat, as even established players would have to fight to control distribution of a new product. Legal industries would have fought back by buying up patents, issuing lawsuits, crafting big-business-favoring regulatory regimes with supportive government officials. But the illegal drug trade could not turn to the legal tools oligopolistic corporations used to keep out pesky, market-challenging innovators. So they did the best they could with the weapons they had. They used violence – or the threat of violence – to marginalize crack entrepreneurs and keep them out of the city's major illegal drug markets.

Given such market constraints, crack crews arrived in Chicago in marginal markets on its periphery. Nascent crack dealers targeted several of Chicago's low-income, predominately black suburbs located south, southwest, and west of the city. These economically banged-up communities had two things going for them: with minimal tax bases they had little effective law enforcement and, relative to Chicago, they had no major, ongoing gang presence. As one suburban law-enforcement official put it, crack entrepreneurs were searching for locations not under the control of the city's major and lethal street gangs; they wanted "virgin soil ... Dealers figure they can come here and start their own thing."[52] The biggest set-up was in the economically devastated and nearly lawless small southwestern suburb, Robbins, which quickly acquired the sobriquet, "Rockville."

Around that time, probably in 1987, Norman Tillman, a Chicago-born-and-raised young man who had moved to Los Angeles and become involved with "Freeway" Ricky Ross's massive cocaine and crack empire, returned to Chicago. His aim was to transport large quantities of cocaine from LA to Chicago so as to set up a major crack-distribution ring. It's possible that he already had made connections with – or even supplied – the crack dealers in Robbins. The first black Cook County District Attorney, Cecil Partee, later argued that the first crack dealers in Chicago's low-income black suburbs were supplied by Los Angeles street gangs – and Tillman, besides operating as a lieutenant to LA cocaine kingpin Ricky Ross, had strong connections to the LA-based Crips, who along with their rivals, the Bloods, played a substantial role in distributing crack in LA and were fast branching out to other cities.[53]

Whatever small forays Tillman and/or the Crips had already made into the Chicago market, Tillman wanted to hit the crack mother lode. He understood that the only way to breach the big Chicago drug market was to find a reliable partner. The Crips had at that time only limited alliances in Chicago. Tillman needed to work with one of Chicago's super gangs who had well-established, fiercely enforced, territorially based distribution networks.

Tillman had connections. He approached old friends in the El Rukns. They told him that they had their own thing and were not interested in his proposition. When they demurred, Tillman, seeing no real option, pressed forward. He began his own operation. "In less than a day," he told an interviewer, "he got a visit from his El Rukn buddies, who told him that not only was he to stop serving [selling crack], he shouldn't be seen again in Chicago unless he wanted to be killed." Authors sympathetic to the El Rukns have suggested that the El Rukns' leadership suppressed crack sales – as their predecessors had done with heroin some twenty years earlier, going so far as to kill a heroin dealer – out of regard for the damage it would do to their communities.[54] When Tillman was asked if the El Rukns "refused to distribute crack because they were protecting the black community, he laughed. He said the El Rukns only wanted to protect their control of the market ... Their decision not to sell crack was strictly business, not moral."[55] Tillman left Chicago and opened up shop elsewhere, at least temporarily. Chicago's crack trade stayed modest and peripheral for a little longer.

Two major market disruptions opened up the crack business in Chicago. These disruptions came, ironically, not from plucky entrepreneurs – there is no Steve Jobs in the story of crack in Chicago – but from federal and city authorities' well-intentioned and largely successful efforts to crack down on some of the most violent and dangerous illegal narcotics operations in Chicago. Beginning in 1985, the feds went after the Herrera Family, the leading narcotics suppliers in the city. Soon thereafter, the Chicago police, in partnership with the FBI, went after the leadership of the El Rukns, as well as several other Chicago gang leaders. In the last half of the 1980s, law enforcement successfully brought some ruthless criminals to justice but they also created a far more open, disorganized drug market in Chicago. Crack dealers rushed in and made their play.

Up until 1987, the Herrera family, which operated out of the Mexican state of Durango, as well as Sinaloa and Jalisco, controlled the supply of heroin and played a substantial role in bringing cocaine to Chicago. With some 2,000 members, the Herrera organization processed its own heroin from the poppy fields that dotted the Sierra Madres and then trucked shipments through El Paso up to Chicago where it was distributed.[56] They'd been using Chicago for their heroin-exporting business since at least the 1950s. Their business had expanded dramatically when the Mafia-allied "French Connection" ring that had smuggled "white heroin" into the United States and Canada through New York City and Montreal had been disrupted in 1972 (it continued operating but out of Mexico City, Buenos Aires, and other areas). This market disruption opened up new opportunities for Mexican smugglers of so-called brown heroin or "Mexican mud." By 1977, the Chicago Police Department estimated that 99 percent of all major heroin dealers in Chicago belonged to the Herrera family. Those dealers distributed to smaller-scale retail dealers, including members of Chicago's major street gangs, dominated by the Vice Lords, the Black Gangster Disciples (later the Gangster Disciples), and the P. Stone Nation/El Rukns, but also including Puerto Rican gangs such as the Latin Kings. In the late 1970s, the Herrera family branched out into the marijuana and cocaine business (they acted as intermediaries for the Colombian cartels), using their well-established smuggling and distribution networks.[57]

The Herrera family also controlled a major share of Chicago's cocaine supply, though not to the degree that they monopolized the heroin trade. Still, cocaine prices in Chicago, until the late 1980s, were much higher than in cities such as Los Angeles, Miami, or New York City, in part due to the Herrera family's ability to control price through market domination. The high price of cocaine in Chicago adversely impacted the crack trade, which depended on low prices. All this began to change in 1985, when federal authorities went to war with the Herrera family in Chicago. In July of that year, some 500 federal agents from six different federal agencies raided the Herrera family's Chicago operations – as well as other Herrera strongholds, including their stash houses in a desolate neighborhood in nearby Gary, Indiana, which had only a dozen years before been a thriving steel town but had become by the mid 1980s a deindustrialized wasteland.

The feds arrested some 120 members of the Herrera ring and used the 1984 Comprehensive Crime Control Act to seize $1.5 million in cash, 31 houses and apartment buildings, gasoline stations, candy stores, restaurants, taverns, jewelry stores, and so many automobiles the Justice Department lost count. The Justice Department stated that all of these assets had been used in the Herreras' drug operation. The heads of the family were jailed and then sentenced to lengthy prison terms.[58] The DEA, now working with the Chicago police, kept after the operation and in July 1988 took down what they believed to be the Herrera family's last remaining stash, a garage filled with 240 pounds of heroin and 120 pounds of cocaine. No Chicago police were involved in the operation. For more than two decades the CPD had done almost nothing about the Herrera family business.

The arrest of the Herrera family did not stop the flow of heroin or cocaine into Chicago, though it did disrupt the heroin business for a while. Other Mexican cartels, which were already invested in smuggling cocaine into Chicago, rushed to take a larger share of the fluid market. Cocaine distributors from other markets, including Los Angeles, also saw new opportunities to take advantage of the supply disruption and price differentials between their price and Chicago's traditionally higher prices.

Thus, in late 1988, the take-down of the Herrera family did not close down the narcotics market in Chicago. Instead, it helped to open it up, as suppliers competed for new distributors and dealers. In the late 1980s and early 1990s, the price of cocaine dropped in Chicago, enabling the sale of cheap crack, and competition over territory intensified.

As the price of cocaine fell in the late 1980s, a robust illegal market developed in both the city and the suburbs. In white areas, cocaine was a highly decentralized business that operated out of bars and taverns and restaurants, as well as through private networks. In Chicago's black neighborhoods, a few well-organized super gangs largely oversaw the drug business. In the mid 1980s, gang members often acted as retail distributors for major African American wholesalers, such as Willie "Flukey" Stokes (infamous in Chicago for burying his murdered drug-dealing son upright at the steering wheel of a mock Cadillac). Or the gangs traded protection to the dealers' own networks in exchange for financial incentives. By the mid 1980s, all of Chicago's major gangs controlled drug-selling territories. Their biggest operations were in and around the massive, lawless public housing developments – the Robert Taylor Homes, Stateway Gardens, Cabrini-Green, and others – that stood as stark landmarks to the city's segregated housing patterns.

In the mid 1980s, Chicago arguably had the most organized street gang system in the United States. Chicago's street gangs, of all races and ethnicities, had been around since the early twentieth century but until the 1960s, they had mostly been social clubs in which fistfights with rival gangs served as their *raison d'etre*. In the late 1960s, a few African American and Puerto Rican gangs began to turn their attention to more profitable enterprises. One of the original members of a major, Stones-affiliated, West Side Chicago street gang, the Four Corner Hustlers, explains: "They're starting out trying to protect a neighborhood ... Well, after you protect the neighborhood, what are you going to do with it? The members of the gang are going to say there's a lot of money in this business: 'We can do cars; we can get a chop shop.' And that money is going to make you want more money. And the most money is in drugs."[59] By the early 1970s, extortion, drug dealing, and other illegal activities put a premium on controlling territory and Chicago's gangs began to compete viciously and violently.

In 1978, to bring some peace to this chaotic and dangerous realm – especially in prison, where rival gangs were forced to live precariously in close quarters – gang leaders crafted an extraordinary Westphalian peace which divided Chicago into two rival factions: Folk Nation, which included the Black Gangster Disciples, and the Latin Eagles; and the People Nation, which included the Almighty Black P. Stone Nation, Vice Lords, Latin Kings, and the Mickey Cobras. These consolidated gangs distributed or facilitated the sale of relatively small amounts of cocaine, as well as larger quantities of heroin, in a highly organized fashion, primarily in Chicago's black and Puerto Rican neighborhoods. The Black P. Stone Nation, then the largest gang, also distributed massive amounts of "syrup" (a codeine-based drink) and huge amounts of "Ts", also known as "Blues," a cheap heroin substitute that was an injectable combination of the opioid Talwin and the antihistamine Tripelennamine. By the mid 1980s, Chicago's major drug-dealing gangs had crafted a lucrative and steady business.

In the late 1980s, these gangs began going through a period of law-enforcement-induced disruption. The El Rukns, in particular, were hit hard, opening up their territory, as well as their business operations.

El Rukn was a storied gang that had gone through several iterations. First known as the Blackstone Rangers, the gang had taken a political turn in the 1960s and had even received several large federal community grants (though they were soon thereafter indicted for criminally misusing the funds). Then, under the continuing leadership of the talented and charismatic Jeff Fort, members embraced Moorish Science, a home-grown African-American-inspired form of Islam. Despite such religious trappings and beliefs, the gang increasingly turned to criminal activities and became a dominant force in the drug industry on Chicago's South Side.[60]

Even as they invested heavily in territorial-based criminal activities, the El Rukns made forays into the wider world. Their most improbable effort took place in 1986 when they used a connection to negotiate a terrorism for-cash-and-weapons deal with the "Brotherly Leader" of Libya, Muammar al-Gaddafi. Though El Rukn leaders did meet with Libyan officials outside of the United States, before any terrorist activities ensued – and it was never clear if the gang members were working a hustle or actually intended to commit the terrorist acts – federal authorities indicted them. Jeff Fort, who was already imprisoned, and four other leaders of the organization were found guilty of conspiracy to commit terrorism.

Other trials targeting the leadership of the El Rukns for other major crimes quickly followed, including murder charges. The special prosecutor in charge of the murder case declared at the end of the successful trial that the El Rukns were finished: "There's just no leadership anymore."[61] He was right. On the streets the El Rukns were in free fall. The remaining leaders of the Mighty P. Stone Nation, which the El Rukns had dominated, had to decide how to keep their members paid, and thus loyal.

Once under rigid hierarchical control, by the late 1980s the Mighty P. Stone Nation was in organizational disarray. Though members still called themselves "Moes" (a vernacular twist on the word "Moors") and called out "Behold the Almighty Blackstone!" set leaders (sets are individual gangs within the larger super gang structure) were increasingly on their own.

As key gang leaders went down by law, the super gangs' relatively orderly narcotics business model came under stress, opening the door to more entrepreneurial activities on the part of ambitious "sets" who felt free to innovate. Un-incarcerated individual gang leaders, supported by their members, began to set up their own operations, searching out new drug connections and new market plays. Outsiders, too, saw that the relative organizational chaos and market flux offered them an opportunity to breach Chicago's boundaries.

The aforementioned Norman Tillman, for example, rushed in. With the El Rukns out of the way, and demand for wholesale cocaine connections high, he returned to Chicago in late 1989 and opened up negotiations with several different Chicago gangs – not at the highest levels of the gang hierarchy but with individual set leaders who were looking to make money in the new, less controlled, chaotic business atmosphere. Tillman soon worked out arrangements and opened multiple crack cookhouses, which supplied numerous Chicago gangs on the south and west Sides with product. He claims that by early 1990 he was wholesaling 50 kilos of crack a week, bringing in $9 million a month.[62] He was not alone. By early 1990, less than a year after Chicago's police leadership declared that Chicago had no crack problem, the city's black neighborhoods were awash in crack cocaine.

Chicago's largest gangs quickly came to accept and then dominate the crack trade. From his prison cell, Jeff Fort gave his blessings to new men willing to step into the breach and keep the Stones strong. Reno Wooldridge was at the top of that new pyramid; operating only below Jeff Fort, aka Chief Malik, and Fort's son, known as Prince. Wooldridge was, in Stone's terminology, the *Kaaba*, a title taken from Islam's most sacred site in Mecca. Title aside, Wooldridge had little interest in Islam. He was, as Stones insider, author, and Chicago street-gang expert Lance Williams declares, "a big-time player in the crack game ... [he] served as one of the middlemen between the Blackstone Nation and other street gangs, local mafias, and other organized crime groups that were plugged into international drug cartels." Wooldridge had made his way to the top of the Blackstone nation not through his prowess as a gang leader but through his cocaine connections. According to Williams: "the new gang chiefs were guys who had enough money to buy their rank and the muscle to impose it."[63]

Beginning in 1990, Reno Wooldridge, who worked closely with his twin brother, Deno, was on a mission to turn South Side sets of the Nation into a crack-selling army. Lance Williams tells a vivid story of how one set with whom he had a long-standing and continuing relationship, the 8-Tray Stones, became part of that army.[64]

By 1990, with the Almighty P. Stone Nation's once feared and respected leadership broken and divided, the 8-Tray Stones had largely gone their own way. Some of the members sold cocaine and crack. But the set leadership was not formally involved and the individual sellers were small-time with no solid drug connections. All that changed in the summer of 1992. One evening, about 50 members of the 450-members-strong 8-Tray Stones were hanging out deep in their territory on 85th and Carpenter when they spotted a cavalcade of 30 cars driving slowly toward them. The procession pulled up in front of them, came to a stop, and in synchronized fashion car doors popped open and four men stepped out of each vehicle – 120 strong. They presented themselves peacefully, shouting "All well, Moe," and with their hands out in the "ritual Blackstone greeting" that ended when each visiting gang member "balled up his fist and pounded his chest over his heart to represent Stone love."[65]

Wooldridge then asked to speak privately with the leaders of the 8-Tray Stones. He told them that it was time for the Nation to reintegrate under his authority. Despite the mighty entourage he had brought with him, he did not threaten the 8-Tray Stones. Wooldridge was not trying to pull off a hostile takeover. Instead he offered the 8-Tray Stones a choice: they could continue as they had been doing, running their territory as they saw fit, but if they made that choice they had to stop calling them-selves "Blackstones" and they would be unprotected from other gangs' encroachments. On the other hand, Wooldridge explained, they could become a part of a new unified Blackstone set that would stretch across a wide swathe of the South Side that Wooldridge was calling, in accord with his privileged rank, the "Holy City of Mecca."

Wooldridge was proposing a merger to the 8-Tray Stones. As members of the superset they would have the unified protection and respect of all of its members. More instrumentally, as part of that superset, the 8-Tray Stones would be provided with large quantities of cocaine, which would be cooked into crack. 8-Tray leaders, like other set leaders, would be granted packages of 2 to 8 kilos of cocaine at a time which they would then process and divvy up to their members for street sales. As Lance Williams concludes, the 8-Tray Stones "got in line with Reno, and as promised, 8-Tray began to eat very well."[66] The 8-Tray Stones, and many other Blackstone sets, were suddenly well-oiled cogs in a massive crack enterprise that stretched across Chicago's South Side. Set leaders were making hundreds of thousands of dollars, while hand-to-hand street sellers generally made $100 to $200 a day. Reno and Deno Wooldridge, at least according to Williams, made millions of dollars.[67]

Reno Wooldridge did not have much time to enjoy his wealth. He was shot dead by an unknown assassin a little over a year after he induced the 8-Tray Stones to join his network. He was twenty-four when he was murdered in the fall of 1993. His twin brother Deno was gunned down eight years later (and to compound the horror, Reno's son, Reno, Junior, was eventually murdered in a gangland shooting, as was Deno's son, "Lil" Deno).

The 8-Tray Stones, too, had little time to enjoy their newfound wealth in peace. Not long after Reno was murdered, two police officers confronted the co-leader of the 8-Tray Stones, twenty-one-year-old Christopher "Loopy" Keys, who was sitting inside his car outside his home. The police claimed that Keys started to drive away, hit one of the officers, and so, fearing for their lives, the other officer opened fire on Keys through the front windshield. Keys died on the scene with multiple gunshot wounds and thirty-one bags of crack inside his coat sleeve.[68] Loopy's death opened up a rift within the 8-Tray Stones and over the next weeks and months the gang imploded; an internecine, murderous war over leadership and control of drug spots tore the 8-Tray Stones apart. Plenty of other sets were more than happy to take advantage of the 8-Tray Stones troubles; crack sales continued unabated on the South Side.

The affiliated sets of the Almighty P. Stone Nation were major players in Chicago's crack trade but they were not the biggest. The Gangster Disciples, run by Larry Hoover from his prison cell, was the most successful crack distributor in the city and, for a while, maybe in the nation. They were also one of the most efficiently organized and highly structured gangs in the entire United States.[69] According to the United States District Attorney in Chicago, the Gangster Disciples were selling $100 million a year in drugs, the bulk of it via crack sales, in the early 1990s. At their peak, some 30,000 people sold drugs, at least part-time, for the GDs in the Chicago area.[70] The GDs sold their drugs all over the city's predominately African American neighborhoods on the south and west sides, but elsewhere in the city and suburbs, as well. They dominated many of the biggest public housing complexes in Chicago, including most of the twenty-eight sixteen-story buildings that comprised the Robert Taylor Homes, which ran for two miles on Chicago's South Side, not far from Lake Michigan. Some 25,000 people, overwhelmingly poor and officially unemployed, lived in what a *Chicago Tribune* reporter, in one of many exposés about the horrors of the project, called "vertical prisons."[71] With its built-in clientele, easily defended spaces, residents' general antipathy to the police, and its history of underground and illegal enterprises, it was an ideal place to sell crack.

The GDs also controlled most of the buildings in one of the only huge public housing projects on Chicago's Northside, the Cabrini-Green Homes, with its 15,000 residents. Despite its location close to affluent, largely white neighborhoods, Cabrini-Green was located in an area that had long been regarded as a slum and was almost completely made up of poor African American families, though a number of working-class families fought hard to co-exist there, as well. Cabrini-Green had the advantage of being close enough to white neighborhoods to draw white patrons to its drug marketplace, though its well-deserved reputation for violent criminality was so fierce that sales to whites were almost always on the project's periphery and most whites never left their autos when making their purchases.[72]

The Gangster Disciples' operations at Cabrini-Green exemplified their general business model. They were rigidly hierarchical in structure, highly disciplined, and resisted all challenges to their territory with extreme violence. According to gang historian Zach Jones, the GDs ran a tight operation there twenty-four hours a day. To keep thieves, robbers, and rivals at bay, heavily armed "soldiers" patrolled the projects non-stop, regularly searched anyone they found suspicious, and even, for a while, enforced a night-time curfew on non-drug-buying residents to keep the selling areas clear for customers during peak late-night business hours. Any gang member who slacked off or dogged his security responsibilities was given a beat down. Every night (weather permitting), all members of the GD crews met in the project's central courtyard and, in full view of residents and any snooping authorities, engaged in rigorous physical exercise. The GDs were a constant menacing, intimidating presence.[73]

Larry Hoover, who referred to himself as Chairman of the Board, organized the Gangster Disciples from the top down. Hoover had been a gangster since he was a child. Born in Mississippi in November 1950, his mother brought him to Chicago in 1955 and he grew up in Englewood on the South Side. The neighborhood had been racially integrated and majority working-class white when Hoover arrived, but not for long. By the time Hoover and the Gangster Disciples controlled the community it was the most racially segregated neighborhood in Chicago – "Not even the ethnic cleansing in the Balkans achieved the level of turnover that white flight in Chicago did," reported a local television channel, looking back at Englewood's rapid demographic changes.[74]

Hoover started his career as a gangster at twelve, when he joined the Supreme Gangsters and before he was fourteen he was its shot caller. Rumors spread that he had killed the gang's founder. By the end of 1968, the gang prodigy was leading a rapidly expanding Gangster Nation. After an attempted alliance with the Blackstone Rangers ended in murderous violence, Hoover led his people into formation, instead, with the Black Disciples, then under the leadership of legendary Chicago gang leader "King" David Barksdale. The Black Gangster Disciples Nation – BGDN – was born. Over the next several years, terrible violence ensued between the BGDs and the Black P. Stones. Barksdale was shot up and eventually died from his wounds. Larry Hoover, meanwhile, focused on expanding and controlling the BGD's extortion and drug-dealing operations. To instill discipline on the streets, he ordered the murder of a local teenager who had stolen narcotics from the gang. Hoover was arrested for the murder, convicted, and on November 5, 1973, just short of his twenty-third birthday, he was sentenced to serve 150 to 200 years in Statesville Prison, which is located about an hour southwest of Chicago.[75]

Hoover's reputation and power actually grew in prison. He led prison strikes demanding better food and conditions. Then, transferred to the state prison in Pontiac, he led a 1978 prison riot to protest against abysmal conditions – three guards died in the riot; Hoover was indicted for the murders, but no one would testify against him. Soon after (and as noted earlier), to stop out-of-control violence between incarcerated rival gang members in the Illinois prison system, he organized a meeting of the incarcerated leadership of most of Chicago's major gangs – not sets, but the actual gangs; e.g., the Vice Lords, El Rukns, Spanish Disciples, Latin Kings, Mickey Cobras, and many others – and helped to institutionalize the great divide between two mighty alliances, the Folk Nation and the People Nation, aimed primarily at keeping the peace within the entire state prison system through a system of negotiation between members.

Beginning in 1981, in a bid to gain better treatment in prison and a transfer to a minimum-security facility – and eventually parole – Hoover orchestrated a good-will campaign. Working with a well-educated and highly articulate GD member, Hoover began issuing a long series of communiqués under the rubric of "Brothers of the Struggle," that instructed gang members inside and outside of prison on how to behave and how to organize: "We as an Organization of young Black Men cannot allow ourselves to stay confined behind walls and locked in cages to slowly grow old and useless. Through Business and Politics, we can build an economical base that will insure us boundless power and wealth. But if we stay uneducated and without political power, prisons and death will continue to be a way of life for many of us."[76] In addition to such exhortations, Hoover instructed his BGD members they must not hurt guards or other prison personnel – unless clearly ordered to do so. Hoover's separate peace with prison authorities and his efforts to educate gang members worked: in 1987 Hoover was transferred from a maximum-security state prison to a minimum-security facility. Hoover now had unlimited phone access to his cronies and wide-open visitors' hours. Running his business had become much easier. The timing could not have been better – the crack trade was on the near horizon.

Even while burnishing his credentials inside and outside prison, Hoover was tightening his control of his gang empire and expanding its criminal reach. In the 1980s, he set up two "boards of directors." He was chairman of each. One was inside the prison system. It kept order and managed the BGD's various inside hustles. The other board ran the BGD's ever-increasing gang membership and street operations. Under the supervision of the outside Board were a number of "Governors" who ran district drug sales.

By time the Gangster Disciples (around 1990, due to various beefs, the Black Gangster Disciples fragmented and Hoover's followers became the Gangster Disciples) were developing the crack trade in 1990, each Governor, assisted by "Regents" and "Coordinators," ran around a thousand "Foot Soldiers." These were the gang members who actually handled the nitty-gritty of distributing and selling the drugs. At times, crack markets were so hot that the gang let independent drug dealers – known as "Neutrons" – operate on their turf. The Neutrons paid a tax for the privilege. Gang revenues from crack sales were so high that Hoover instituted a special "political" tax on all drug sales that went toward a kind of gang-affiliated political-action committee, called 21st Century V.O.T.E. Hoover used the money to gain the support of Chicago black politicians, including the city's former mayor, Eugene Sawyer, and several aldermen, as well as a number of well-known ministers and community leaders, all of whom began lobbying for Hoover's release from prison. In 1993, Hoover added another levy on the drug sellers; he called it "One Day a Week" or "Nation Dope." Dealers' proceeds from one day a week selling crack – or whatever narcotics they marketed – would go to Hoover's personal account. Governors were instructed to inform all interested parties that if they refused they would be killed: "One day a week ain't much to ask for your life."[77]

In 1993, Hoover put some of his wealth to work. In the months before his August parole hearing he orchestrated a major effort to persuade the Illinois Prisoner Review Board to release him from custody. To rally supporters and to demonstrate the Gangster Disciples' political power, Hoover sponsored a picnic on a farm outside of Chicago. Ten thousand gang members and their families attended. A petition with 5,000 signatures, which included a number of the leading black politicians in Chicago, was presented to the Board. Alderman Virgil Jones was one of several who wrote individually to the Board, "I feel that after two decades in the Illinois Penal System Larry Hoover has shown that he understands what it means to be a productive member of society ... Larry Hoover has shown that he can be a positive role model for young men and women in the African American Community."[78] Gang scholar George Knox argues that certain individuals were paid up to $50,000 each to testify on Hoover's behalf before the review board. Law-enforcement authorities – which were at that time four years into an investigation of the Gangster Disciples' drug operation – heavily supported by articles in the *Chicago Tribune*, made the case against Hoover's parole. Hoover was not released, but the struggle continues; in 2018 renowned rapper Kanye West, who was raised in Chicago, visited the White House and asked President Donald Trump to pardon Hoover.

Hoover's empire came crashing down in 1995. Federal authorities brought a fifty-count indictment against him. Thirty-eight of his main men, many of whom had loyally reported to him at his minimum-security facility, were charged as well. The feds had used an ingenuous trick to gain information on the gang. For six weeks in 1993, a listening device had been inserted into the laminated visitors' badges that Hoover's people had been required to wear when they met with Hoover. Recorded conversations revealed a bevy of crimes that went back twenty-five years. Federal authorities also argued that Hoover and his people had used 21st Century V.O.T.E. to launder substantial amounts of money. Save the Children, Inc., an organization run by Hoover's wife, that sponsored a bevy of hip-hop concerts that were supposedly used to fund community activities, also came under indictment as a drug-money-laundering operation.[79] Hoover and dozens of his lieutenants received lengthy prison sentences.

Perhaps more significantly, Hoover was removed from his Illinois prison and in 1997 sent to the United States Penitentiary Administrative Maximum Facility in Florence, Colorado. At the "supermax" facility, outside communications were severely limited and Hoover was, after running his organization from prison for nearly a quarter of a century, cut off from his people. The Gangster Disciples, of course, were not finished, nor was their control of huge swathes of the illegal drug trade but the extraordinary order and discipline Hoover had brought to the sale of crack and other narcotics in Chicago would devolve in the years that followed, unleashing, in general, new waves of violence.

* * *

Chicago and New York represent just two ways in which crack cocaine came to market. Neither city, however, was the biggest player in the crack trade. Los Angeles probably holds that distinction – not because of the extent of its crack sales (though it did sustain a robust marketplace), but because it supplied the cocaine that fed the crack trade in many other US cities. According to federal authorities, by 1989 LA street gangs – Bloods and Crips – were supplying forty-two cities with the cocaine that sustained their crack markets.

LA had a big cocaine trade by the late 1970s, but it became America's cocaine capital in the mid 1980s because of an external disruption in US supply networks. In the early 1980s, federal authorities targeted the Colombian cartels' supply routes and distribution networks in South Florida. Rather than give up and find a new way to make a living, Colombian suppliers worked with Mexican narcotics trafficking organizations – experienced in bringing heroin and marijuana into the United States – to transport their cocaine. LA offered opportunity. It was conveniently located near the border, it was economically bustling, and it had a heavily trafficked and decentralized highway system. Thus LA became the Mexican smugglers' cocaine hub. As an exasperated DEA agent explained, thwarting the illegal drug business is like "squeezing a half-inflated balloon … When one route into the country is plugged another sprouts." Tons of cocaine came in by the truckload and by 1985 the price of coke in LA had dropped below the price in Miami. Relatively cheap coke from LA fueled crack startups here, there and everywhere.[80]

Big-time players abounded in LA. "Freeway" Ricky Ross became one of the best known, though not solely because of the extent of his sales. He famously claimed that his crack operations were supplied by a CIA-protected Nicaraguan cocaine dealer, and thus – according to this reasoning – the federal government was behind the crack trade. There was a touch of truth to his claims: his Nicaraguan connect was, for a time, connected to the Reagan administration-supported Nicaraguan Contras, who were very much protected by the CIA. Still, the coke that Ross bought from his Nicaraguan connect was just a small bit of the massive loads of Colombian cocaine the Mexican cartels were delivering to LA.

A less-publicized crack and powder cocaine kingpin, Brian "Waterhead Bo" Bennett, was more representative of the LA trade. Bennett had a direct connection with a major Colombian importer, Mario Ernesto Villabona-Alverado, who regularly brought a ton of cocaine to LA every month. Bennett, in turn, supplied a multitude of crack houses run by LA gang members; he used those same gangsters to run cocaine, destined for the crack market, all over the country.[81] In LA, crack cocaine was a multi-tiered, import–export business that made poor men millionaires and created national criminal networks that surpassed the gory exploits of the glorified gangsters of 1920s prohibition-era America.

By the early 1990s, the US crack cocaine industry had operations in every major city, many towns, and plenty of suburbs. In this process, business rivalries and flexible alliances created new ethnic relations. Black-only gangs such as the Black Gangster Disciples opened their ranks to members of all races in order to expand their crack-distribution networks. In different cities and regions, Puerto Ricans, Dominicans, Mexicans, Haitians, Jamaicans, Colombians, and African Americans sorted out the crack business, sometimes amiably but more often violently. And while no whites seemed to have operated as crack kingpins or major distributors, they too, played their parts, dealing and most certainly buying.

The crack business made a lot of people who lived well outside the bounds of legitimate law-abiding society rich – at least temporarily. But to make the millions that made those men rich, a lot of customers had to be found.

CHAPTER 3

Crack Up: The Cost of Hard-Core Consumption

I N PHILADELPHIA, A CITY THAT ARGUABLY HAD MORE CRACK
users, per capita, than any other, a dealer mused about his clientele:
"The girls like 'the girl' [crack], the boys like 'the girl' … That glass dick
[the crack pipe]. They puffin' away for the genie in the glass bottle. Ha-
heh."[1] By 1991, more than four million people had smoked crack.[2]
Whites made up the majority of those people. Even though pretty
much every mass media story and politicians' claim emphasized the
addictive power of crack, the vast majority of people who smoked crack
did not become addicted to the drug. Most smoked recreationally, rarely,
or they tried it once or maybe a few times and then stopped. But the
biggest consumers, the people the crack crews depended on for their
profits, those were the addicts, the people, as the Philly crack dealer put
it, who put their lives in the hands of the "genie in the glass bottle."

In 1990, the federal government determined, about half a million
people smoked crack chronically. Some hit the pipe every day. More
binged. They smoked crack for days at a time, sometimes for as long as
they could find a way to pay, and then stopped until the next time. They
might go for a day, a week, or even a month without crack. Then they'd
binge all over again.[3]

Poor people – most especially urban black poor people – made up the
majority of heavy users.[4] Historically, poor women, as compared to men,
had avoided hard, habit-forming drugs. Not crack.[5] As the Philly dealer
noted, crack dealers had a customer base that crossed the gender line.
The number of hard-core crack users skyrocketed between 1985 and
1990 and stayed strong until the mid 1990s, even as the number of
recreational users of powder cocaine declined by nearly half.[6] As white,

78

Figure 6 Smoking crack: A woman smoking crack in Brooklyn in 1991. Women took to crack cocaine in tragic numbers. (Andrew Lichtenstein/Corbis via Getty Images.)

wealthier users of powder cocaine began to turn away from their decade-long indulgence, poor people increased their demand for crack's brief but overwhelming rush.

Those who succumbed to their need for crack's monstrous high would often do almost anything to get it, ravaging their families, their communities, and themselves. Many of crack's most devoted users were cut off from the mainstream economy. So, to pay for their rock, they did what they could. Some women, and some men, too, traded sex directly for crack. Many robbed and thieved. Often they started with their family and friends. Women often turned to prostitution. Crackheads, to use the pejorative term of the times, were a boon to the criminal economy.

* * *

People became crack customers because they wanted to get really high, really fast, in a very specific fashion. Few people who smoked crack were unfamiliar with getting high. Almost all crack users had used other illegal drugs. They were already good drug customers. But there was something

Figure 7 Crack house interior: A crack house in Baltimore. Amidst all the debris, note the crack vials littering the floor. (Peter Moskos.)

about crack that really appealed to a subset of people who liked to get high.

Crack hits the brain hard. "A bell-ringer," some report. The crack high is a powder coke high but – wham – it comes on much faster, it is more compressed, and it is more intense. Heart rate accelerates, as does breathing and blood pressure; you might feel jittery. For a few lovely minutes, crack wipes away despair and boredom; euphoria rules the mind. Whatever your level of pulchritude and fitness, you feel sexy and ready for action. You feel vibrant and sharp, even if others might find you confused, confusing, and maybe kind of crazy. The first hit is usually the best and the first high usually lasts the longest. Because you come down fast, most people immediately want more to keep the good feeling going.[7]

At the height of the crack years, an intellectually astute, white middle-class journalist heroically smoked a few hits of crack so he could explain its effects to other people of his sort, most of whom were unlikely to try it for themselves. Mostly, Jefferson Morley described what others have recounted, albeit in a wittier fashion:

Smoke a rock and, for the next 20 minutes, you will likely appreciate
sensuous phenomena ranging from MTV to neon lights to oral sex with
renewed urgency ... the crack high combines the best aspects of marijuana
and cocaine ... spacey and intense ... you may notice that your world looks
just fine, as do various of the women (or men) in it. Reality isn't real and all
that was formerly a possibility is now on the verge of actuality. You'll want
to turn up the music and maybe your sexual aggression quotient. You'll
gain new insight into why crack is so popular among women.

Morley goes on to guess at why crack might appeal, in particular, to
people who had been locked out of the economic boom times of the
late 1980s and early 1990s: "You can be a moral tourist in the land of crack
and still get a sense of how the drug can make sick sense to demoralized
people. If all you have in life is bad choices, crack may not be the most
unpleasant of them."[8]

Crack's hard-core users describe their high with a similar sense of
exaltation. And, as Morley suggested, the more self-reflective at least hint
at the desperation they hope crack can keep at bay. "Alice," a poor black
woman in Atlanta, told a Dutch drug researcher about her first time: "It's
like you get to go to heaven for a second." But she adds, "No kidding, I
thought I was gonna die, but a pleasant death." Another chronic user in
Atlanta told of similar feelings: "The first time was a real spiritual experience for me." But that feeling of holy elevation did not, she recounts, last.
The more she smoked the less crack gave her: "Now I need a rock so I can
keep on going. It went from crack making me feel good to crack being
the medicine for the pain I caused myself to have."[9]

Plenty of chronic crack users spoke little of matters spiritual or elevat-
ing. They just really liked the high: "I liked it. It gave me a real, real heavy
head rush, real heavy head rush."[10] Another: "The only reason I get high
is because I love it ... It's a brain thing. It's thick. Once you take that first
blast, then the whole night is going to be a total adventure into madness.
It's just a thing, you have to have more."[11] Heavy crack users believed that
crack's high was better than what they could get from powder cocaine
and it was better than marijuana, drugs almost all serious crack users had
used – and many continued to use – regularly before turning preferen-
tially to crack.

In the late 1980s and early 1990s, politicians, the mass media, and even a surprising number of drug and public-health experts declared that crack use had become epidemic in the United States. It wasn't, at least not in the normal sense of the word. Two of the most sophisticated scholars of the crack years, sociologists Craig Reinarman and Harry G. Levine, argue that, obviously and overwhelmingly, broad swathes of Americans never used or even considered smoking crack cocaine. So, at the national level, crack was no epidemic. Despite widely shared fears, it did not spread like a "plague" to the middle class or to white suburbia or to working-class people of any description. But, Reinarman and Levine write, "An 'epidemic of crack use' might be a description of what happened among a distinct minority of teenagers and young adults from impoverished neighborhoods."[12]

Crack hit certain neighborhoods, almost always poor or economically declining neighborhoods, like a bomb. Corey Pegues, the erstwhile junior crack dealer discussed earlier, does not mince words in describing how crack blew up his poor and working-class African American community in Queens: "Before crack, there were kids in the park. People in the front yard. Barbeques in the summer. Crack hit, and it just went ... Families stayed indoors, kept their kids at home."[13] A large majority of people in South Queens never smoked crack, but enough became chronic users to tear apart the community.

A veteran of the crack scene in Atlanta describes the impact of crack on her neighborhood in almost identical terms. But she emphasizes an uncomfortable, if not surprising, truth: by the mid 1980s, crack's hardcore users tended to fit a racialized – and age-specific – economic profile. "It was a black and white neighborhood," she says. "Very peaceful. Very quiet." The white residents who lived in that inner-city Atlanta neighborhood at the advent of the crack years were almost all older people, working-class retirees who had been in the community for decades. They did not smoke crack. Their black neighbors tended to be younger and poorer. From their ranks came the hard-core consumers of crack. "After the crack came in," she continues, "they [the crack users] started breaking in the white folks' houses. They wanted them a hit so bad that they would walk up on the porch and walk on in them folks' houses and come out with what they want and tell them, Don't move! ... The children couldn't go out and play no more, it had got just that bad."[14] Crack, potentially, could be smoked anywhere by pretty much anyone. But its habitués, the people who turned their lives over to crack, tended to be poor and they tended to be black and they tended to live in communities that were in economic decline.

When crack cocaine first came onto the market, it was not primarily a drug used by poor people of color. In New York City, for example, people started buying crack commercially in late 1983. According to the DEA, crack's first customers were overwhelmingly white and at least middle class. Most of them were from Long Island, suburban New Jersey, and wealthy suburbs. Mostly, they were the same people who had been coming into the city regularly to buy powder cocaine, mainly from Dominican dealers in Manhattan. They were not casual consumers of cocaine; they were heavy users chasing an intense high. Some of these white "coke-heads" became "crackheads." But by mid 1984, as crack became much more widely available and cheaper in New York, the customer base expanded and radically shifted to poorer neighborhoods and by 1986, the DEA's official history recounts, "crack had a stranglehold on the ghettoes of New York City."[15] Young whites, middle class and otherwise, continued to use crack all through the 1980s and 1990s (and still do today) but the steadiest customers, "crackheads," were disproportionately young black men and women.

Consumer demand for crack cocaine, like all drugs, has a specific history. As was recounted in Chapter 1, at the advent of the twentieth century, white, middle-class people used opioids, including heroin, in numbers vastly disproportionate to poor African Americans. Today, rural and small-town whites have made illegal opioids a big, roiling market, although in the post–World War II decades heroin was predominately an African America and Latino drug. In the late 1960s, young white, well-educated people wanted "mind-blowing" drugs; they smoked marijuana and tripped on LSD. Today, suburban teenagers, looking to connect, roll on Ecstasy or "Molly." In different places, at different times, among different groups of people, different illegal drugs take root and prosper. And almost always the demand for that illegal drug among that particular segment of the intoxication market rises and then falls. Explaining why a certain illegal drug gains – and loses – popularity among a certain market sector is no easy matter and always contains a large amount of speculation. Social scientists and other experts do offer some compelling explanations for why crack cocaine use rose in the mid 1980s and became locally "epidemic" in poor black neighborhoods through the mid 1990s.

Scholars Craig Reinarman and Harry Levine make a simple, if somewhat opaque, argument: "the devastation attributed to crack use in the U.S. is largely a consequence of U.S. social and economic policies and how those shape the social settings of use and the mind-sets of users."[16] Ethnographer Philippe Bourgois makes a similar, if clearer argument: "Crack as a preferred drug of abuse only appeals to desperate population subgroups who are victims of extreme forms of structural violence. This explains the tragedy of the US epidemic where chronic intensive crack use continues to devastate urban African Americans and Puerto Ricans."[17] These scholars mean that the reason crack hit some people and some communities so hard is not simply because crack is rough stuff, though it certainly can be. They claim that crack became so popular and then so problematic in poor communities because most of the people drawn to chronic crack use were already in deep trouble of all kinds, before they took their first hit. That trouble – economic, educational, psychological, cultural ... the list goes on – was shaped by the callous and racist society in which they lived. And then once these troubled people started using crack, most every kind of authority, from the police to social workers to local prosecutors, mostly made their lives worse rather than trying to help them.

To bolster their claim, Reinarman and Levine draw on studies of crack cocaine use in other nations. They point out, for example, that if crack use was merely the result of a combination of its availability, its inherent charms, and its addictive or habit-forming qualities, then it should be most widely used where it would be easiest to get; in the Netherlands, for example, where drug laws in the 1980s and 1990s were minimal and cocaine was widely available. But few people in the Netherlands were drawn to crack. The inherent qualities and plausible availability of the crack, in other words, did not produce its popularity among a given customer base at a particular time in a given place. People smoked crack and, more importantly, people became chronic users of crack because they felt like the drug gave them something they specifically desired; because they lived in a place where savvy entrepreneurs made sure that crack was easy enough to get; and because they operated in a society and a culture where crack use seemed a reasonable response to their needs.

The furious rise of crack in the 1980s in poor, primarily black neighborhoods in America's cities – and not in the socially progressive, welfare-state-oriented, more economically homogenous lands of the Dutch – is not exactly shocking. Many of these same dragged-down neighborhoods had been torn apart by the ravages of prior, localized hard drug epidemics. In the late 1960s and early 1970s, it had been heroin. As Eric Schneider wrote in *Smack*: "Heroin was a city-killing drug, and in the early 1970s the American city appeared to be on its way to the morgue."[18] In those years, New York City was the epicenter for heroin use, with approximately half of all of the nation's addicts; three-quarters of those addicts were low-income African Americans and Puerto Ricans.[19] As the drug-selling activities of Chicago's major gangs in the mid 1980s demonstrated, heroin was still a force to be reckoned with in the illegal inner-city drug marketplace. Heroin offers a very different kind of high than does crack cocaine but they share the same ability to bring a sense of both euphoria and oblivion. And while a disparate crew of people might find a high that combines both euphoria and oblivion rewarding, those in hard circumstances are its likely audience.

A team of crack experts argues, "Historically, from the so-called 'gin-epidemic' in the slums of the eighteenth century London to the 'heroin epidemic' of urban America in the 1970s, the worst drug problems have always been concentrated amid profound and preexisting suffering."[20] Speaking specifically about the call of crack, they conclude, "Very few people who have good choices available have opted for crack very often or for very long."[21] Some rich people did smoke crack and a percentage of them became absolute fiends; they tended to be devotees of its intense high and were overwhelmingly serious drug users. But mostly, crack users were people who were suffering from a sense of desperation, many of whom, in a different era, might have sought some other high-powered form of drug-induced escape, such as alcohol or heroin.

Crack sellers' good fortune or genius was that the particular hard-edged high they provided could be sourced and manufactured easily;

sold cheaply, securely, and often openly; did not require off-putting and dangerous needles (especially important as hard-core drug users realized that AIDS was being spread through shared needles); and worked very fast and very intensely. It was not every hard-core intoxicator's favorite high – heroin use did not disappear during the 1980s and 1990s – and hard-core alcoholics vastly outnumbered and, in many measures of personal devastation, outperformed crackheads. But during the decade of the middle 1980s to the middle 1990s, roughly, crack did hit the steady need of several hundred thousand people to lose themselves in a brief, spectacular, repeatable high even as it often alienated them from everyone who did or might love them and robbed them of their dignity and their health.

For affluent people in the United States, the fuel of desperation that fed crack's rise in America's urban ghettoes was a mostly unimaginable mystery. White Americans, in particular, wanted to believe that America, in the mid 1980s, had turned the corner on its social and economic ills, including the nation's inglorious history of racism. A large majority of them embraced Ronald Reagan's 1984 campaign slogan, "It's morning in America," and became misty-eyed watching the president's ads with their images of small-town newspaper boys and happy couples wedding – "This afternoon, 6500 young men and women will be married. They can look forward, with confidence to the future."[22] In some ways, America surely had turned a corner, at least as compared to some of what had come before.

The national economy, by the mid 1980s, was improving and would, over the next dozen years, become much stronger. Official unemployment figures had dropped from the disastrous pre-crack level of 9.6 percent in 1982 (President Reagan's "morning" took a little while to dawn) to just 5.3 percent in 1989 when crack was hitting poor urban communities hard. And, more pertinently, the kind of blatantly declaimed racial discrimination that had locked black Americans out of the vast majority of good paying jobs from the time of Emancipation through the decades of civil rights struggle was illegal and increasingly rare by the 1980s.

A majority of white Americans in the 1980s pointed to the equal opportunity laws that had been passed in the 1960s and after and declared that racism was dead and that now it was simply up to every individual, regardless of their skin color, to get on with the game of life. In 1964, Ronald Reagan had vehemently opposed the Civil Rights Act that outlawed employment discrimination but in 1986, President Reagan, like most whites, had officially gotten on board. He celebrated – if cautiously – legal equality: "We are committed to a society in which all men and women have equal opportunities to succeed, and so we oppose the use of quotas. We want a color-blind society." Reagan and his supporters insisted that all that remained for that equal opportunity to be realized was for people to work hard and demonstrate their merits. President Reagan, who had scorned Martin Luther King while he was alive, dutifully quoted his famous "dream" in the middle of his second term in office, cheerfully declaring that the time had come for all people to be judged "not by the color of their skin but by the content of their character."[23]

Such sweet-sounding sentiments were not rare in America's public rhetoric during the 1980s, when crack cocaine came into play. And real progress, material progress, had been made in realizing the dream of racial justice that had animated generations of people who had endured and fought white supremacy in all its protean forms. Still, few African Americans, even those who had found economic security and opportunity in post-1960s America, believed that all was well in Reagan's America. At the onset of crack's rise in America, striking majorities of black Americans believed that their nation's leaders did not have their best interests in mind.

Black Americans were well aware that the Reagan administration was gutting some of the social provision measures that stabilized poor neighborhoods, especially desperate inner-city black communities. Most obviously, the Reagan administration decimated America's public-housing programs, cutting their budget by some 76 percent between 1980 and 1988. The federally maintained operating budget of the Chicago Housing Authority, which oversaw the city's massive projects, such as the Robert Taylor Homes and Cabrini-Green, fell 87 per cent during that time.[24] These were the same projects that would become the lawless havens of Chicago's dominant crack-selling gangs by the end of the decade.

Even as President Reagan was assuring Americans that he believed in equal opportunity for all, an astonishing 56 percent of African Americans surveyed told a pollster, simply and straightforwardly, that they considered their president a racist (and only 31 percent said he was not). Just 23 percent said they approved of Reagan's overall performance.[25] Relatively few black Americans believed, in the 1980s, that it was morning in America.

Such relatively unified political sentiments revealed African American frustrations with the pace of racial progress in the 1980s during the Reagan years. But they hid, in some ways, the great changes that continued to sweep through black America in both the 1980s and 1990s. Sociologist Elijah Anderson, writing about a black neighborhood in West Philadelphia in the 1980s that would be particularly hard hit by crack use, recounts the powerful changes afoot during those years: "In the past blacks of various social classes lived side by side in segregated Northton ... Because of recent openings in the opportunity structure of the wider society ... Northton has experienced an outflow of middle- and upper-income [African American] people."[26] Those left behind, Anderson argued, tended to be those unable to avail themselves of these economic opportunities. These residents, he wrote, had become mired in "a local underclass ... This underclass of Northton is made up of people who have failed to keep up with their brethren, both in employment and in sociability. Essentially they can be seen as victims of the economic and social system."[27]

Anderson's use of the term "underclass" was common, though still controversial, when he deployed it in 1990. Some critics of the phrase worried that "it blamed the victim" for the awful effects centuries-long racism and white supremacy had rained down on African Americans. Generally, that was not scholars' intent, though as the term spread, some people did definitely deploy it to argue that poor black Americans in the 1980s were personally responsible for whatever harm had befallen them. Most careful scholars meant something different. They deployed the term underclass to describe a phenomenon that rattled many experts' expectations about racial progress in the United States in the post-1960s era. Why were so many African Americans still living desperate lives even after the most obvious forms of legal racism had been outlawed? How could social scientists explain the very real progress of some African Americans during this era, even as others floundered and lost ground? Out of their debates came the term "underclass."

Most basically, when experts used the phrase underclass they were describing people living in areas of concentrated poverty, in which intergenerational poverty and lack of legal employment was normal, and where single-parent families, criminality, and substance-abuse problems were common. Crack would take root in such communities. One of America's preeminent sociologists, William Julius Wilson, had laid the groundwork for this analysis in his 1978 book, *The Declining Significance of Race: Blacks and Changing American Institutions*.[28] In it, he argued that the changing nature, and more importantly location, of working-class jobs – out to the metropolitan periphery and also away from the industrial Midwest and northeast and down to the "Sunbelt" – at the very same time as anti-discrimination laws had opened up workplace opportunities for African Americans – had isolated less well-educated and less well-prepared black inner-city residents from economic opportunities. While better-educated and better-situated black Americans were able to adapt to this new job market and even prosper within it, too many others had suffered too deeply from segregation, discrimination, and other forms of racism to take advantage of the legal changes the civil-rights movement had wrought.

In 1997, looking back at the decade that had ravaged too many low-income black communities, Wilson, an African American, had a telling conversation with Henry Louis Gates, Jr., who was one of America's preeminent black public intellectuals. He argued that African Americans had been the hardest hit by the de-industrialization that had restructured the American economy in the 1970s and 1980s; that because of a long history of racist repression, far more had entered that challenging era poorer and worse educated than whites. As a result, too many were ill equipped to adapt to new opportunities and to gain the kinds of skills the new post-industrial jobs economy depended on. These structural impediments were worsened by the disconnect between where blacks had been forced to live by prior decades of rigidly enforced housing segregation and where the new job opportunities were proliferating. Pointing to the "historic core of the black belt in Chicago" he noted that in 1950, when unskilled and low-skilled industrial work inside Chicago, close to those neighborhoods, was plentiful, 70 percent of black men aged fourteen and over were gainfully employed (though, it must be said, in poor-paying jobs). But by 1990, in those same neighborhoods, far from where the new jobs were, only 36 percent of black men aged sixteen and over had legal jobs.[29] In Chicago's roughest public-housing projects the statistics were even more daunting with 90 percent of the adult residents without legal work and largely dependent on welfare and other social services.[30]

Wilson is quick to note that civil rights laws had benefited a sizeable number of African Americans. He insisted that, "If you talk about the overall socioeconomic status of the black population, we are better off because we have a higher percentage of blacks in professional positions, more black homeowners than we had back then, more black college graduates. No question about it." Wilson's larger point was that there had been "a crystallization of the black class structure." Black America, he pointed out, actually had more income inequality within its ranks than did white America (even as black Americans, in every income quintile, on average, made less money than did whites, with continuing racism a critical factor in that disparity).[31]

All did not share Wilson's focus on how changing job markets had produced an "underclass." Urban ethnographers, who often lived closely for long periods of time with their subjects, saw other factors, even as they never fully discounted the obvious changes in the nature and place of work in 1980s and 1990s America. As noted earlier, Philippe Bourgois, who lived amongst crack dealers and crack buyers in New York's East Harlem, agreed that many of his new friends and acquaintances claimed that they wanted to do the kind of construction or industrial work they believed their male relatives had once enjoyed. But he is quick to point out that in New York, at least, there was other steady work – service and back-office work, generally – available for young men of color. They just didn't want to do it. Many were unwilling to observe the kind of servile conventions they believed, with reason, such work demanded, especially if it meant taking orders from women. They preferred the rough and tumble life of the streets. At least to an extent, they preferred to be members of a lawless, violent underclass to being law-abiding, disciplined low-status service-sector employees.[32] The journalist Ken Auletta, in his 1982 book *The Underclass*, which brought the term into widespread public use and debate, emphasized this piece of the puzzle. He claimed that inner-city young people were simply in open rebellion against the norms of American society and relished joining a criminal sub-culture.[33] Other scholars, especially on the conservative side of the spectrum, echoed this "dysfunctional" behavior model as well, to explain the rise of an "underclass."[34]

Elijah Anderson, who spent years with people caught up in what he calls the "code of the street," generally accepts the utility of calling a segment of inner-city residents members of an underclass. In so doing, however, he offers a nuanced, dynamic, and convincing argument for its rise and for its relationship to the widespread use of crack among the young black urban poor.

> In cities like Philadelphia certain neighborhoods have been devastated by the effects of deindustrialization ... With widespread joblessness, many inner-city people have become stressed and their communities became distressed. Poor people adapt to these circumstances in the ways they know, meeting the exigencies of their situation as best as they can. The kinds of problems that trigger moral outrage begin to emerge: teen pregnancy, welfare dependencies, and the underground economy.[35]

The underclass, Anderson argues, has a history that reveals both economic and cultural causes and crack fit nicely – if tragically – into both sides of the story. By the mid 1980s, according to Anderson, the localized crack epidemic in poor black communities was driven by a supply-side pressure: people in those neighborhoods needed a way to make a living and becoming a dealer appeared to be a way to do just that. But the rise of crack was also driven by demand: poor people looked to escape their dire situation by embracing expedient measures that offered short-term pleasure. These were people in need of the quick, intense reward of intoxication. Crack fit the bill, in all regards.

Crack dealers' most dependable customers, then, were poor people who lacked steady – or any – legal employment. This disjuncture between what the customer wanted – binge-able amounts of crack cocaine – and the economic resources they had to get it, created an obvious problem.

For those poor people who regularly smoked crack, coming up with the wherewithal to pay for their habit was a grind. Crackheads were on a constant hunt for money or for anything of value they could trade for crack vials. Rarely did they go far afield to come up with what they needed to get what they wanted. People living even just a couple of miles from where crack *was* epidemic had little to fear. Crack fiends tended to hunt close to where they scored. They took from family, from friends, from neighbors. They scourged their communities.

Families of hardcore crack users suffered the most. Not only did they have to watch someone they loved turn feral and desperate, they had to confront a child or a sibling or a mother or a father who would thieve from his or her own family to score crack. Their very own blood had become, as the saying went, "backstabbers," who would lie and deceive and betray the people who loved them – who they loved – to get what they needed to buy more crack. Again, in Corey Pegues's words, "Fiends were breaking into cars for stereos, breaking into neighbors' cribs for television and VCRs, stealing their mom's jewelry, their kids' record player, anything they could trade for crack." He tells a terrible story of trading five jumbo vials of crack to a drug-hungry neighbor for a 32-inch color television. That same day, the man's mother came over and asked if she could please have her television back. Corey lied and said he didn't have it. Then, in a mixed-up rage, angry at the crackhead for stealing from his own mother but also angry because he had made Corey act like a person he didn't want to be, Corey and a friend beat down that mother's desperate son: "We fucked him up bad, like kicking a stray dog. We beat him unconscious and left him lying on the sidewalk in front of my house."[36]

Pegues's story of mother and son was not unusual. Many crack fiends began, at least, their hunt for assets to buy their drugs with what they or a loved one had to offer their dealer. As the manager of a Detroit crack-house reports: "Men would come in with clothes from their girlfriends or wives, or gold or diamonds or furniture, appliances, VCRs, cars, – anything."[37] Some dealers, those who were well connected in the underworld, preferred barter to cash. With the right fence or relationship with crooked storekeepers or black-market consumers (especially of weapons), they could increase their profits over straight cash deals. Larry

Chambers, who became one of Detroit's biggest and fiercest crack distributors, established a formal barter system to enable his steady customers to finance their crack sales flexibly: "a new nineteen-inch color television was worth five five-dollar rocks; a handgun no more than six rocks; an Uzi [!] no more than twenty rocks; a black-and-white TV one or two rocks." He also accepted jewelry and most anything else he could sell profitably or use in his own business – mostly guns.[38] People beggared their families and, of course, themselves, to get their next hits.

Neighbors, too, faced the brunt of crack addicts' need for something to buy or trade for crack. On the blocks surrounding the crack dealerships at 105th and 107th Street on Manhattan's Upper West Side, streets gleamed with individual mounds of shattered, pebble-like automobile window safety glass. Addicts smashed a driver-side or passenger-side window, unlocked the door, and busted out the car radio/CD player. They could pull off the whole operation in a couple of minutes or less. They traded the entertainment system for a (very) few hits of crack. Of course, if anything else of even minimal value was left in the car that was taken, too. Some people had their car window shattered for an umbrella or even an ice scraper. By 1990, few car owners replaced their stolen sound systems. People left their cars unlocked and taped cardboard signs to the side windows. In big block letters, they wrote: NO RADIO NOTHING IN CAR, hoping that they would not have to replace their windows again. The unlocked autos were a magnet for homeless people and people looking for a private place to smoke crack.[39]

Men also robbed and mugged people, looking for cash, watches, and jewelry. In East Harlem, crack addicts targeted undocumented Mexicans, knowing that they were unlikely to go to the police. One addict who, like many crack-era muggers, used the "007" rocker-bar locking folding knife favored for its long blade and easy release in committing his attacks, explained. "Everybody be ripping them off; they easy prey 'cause they illegal most of them ... Mexicans be fucked up with crime in New York."[40]

Older neighborhood women, too, were handy victims. In low-income Philadelphia neighborhoods, street hold-ups and purse snatchings perpetrated by crack users were so bad, women had to have a strategy to get by; they hid their purses under their coats, didn't wear their jewelry walking down the street, walked fast, and did their best to befriend the young men most likely to rob them. They hoped a personal relationship would make the young men too embarrassed to harm them. It did not always work.

An angry West Philadelphia man, talking to the ethnographer Elijah Anderson, remembered how his vulnerable, good-hearted mother handed out cough drops and kindness to the crack fiends in his neighborhood: "It's a deterrent for some, but for others, even that don't matter. They'll snatch your bag. They'll run around the corner, and they live around the corner. And they know damn well you know them, 'cause you see 'em sitting on the steps. They don't care. 'Cause they need that money right now."[41]

In poor neighborhoods, most anything, even of limited value, was likely to be fodder for a crack fiends' need for resources: car batteries, copper wire, children's bicycles, rusty barbeques. A woman remembered with disgust coming out her front door and seeing that "the pipers stole the flowerpot cemented onto our porch."[42]

Women who became habituated to crack often used sex to pay for their rock. They turned tricks. They traded sex for rocks. They made deals with the men who ran crackhouses to provide free sex to their customers in exchange for a steady supply of rocks. Few women who were not already prostitutes wanted to use sex to get their crack. Or, at least, they did not start with that plan. It was usually a process, a step-by-step movement, though often not a long one, from one sort of exchange of resources to another.

A woman in Atlanta explains why she used sex to get her crack: "I wanted it and I didn't have no money." Turning to sex was her last resort: "The first thing I started doing was looking at my stereo and my VCR. That went first. I started taking everything out the house before I started turning tricks. Because I was one of the types that said I wouldn't let it get me that bad; I wouldn't go that far." Her dealer gave her less than ten cents on the dollar for her possessions. In just a couple of days she had nothing material left to trade: "I had took everything out of the house." But she was riding high and did not want to stop: "So I had to turn my first trick. I felt so cheap because I did it for just enough to get me a sack [of crack] with. I felt so used and so cheap."[43] Nonetheless, she kept at it.

Many young women simply traded sex for crack, though their relationship with the men who provided them crack was often not dissimilar to prostitution. In crack circles, such women were pejoratively called "strawberries," a slang term for their genitalia. One woman explains: "I would tell him, 'I want one nick to smoke now, two to smoke before we have sex, and two afterwards.' Each nick is five dollars' worth [a total of], twenty-five." Even as they had sex, she would be smoking: "While he was performing on me, I was fixing my shit [dope] up. It was very difficult to do. I would have to say stop for a minute or slow down so I could take it [dope] out of the bag. Then afterwards he would give me another two."[44]

Danger was endemic for women whose crack habit had made them vulnerable sex workers. The most focused and monstrous form of that violence occurred in South Central Los Angeles, one of the nation's crack epicenters. From 1984 through 1993, at least five serial killers targeted crack-seeking women in the area. They used the promise of crack to lure them to their deaths. More than a hundred women were killed, almost all of them African American – and while not all of the women were crack-using sex workers, the overwhelming majority were.

The Los Angeles Times reported that crack had changed sex work in the city, making it much more dangerous. "Hundreds of addicts became 'strawberries' – trading casual sex for small rocks of crack," the *Times* explained. "In previous years, prostitutes had been offered some modicum of protection by their pimps or at least by working in the area's many cheap hotels. Now, driven by addiction and expediency, many forsook any notion of safety, taking clients to abandoned houses, vacant lots and dead-end alleys, which is where their bodies began turning up."[45]

The Los Angeles Police Department, at the time, did relatively little to investigate these murders or explore the connections between them. The LAPD felt besieged by a record number of murders and violent crime during this period, a sizeable amount of it linked to the supply and distribution side of the crack trade. Black residents believed that the LAPD was, in fact, indifferent – or worse – to the plight of poor black people, especially poor black crack-hungry women who were perceived as "dregs of society." "It was us against them" during those years, states a prominent racial-justice attorney.[46] It was in 1991, in the middle of the crack years, with all the violence that era encompassed, that a band of

LAPD officers were videotaped mercilessly beating a defenseless Rodney King; it was the acquittal of those officers in 1992 that launched the massive South Central riot that resulted in 63 deaths and some $1 billion in property damage. Crack, poverty, and racism had created a whirlwind of violence in South Central Los Angeles that exploded in all directions. Somewhere at the center of that storm were those vulnerable, desperate women whose murders, despite outcries and organized efforts by the black community, went unsolved for decades.

Women, who became hard-core crack users, often did not just put themselves at risk. If they got pregnant – and their crack-associated sexual practices meant that they often did – they greatly increased the chances that they would harm their fetuses due to poor nutrition, general neglect of the health of their gestating baby and of themselves, and their exposure to sexually transmitted diseases. Fetal death rates among black women went up 25 percent during the peak of the crack years – no similar increase occurred among white women. The number of low birth-weight babies born to poor black women also spiked dramatically during those years (and declined markedly in the late 1990s), putting those babies at risk of a variety of bad health outcomes.[47]

Then, too, to put the matter bluntly, women who binged regularly on crack rarely made for good mothers. For poor black women who had children without the steady support of the birth father in the family, adding crack to the mix often proved devastating. One of the more tragic statistics to emerge from the crack years was the massive increase in the number of poor African American children who were put into the foster care system. Overall, the number of African American children placed in foster care doubled (the white rate stayed steady).[48] Specifically, the number of children exposed to cocaine who were placed in foster care rose from 17 percent in 1986 to 55 percent in 1991 – with crack use by the children's mothers the almost sure cause for this explosive rise. And the number of children who were reported abused or neglected by their parent or parents rose from 1.1 million in 1980 to 2.9 million in 1994. In New York City in the early 1990s, social service authorities stated that a parent or caregiver abusing drugs was responsible for 75 percent of all child abuse and neglect. Crack was the primary drug of choice among the abusers and neglectors.[49]

During the height of the crack years, medical authorities, politicians, and a host of other experts repeatedly declaimed that crack-addicted mothers were giving birth to a generation of "crack babies" who were permanently brain damaged by their gestational exposure to crack. These babies, they declared, were doomed. The experts, it turned, out were wrong. Crack consumption did have adverse effects on the newborns but the damage done by the drug itself was rarely permanent. The actual, much more serious problem for such babies and young children was growing up in the chaotic, dangerous, neglectful, too often loveless home of a crack-addicted mother.[50]

Most poor women who became steady crack customers mourned what their drug use had done to their families. A twenty-four-year-old woman in Philadelphia told the ethnographer Elijah Anderson:

> Right now, I'm really disappointed in myself, in what I'm doing to my babies. I lost my babies. I have three kids; none of them are in my custody. I voluntarily gave them up to my sister. I told my sister I don't want to see my baby no more, because she don't deserve to see me for what I'm doin' right now. It's hurtin' me that I said that and I want to go see her, but I can't let her see me like this ... 'cause as long as I'm out here [in the street] all I want to do is keep getting high, just keep getting high.[51]

Sisters, mothers, and grandmothers found themselves caring for the children of their crack-addicted family member, often gaining legal custody. One forty-year-old grandmother spoke for many who took on the care of their crack-addicted daughters' children: "There's no sense getting upset. This is what you have to do. If you didn't see any sense in it, you wouldn't be doin' it." She admitted, "I get tired sometimes. Sometimes I get frustrated, but I don't dwell on it, you know, I can't dwell on it. Right now the most important thing is these children."[52] Few non-drug-abusing family members of crack-addicted mothers could fully forgive those who had chosen crack over their own children but many did what they could to shower love on the boys and girls who had lost their mothers to the lure of the "pipe."

People who lived in poor, inner-city communities were often horrified by what crack did to their neighbors, their friends, and their loved ones. It angered them. And it scared them, too. On their streets, crack seemed to be everywhere, and so cheap anyone could afford it, at least at first. It was so tempting.

Clifford Bey had all of those feelings in the mid 1980s when crack started to appear in Chicago, when it was still a drug that could only be scored on a few streets on the South Side.[53] Bey appeared to be the kind of man who might be an early adopter of the new drug – and, possibly, a dealer, as well. He was back in Chicago after a long absence. He had been incarcerated for nine years. When he had been sent to Marion, a federal penitentiary in Illinois in 1975 no one smoked crack; few in his community even snorted cocaine, given its high price. It was $50 a spoon when he left, meaning that in his part of town it was a drug primarily indulged in by pimps and other free-spending underworld characters, as well as by high-flying entertainers and other notables of the night-time scene. But when he was released in late 1984, he knew about crack – fellow inmates had talked about it. For men who had been imprisoned before crack cocaine hit the streets, "rock" could issue a siren call. When convicts got out, they had few legitimate opportunities available; crack offered sweet temptation both as a business and as a release from the frustrations of an ex-offender's lot in life.

In the late 1960s and early 1970s, while Bey was working day-jobs and playing music professionally, he had gotten involved with some unlawful activities – "listening to the wrong voices." He knew many of the men who became gang leaders in Chicago. The police pressured him to cooperate with them regarding neighborhood issues. After he refused to cooperate with criminal investigators – to snitch – the police put a bulls-eye on him and, eventually, he was arrested and convicted for an armed robbery, a crime he adamantly insisted he did not commit. In prison, he associated with many of Chicago's leading black gangsters, including Larry Hoover. They were friends. For a while, Nicky Barnes, the legendary Harlem heroin dealer, occupied the cell next to his at Marion. Though gang unaffiliated – a prison rarity – he got along with everybody. On leaving prison, Bey was well connected. He knew he could pursue criminal opportunities. Still, he intended to take a different path.

Bey had used his time in the penitentiary to rethink who and what he wanted to be. He had become a devout believer in Moorish Science (this was shortly before Jeff Fort, leader of the Blackstone Nation, made a similar allegiance). His faith had given him principles and a belief in the honor that came from being descended from strong people of Moorish ancestry. Bey had vowed that he would "go to the school house to get something that was going to assist me, instead of the jailhouse that was going to destroy me." He had "taken the profanity off the end of my tongue" and intended to be an upright man who never again risked incarceration.

Bey's vow was tested just a couple of days after he was released from prison. He was back in his South Side neighborhood, standing on a corner waiting for a bus, when he spotted a friend he had not seen in nine years. Bey was excited. Here was a piece of good fortune. His friend, Terrance, "had the strongest line you could have." Bey hoped his friend could help him move forward. Instead, Terrance offered him something else: "Look," he said, "I stay right down the street in the basement. I got some crack. It's the bomb." Terrance, the kind of man who always knew what was happening, was very early in on crack and wanted to bring Bey with him, first into smoking and then into trouble.

Bey was furious and sad, at the same time. Instead of a helping hand, he was being tempted: "Terrance, I've been gone nine years, man, and you mean that's the best you got to offer me, some crack?" Bey refused. He did not smoke that crack and he did not become a dealer, either. But it wasn't easy: "People don't just go to prison for years and sit there and suck up that abuse, that racism and all that other garbage down there and then get out and decide, that's all right, we're going to walk the chalk line." Shored up by his faith and years of self-reflection, Bey felt that "one in a thousand saw it like I did."

In 1990, at the height of the crack epidemic, some 405,000 offenders were released just from state prisons.[54] With their prison records, they faced a huge disadvantage in the legal employment market. Without the dignity and money a legitimate job offered, they were prey to the solace drugs could provide. Ex-offenders were not only potential dealers, they made an excellent crack customer base – and, of course, many had used drugs before being imprisoned. In 1989, about 50 percent of people who ended up in local jails admitted that they had used crack or powder cocaine before being locked up; and one-third of convicted state inmates told authorities they were under the influence of an illegal drug when they committed the crime that landed them in prison – with crack and powder cocaine being the most common drug of choice.[55] Crack, cheap and easy to find, was there waiting for ex-offenders who had no clear path to a better life. Crack dealers were only too happy to provide it to a ready-made set of new or returning customers, almost all of whom had some experience in gaining the wherewithal they needed to keep the rocks coming.

Clifford Bey watched people in his neighborhood turn to crack. He, like many others, believed that it took just one hit on the crack pipe to hook a person and then destroy their life. While medical science said that was not the case, Bey and many others witnessed friends and loved ones become crack fiends after a single session with crack. It was devastating to watch and there seemed to be little, if anything, to do about it. Even crack dealers recoiled – and marveled – at how quickly people went from crack initiates to full-fledged fiends. A Philadelphia dealer swore, "I've never seen a person walk away from the pipe."[56]

Because crack dealers believed that most crack seekers were likely to be or quickly become repeat customers, some, at least, treated their clientele with some modicum of respect, or at least business-like efficiency. Crack users usually had at least the possibility of finding a new dealer if they felt they were being treated too poorly, though most simply focused on the price and the quality of the rock they were buying. Still, one major Detroit dealer, the infamous Larry Chambers, told the men who worked as doormen at his crackhouses to treat his clientele decently, even warmly, no matter how broken-down the figure before them was: "When a crackhead comes to you and his woman is on his back, his babies don't have no Pampers, he hasn't eaten in two days, and he's about to spend his last five dollars on crack, you have to make him feel good about spending his money."[57]

A small-time crack dealer in Philadelphia offered his men similar advice. His clientele was almost entirely the homeless men who gathered around the Sunday Breakfast Club shelter just north of Center City. These were men who had little dignity left to them. The crack crew boss often gave his hand-to-hand men pep talks, aware that there was not much glamor in selling crack to men who appeared to be filthy, often emaciated derelicts. He instructed them, in so many words, to be civil in their interactions; that it was good business to treat their down-and-out customers decently, so long as they didn't try any kind of hustle. His salesmen, as a result, often joked good-naturedly with their customers.[58]

While crack customers had no formal protections against dishonest or mean-spirited dealers, they could take their business elsewhere. They were consumers, who more often than not, were frequent purchasers in a big competitive market. As a result, at least some dealers treated them with a modicum of decency; some even offered their customers the kind of deals they might have expected at a supermarket. Larry Chambers, in Detroit, not only had his people provide good customer service, he sometimes advertised specials – literally having neighborhood kids hand out coupons that promised during slow times, "BUY ONE [rock], GET ONE FREE" or, when business picked up, "BUY NINE AND GET YOUR TENTH FREE." His loyal customers were told that if they brought in a new customer they would receive for free as much as the newcomer bought.[59]

More often, crack customers demanded more depraved kinds of rewards. Many crack houses, as noted earlier, featured sexual come-ons, such as freely available or extremely cheap "strawberries" to lure male customers. As one woman, who spent years in Atlanta's crack scene, recounted: "Every kind [of crack house] there is [sex available] ... One room they be having sex. Another room they be freaking, like standing on the table, butt naked, dancing. Another room, they be fucking and sucking."[60] Men relished their buying power. Especially for men who did not have steady jobs or other attributes of traditional economic success, being able to access women sexually by buying cheap crack was a boon.[61] The crackhouse customer, even if very wrong from a mainstream cultural perspective, was always right.

Then again, plenty of crack dealers, especially those who operated on the meaner streets, treated their repeat customers less like bona fide consumers and more like desperate down-and-outers, which many were. An ex-addict angrily recalls his experiences scoring crack in East Harlem from the Purple City Crew: "Going through Purple block, they had pit bull dogs guarding they stash ... [They] wouldn't take no change, no dollar bills, see they treated people like dirt ... they treated people like this was the slave times." One of the Purple City dealers agrees: "We started bustin' niggas' asses if they didn't want to line up. Fuckin' dollar, two dollars, putting our foot up they ass." To better mock their customers, these dealers, and others demanded that their customers line up in what they called, "a cheese line." Instead of giving up a piece of their dignity for publicly distributed free food, these poor folk had to toe the line to get their crack.[62] In the eyes of some of the young men who made their living off of their neighbors' desperation, crack customers were certainly not to be respected, understood, or even to be pitied; they were just a source of income.

CHAPTER 4

Crack Money: Manhood in the Age of Greed

THE CRACK INDUSTRY WAS, NO DOUBT, A TOUGH TRADE. Most dealers had to harden their hearts to the harm they were doing to people they knew, to the communities in which they lived. Going to prison, for a while, maybe forever, was a part of the business model. Crack dealers got shot and they killed each other. People died at age eighteen or twenty-one or twenty-five.

But the rewards of success in the industry were just as real. Hand to hand sellers sported the latest footwear, wrapped themselves in gold, and partook of a brotherhood that gave them a sense of belonging and allegiance too rare in their atomized world. Many were young men who saw no mainstream way to reveal their talent or courage to the women in their neighborhoods or to the wider society in which they struggled to survive with dignity. On the streets, other options presented themselves in the hard world these young men made.

Crack dealers of a certain stature were often local heroes, "hood" celebrities, urban style-setters. They played to those roles; it was good business and for many, it just came naturally. In large part their status came from their largesse and the glee they took in self-fashioning. They had money to burn and they spent their fortunes in full public view. They were at the heart of what was happening, mixing and matching with the avatars of hip hop at its moment of ascendance. Crack dealers and the crack scene, with its fat rolls of money, gave flavor and fancy to inner-city dreams. They modeled a way of life – fast and violent and without restraint – that resonated across youth culture's permeable boundaries of race and class.

At the same time that white Wall Street hustlers and commodity traders and real-estate speculators were touting their clichés – "greed is

Figure 8 Christopher Wallace, aka Biggie Smalls, aka the Notorious B.I.G.: Biggie came up in the drug underworld and rapped about his experiences, achieving extraordinary success as a hip-hop artist in the 1990s. He was gunned down in Los Angeles in 1997. (Clarence Davis/NY Daily News Archive via Getty Images.)

good" – and leasing their Porsches and Ferraris, black crack dealers took to conspicuous consumption like a run-away freight train. At a wider cultural moment increasingly unmoored from restraint and the virtues of honesty and fair play – think of Donald Trump's tawdry tabloid 1980s exploits and his 1987 best-selling homage to deceit and exploitation, *The Art of the Deal* – crack dealers, too, played by rules of their own making. They set their minds to building inner-city empires that would give them the wherewithal to act out their fantasies for all to see.

The men who ran crack crews or served as muscle were often still teenagers. At twenty-five, they were veterans of the game. They were interested in young men's diversions. Tonia Taylor-Bragg, aka Ms. Tee, a paramour to some of Harlem's flashiest dealers, brags: "Their hustle game was tight. It was all about looking fly, getting bitches, flashing the flyest jewels, and non-stop flossing."[1] Most squandered their money in ways almost too absurd to believe. A few struggled to channel their ridiculous wealth into avenues more productive. They were self-styled gangsters, boldly proclaiming their manhood in what ways they could in a desperate time. Most of them understood that they were living in a moment that would not last. Mostly, but not always and not forever, they were all about getting money and spending it.

* * *

In 1986, the Chambers brothers, Detroit's most daring and successful crack dealers, returned to their family home in the rural hinterlands of the Arkansas Delta. They had come back for their little brother's high school graduation. The brothers arrived in one of the poorest counties in America in a cavalcade of five mint white Cadillacs. Their biographer, William Adler, describes what happened when they pulled up to Lee Senior High School: "they were mobbed like movie stars arriving at a Hollywood premiere. Parents' cameras snapped, recording the event for posterity; teenagers squealed and pressed against the cars."[2] A teacher, nonplussed, watched the men inside the cars roll down their windows and throw handfuls of money into the worshipful crowd.

When Billy Joe Chambers, the driving force of the brothers' crack empire, returned to Lee County for his little brother's high school graduation, he was twenty-three years old. He had left Lee County to settle in Detroit just seven years earlier. The house he had grown up in had no plumbing; it didn't even have glass windows, just tacked-up pasteboard in the winter and open frames in the summer. The house had four rooms and Billy Joe had thirteen brothers and sisters. Growing up, sometimes, they did not have enough food to go around.

When Billy Joe came back in 1986, in the backseat of a new white Cadillac, he had stacked up enough money from his drug business to rank as one of the wealthiest men in the entire state of Arkansas. He was a self-made multi-millionaire. William Adler writes, "It was proof, really, that a person could achieve almost anything in this country, as long as he really wanted it and was willing to work for it."[3] No doubt, that is how most of his erstwhile neighbors and the high school kids who mobbed his shiny luxury vehicle saw it.

There was nothing new about the gangster hero in America's poor or marginalized communities – or about the ambivalence those communities felt about their notorious outlaws. Jews in the middle decades of the twentieth century had traded stories about Arnold Rothstein, "Greasy Thumb" Jake Guzik, Meyer Lansky, and Murder Inc. boss, Louis "Lepke" Buchalter, the first Jew to be executed in the electric chair. For Jewish boys and men, in particular, often stereotyped as a soft, bookish people victimized and outnumbered by anti-Semites everywhere, a few "tough Jews" were a balm to wounded masculinity. Italian Americans wrestled, too, with the meaning and legacy of the Mafia and its chieftains, the "made men" who were often the best-known representatives of their ethnicity in the United States.

The British Marxist historian Eric Hobsbawm, great champion of the underdog, coined a phrase several decades before the rise of crack king-pins to explain the powerful hold a certain kind of criminal has on the imagination of the people from whom he rises: "social bandit." Think Robin Hood, Jesse James; or for those who know their Australian history, Ned Kelly. Hobsbawm writes, in an oft-quoted passage: "The point about social bandits is that they are peasant outlaws whom the lord and state regard as criminals, but who remain within peasant society, and are considered by their people as heroes, as champions, avengers, fighters for justice, perhaps even leaders of liberation, and in any case as men to be admired, helped and supported."

Not all crack dealers were seen as "heroes" by the people they lived amongst. Certainly, many of their neighbors despised and feared all of them. But as many a hip-hop artist attests, notorious crack dealers were figures of renown and respect to at least some of the people who observed them close-up. Young people admired their flash, their grit, and their determination to live boldly in a society that gave poor people, especially poor black people, ever so few means to achieve greatness. The violence they used to get and keep what they had only magnified their reputations in the eyes of their admirers. It added to their legend. It even could prove seductive to the right kind of woman. One consort of a murderous dealer reminisced, "I wasn't happy that people were getting killed, but being with someone that everyone feared gave me a kind of rush."[4]

Attracting women was a prime reason dealers took on risks to stack up cash. In poor communities, where many young men could not legitimately pay their own way, let alone support a family, crack dealers were a good catch, even if only in the short term. Dealers knew it. "Flossing" – ostentatiously displaying the flashy things that money bought – attracted young women. And dealers were willing to part with some of what they earned to reel those women in. They showered the young women in their orbit with gifts. A Washington, DC jeweler remembers one major dealer who'd come in regularly and buy multiple pairs of expensive large gold earrings: "He'd come here and buy dozens of them for all those girls."[5] To quote, again, the blunt-talking Ms. Tee, who dated several of Harlem's high-rolling crack dealers: "No matter what a dude looked like, if he had cash he was guaranteed to get any bitch he wanted. That 'fine' shit don't mean anything ... That cash flow is all that mattered."[6]

The ethnographer Elijah Anderson mournfully agrees with Ms. Tee. He writes that in "impoverished neighborhoods ... A streetwise young woman is likely to require that the man in her life 'have something' before he 'spends her time.' He must be prepared to show his love by buying her material things ... Hence many young men become strongly motivated to obtain 'crazy' money,' and legal means of doing so may be too slow or nonexistent."[7] Successful crack dealers, as a result, had their pick of young women in the economically precarious neighborhoods in which they worked. That was a powerful incentive for many dealers, who were often just teenagers or young men in their early twenties.

Being in demand because of their wealth did not, alas, produce chivalrous behavior. In the words of the one and only Donald Trump, "when you're a star, they let you do it. You can do anything ... Grab 'em by the pussy. You can do anything."[8] Crack dealers were, in the eyes of many, the "stars" in their neighborhoods. Ms. Tee concludes: "[A] lot of girls in the hood aspired to end up with a drug dealer with a lot of money and a nice car ... We wanted fast money."[9] That mercenary attitude on the part of some of the women who "dated" drug dealers, combined with the promiscuous entitlement some of those same dealers brought to their sexual relationships, did not make for a lot of enduring romances. The one-time crack dealer and hip-hop emcee Snoop Dogg, voiced an extreme version of this sort of disrespect in the 1992 Dr. Dre break out track, "Bitches Ain't Shit," where Snoop gallantly rhymed about "bitches," "hoes," oral sex, and the need for women to vacate the premises as soon as their sexual duties were accomplished.

Flossing wasn't only about enticing women. For dealers of weight, it was a genial "fuck you" to everything and everyone who said that what they did could not be done. For young black men who came up hard the flash – the bling – was a statement of achievement. What money bought was, for the kingpin and his crew, a bounty of luxurious plenty and royal good times in a life that was never supposed to bear any such fruit ... even if it was unlikely to last.

Rayful "Slim" Edmond, powder and crack cocaine king of Washington, DC in the late 1980s, was one of many who set the standard. Edmond started off distributing cocaine; his mother and father had got him into the trade and allegedly he came from a long line of street hustlers. When crack hit, his business blew up. He arranged to buy cocaine directly from the Crips in LA (working with the aforementioned Brian "Waterhead Bo" Bennet), who were supplied by the Cali (Colombia) Cartel. Edmond bought up to $3 million at a time and distributed around 1,700 pounds of cocaine a month. The coke was then distributed to street sellers who cooked and packaged it – Edmond and his people happily sold both "hard and soft candy." By early 1989, Edmond's crew brought in up to $2 million a week. Money piled up. At one point, Edmond claims he had $15 million in cash stacked in his house. He was in his early twenties.[10]

Edmond checked every box when it came to conspicuous consumption. While careful to keep his distance at all times from the product that made him wealthy, Edmond loved to flaunt his good fortune. *The Washington Post* reported, "Edmond was something of a walking advertisement for his organization."[11]

Edmond had a thing for luxury autos and jewelry. He had a Porsche and he had a Jaguar convertible with gold-inlaid hubcaps. When he wanted to bring along an entourage he drove a perfectly detailed white Range Rover. His stable included Mercedes and BMWs. He had so many cars he let his lieutenants drive around in the extras. On his wrist he wore a $45,000 diamond-encrusted Rolex and around his neck, when he wasn't weighed down with gold, he favored a $15,000 diamond cross.

Edmond also led the way in moving away from tracksuits and branded athletic wear. He favored custom-tailored designer outfits. His preferred men's store was Georgetown's exclusive Linea Pitti, where he would casually spend four or five thousand dollars on a lazy afternoon. According to federal prosecutors he and his men spent over $460,000 at the store (forerunners to Trump's 2016 sartorial campaign strategist Paul Manafort!), paying strictly in cash (store owner Charles L. Wynn was found guilty in 1991 of laundering huge sums of cash for Edmond).[12] Edmond and his entire crew dressed only in the finest. His chief enforcer, Antonio "Yo" Jones, recollects: "The entire crew started rocking the likes of Hugo Boss, Valentino, Ralph Lauren, and top of the line Versace shit … not that colorful lame shit." Underworld chronicler Seth Ferranti draws the right conclusion: "When they stepped out it was like a walking advertisement for drug dealers, young black millionaire, have money, get paid. Everyone in the hood wanted to be down with the Rayful Edmond show."[13]

Edmond, like several of his peers, also went in big for the Atlantic City and Las Vegas scene. He loved to gamble. He thought nothing of dropping $100,000 playing craps. He also attended, like many other major crack dealers, the big fights held in both gambling towns. The rows near the ring were filled with young black men and their women friends, outfitted spectacularly in furs and diamonds; professional athletes mixed with the drug lords. It was at the legendary April 1987 Sugar Ray Leonard–Marvin Hagler title fight in Vegas that Edmond first met his LA connects. Major cocaine brokers flocked to the big Vegas fights, looking for new clients, such as Edmond.[14]

Rayful Edmond spent a lot of money on himself but that was not the whole story. The "social bandit" Robin Hood piece was there, too. Edmond loved his suits, jewels, and cars. He did lavish gifts on the women he wanted. But Edmond was a community benefactor, as well. Some of his largess was of the old school John D. Rockefeller kind. In the early twentieth century, Rockefeller, at the advice of his public-relations man, had given away shiny dimes to children. Edmond gave away $100 bills. He professed to love kids and for all to see he put his money where his mouth was. More than twenty years after the fact, a recipient of his generosity fondly recalls, "I remember Slim pulled up in my hood and gave all us lil' niggas $100 a piece and told us to take our lil' asses to school. I was like 7 years old then and to me he was a star because he was getting out a limo."[15]

Like other major players, Edmond and his crew made sure that the neighborhood in which they operated stayed on their side – in other words, quiet. Like an old-time political ward boss, he gave away turkeys at Thanksgiving time and even bought meals for the homeless who bedded down in the streets around his main selling ground. His chief enforcer, Yo, claims that they moved their main drug spot away from the streets across from Gallaudet University (and just a few blocks from where some of the most devastating arson and looting took place after the assassination of Martin Luther King in April 1968) and into a maze of nearby alleyways as a nod to the community: "We decided to use the alleys to prevent the kids from being exposed to the criminal activities that we were involved with. The neighborhood loved and respected us for that move."[16] Yo also insists that he and the other muscle assured that the neighborhood stayed – putting aside their drug sales – crime-free: "We became one with the neighborhood and made sure everybody stayed safe."[17]

Edmond also played a major role in his city's number one sport: basketball. Like a number of his peers in Chicago, Detroit, New York, Philadelphia, and elsewhere, he was a fanatical basketball supporter. Edmond, himself, was an outstanding player – he could have certainly earned a college scholarship but even in high school he put hustling first. Still, he loved to play and he loved to watch. By the time he was twenty he sponsored his own teams in high-level city leagues and tournaments. He assigned himself the role of player-coach.

Edmond regularly entered tournaments that raised money for DC kids, such as the Police Boys and Girls Club. The tournament organizers knew what they were allowing. In fact, they were aware that drug dealers sponsored many of the teams and played on them, as well. The program director of the Boys and Girls Club explained: "A lot of times they'll drive up in the new Cherokee Jeeps or the BMWs ... We allow them to play to keep them off the streets. The more time they spend with us the less time they're out there." Another tournament representative just shrugged off the situation: "For the drug dealers playing basketball is like a doctor playing golf ... They do their business, then they go play basketball. That's their recreation."[18]

Edmond was a huge hit with the fans, especially with the children who flocked to the games. The Boys and Girls Club program director told a reporter: "When Rayful played the gym was always packed with little kids who followed his team … Rayful was a big name – a big name. His teams were always good, and the kids looked up to him."[19] Edmond recruited talented players for his teams, as did the other drug-dealer-led squads. Two of Edmond's best players sold drugs for him. Allegedly, he paid his other stars $1,000 a game. Basketball was a serious business for Edmond, who showed up game-time *sans* jewelry and other finery – he came to play. Though he did drive up in his Porsche or one of his other high-end vehicles, mesmerizing the kids at the gym who watched his every move.

In late summer 1988, Edmond played in an NCAA-sanctioned summer league. Because of the NCAA imprimatur, Edmond played alongside a bevy of college stars, including future NBA Hall of Famer Alonzo Mourning and the future first-round NBA draft pick John Turner, both of whom played for the Georgetown Hoyas. Edmond befriended both young men and when the Hoyas season started he became a regular attendee, bringing along members of his crew to watch the games and then take his friends out afterwards to celebrate. Yo Jones recalls, "Both were damn good youngsters … They would just hang and talk shit with us. We never involved them with any negative bullshit, out of respect."[20]

The relationship did not please Georgetown's towering coach John Thompson. DEA agents had tipped off the coach about Edmond's livelihood and he warned his players to stay away from the drug dealer. Mourning agreed but Turner, who had grown up in DC and had been acquainted with Edmond for years before becoming his friend, balked. He insisted that Edmond was a good guy and that he didn't know anything about any drug dealing. In February 1989, the DEA interviewed Turner in Coach Thompson's office and he admitted that he sometimes drove around in a Mercedes that was owned by Edmond's crew and that Edmond bought him clothes and meals. Thompson threw him off the team. High-level basketball players and major crack dealers, often young men of very similar backgrounds, were a volatile mix.[21]

Basketball gyms and outdoor hoop courts were not the only place where crack dealers and other young black men of talent met up. As anyone who knows the least bit about the hip-hop scene in the 1980s and

1990s understands, crack crews and hip-hop artists often intersected. And sometimes they were interlocked – some hip-hop artists were crack dealers and some crack dealers were aspiring hip-hop artists.

In Rayful Edmond's world, the two scenes banged into each other at places like Chapter III and the Metro Club.

Chapter III, in particular, was a breakout spot for Washington go-go groups and rappers. A well-to-do black clientele flocked there. Len Bias, the Maryland basketball great who was on his way to the Boston Celtics before he died of a cocaine overdose, spent a lot of time there.[22] As well, the DC police attested, the club was popular with "several persons believed to be the District's largest cocaine dealers." The result of so many dealers showing up, usually on the same nights, was that it became "a favorite site for the rival groups to settle scores." In late 1987 and early 1988 alone, fifty-five violent incidents occurred at or around the club. That included gunfights. A DC homicide detective commented on the violence at Chapter III: "There aren't any fistfights in the city anymore. People just kill each other."[23]

At the cusp of the 1980s and 1990s, every major city had clubs that attracted the burgeoning, overlapping hip hop and crack dealers' scene. New York probably had the most intense and prized set of clubs. The Grand, Club USA, Country Club, Club 2000, and the Tunnel were among the most celebrated among those favored by the city's crack crews out for a good time.

Starting in 1993, the Sunday night party, "Mecca," at the Tunnel became the main spot where rap artists mixed with drug kingpins and their crews. As the documentarians behind "Hell up in East Harlem" narrate, the dealers and the artists "congregated to show off their wealth, meet women ... Violent altercations were common."[24]

The Tunnel was in an old, 80,000 square foot warehouse in Manhattan in an anomic part of Chelsea on the far Westside, at 12th Avenue and 27th Street. Funkmaster Flex DJed. He was one of the biggest hip-hop DJs in the city. People lined up down the block to get in. Crack crews from all over New York showed up, mixing with the rap artists, record-industry executives, and three or four thousand other people, few of them white. DJ Flex recalls: "You would have one crowd that would come at 10:30 p.m. and leave by 1:30 a.m. because they had to go to work. Then all the money niggas, all the drug dealers and the fly chicks would come at 1:30 a.m., 2 a.m., and be there till the end at 4 a.m."[25]

Chelsea was nobody's territory so everyone felt welcomed … kind of. Prodigy of Mobb Deep, the gangsta rappers who came out of the public-housing projects of South Queens, explains: "We would have connections at the door, and they used to meet us in the bathroom with a backpack full of shit: razors, screwdrivers, guns. I'd pass out the shit to everybody, then we'd go have fun. It was just to protect ourselves."[26] For the Mecca party, Tunnel employed up to ninety security guards, many of them ex-offenders, men from the different boroughs who knew who was who, in an attempt to keep the mayhem down.

In the long deep space of the club, crews from the different boroughs would stake out their part of the floor. Violence was a constant threat. The rapper Jadakiss, who started selling drugs as a twelve-year-old before he committed to his art, remembers: "All the way in the back was love – all the people that were really enjoying the music were there. But to get to the back you had to walk through a long line of Brooklyn niggas, all types of incredible shit – you never knew what was going to happen. You could get your chain snatched, you could get slice[d] with a razor, anything."[27]

Sean Combs (Puff Daddy) was at the center of the action at the Tunnel in those days. Founder of Bad Boy Records in 1993, Combs deliberately situated himself at the intersection of hip hop and the crack-dealing gangster culture that terrorized and enthralled Americans.[28] Combs's premier rapper, then, was Christopher Wallace, better known as The Notorious B.I.G. or Biggie Smalls. Biggie had been an authentic gangster before he learned how to make his living rapping. Out of Brooklyn, he had started dealing drugs when he was twelve and in 1989 was arrested on weapon charges. In 1991 he was arrested again, this time for dealing crack – he served nine months in a North Carolina jail. In 1992, Combs signed Biggie to Bad Boy Records. Biggie created his art out of his experiences, including the iconic "Ten Crack Commandments" (1997) that outlines his street philosophy.

At the Tunnel, Combs surrounded himself with hard men – "wolves" – to keep his personal situation on an even keel. It didn't hurt his reputation, either, to be surrounded by people who could outgangster the gangsters, if need be. Combs was never one to let false humility get in the way of his self-promotion: "The Tunnel was mine at the time. Let's not get it twisted. I was ordering garbage buckets full of champagne. The bar is where I would stand and walk around. My feet would not touch the floor."[29]

Crack dealers and newly rich hip-hop artists and producers would compete with one another, seeing who could spend the most money in the most visible ways. Tunnel mainstay and then music executive Joie Manda laughingly recalls the scene: "At the bar, you'd say 'Give me a bottle of Moët,' and you would pay cash. 'Give me a bottle of Cristal, give me a bottle of Dom – no glasses. Watching a thousand people holding bottles of Cristal, Dom Perignon, or Moët at one time was kind of amazing. The club constantly sold out of champagne."[30] The champagne *bon vivants* wouldn't let the staff clear away the empties, lining them up, instead, on the bar for all to see. Crack dealers from Purple City and other East Harlem crews sometimes dropped ten thousand dollars in a single night at the club.[31]

The Tunnel was run by Peter Gatien, a white man who was forty when he opened the club in 1992. He believed in hip hop and had nothing against anybody who made his or her living in the drug trade. But he was a professional nightclub operator. Other than Sunday night, his club primarily drew white people. The same way he had one night a week dedicated to hip hop he had other nights at the Tunnel aimed at drawing in gay men. He was a businessman.[32]

Other clubs, as well as a range of hip-hop-based businesses, were much more directly tied to the burgeoning crack scene. In particular, they were tied to crack money. Kingpins, looking to clean their illegally gotten gains, saw the interconnected world of nightclubs and hip hop as a sensible and comfortable place in which to invest.

Sticking with New York, one of the most notorious and popular dealer-owned nightspots was Club 2000, in Washington Heights. Wainsworth "Unique" Hall owned it in the early 1990s. Besides running powder cocaine and crack in Harlem, Unique ran a drug pipeline to the Norfolk area of Southeastern Virginia. His brother, in Tidewater, then cooked the cocaine into rock and distributed it throughout the area. According to one of his women friends – and Unique was notorious for having many women friends – "Unique was definitely taking care of business in the streets."[33]

Part of the challenge for Unique, like all of his compatriots in the powder cocaine and crack-distribution industry, was what to do with his stacks of cash. Like most everyone else, he consumed conspicuously, with a particular love for cars. He was one of the kingpins who favored customizing his flight of luxury vehicles to make them even more ostentatious. One of his favorite cars was a white Mercedes that he had tricked out (by a legitimate car customizer who specialized in working with drug kingpins) with white leather upholstery and mint green piping – the contrasting piping on the front and rear seats became, for a while, a sign of high style in drug-dealing circles.[34] But Unique also wanted to launder his cash and use it to generate a legitimate revenue stream. A gifted and industrious entrepreneur, he turned to the club and music industry.

Owning a club was a natural fit for Unique; he loved to party and people loved to party with him. A sweet-talking Jamaican, he smoked blunts morning, noon, and night and was happy to smoke out anybody in his vicinity. Club 2000 was a gathering place for Dominican, Puerto Rican and African American dealers, as well as a who's who of the early 1990s hip-hop scene, including Sean Combs, the Wu-Tang Clan, Fat Joe, Queen Latifah, and many others. Assaults, gunfire, and general mayhem were par for the course. Neighborhood residents complained constantly about "the noise, the drinking, the drugs and the traffic" and the simple fact that no one within blocks of the club could get any sleep at night.[35] While trouble was no stranger to Club 2000, Unique worked to make his club a spot where people of different ethnicities could mix and mingle, unified by a love of good music.

Unique also owned and operated a music studio, Mecca Audio. He had an underground hit in 1994 with the vinyl 12", "My Dick Gets Hard/ Alright," which Unique co-produced. Unique was a good businessman, both in the legit and the illegit ends of the economy.

Unique had one other money-laundering trick shared in by many of his peers. He bought a lot of expensive jewelry. In his case, he wore very little of it, keeping most of it in a large Ziploc bag, perfect for a quick getaway if necessity demanded it. As he saw it, the jewelry "was his money bag in case shit ever got thick."[36] Hall never got a chance to sell off his gold and diamond stash of jewelry. He was arrested and then convicted in

June 1994 of being a drug kingpin. He got life in prison. The whereabouts of his Ziploc full of jewelry remains in question.

Unique was far from the only drug dealer who invested some of his illegally gotten gains in the hip-hop scene. In Los Angeles, Quintin "Q" Stephen, an Eight Trey Gangster Crip (the set was infamous for brutally beating up truck driver Reginald Denny during the 1992 LA riot) and a much bigger distributor than Unique, invested some of his proceeds into Nu U Productions, a recording studio in Hollywood. Supposedly, he was going to produce rap artists. In the early 1990s, in association with fellow members of the Eight Trey Gangster Crips, Stephen distributed more than $10 million in crack and powder cocaine (which was overwhelmingly cooked into crack) in LA, Denver, Seattle, Birmingham, and several other sites. Stephen's crack ring was both energetic and lucrative. Nu U Productions not so much. While a reasonable-looking front for laundering his drug proceeds, Stephen had no success in the rap game. Nu U Productions disappeared when Stephen was arrested in 1995.[37]

If Unique was a relatively small-time player in the hip-hop world and Q barely made a dent, Shawn Corey Carter, better known as Jay-Z, did a whole lot better. From an early age, Jay-Z wanted in on the music industry. By the time he was a young teenager, living in Brooklyn where he had been raised in the Marcy Projects, he'd become a gifted rapper. But in the mid 1980s, he was not yet making a living with his art. At eighteen, he did what many an aspiring artist had to do. He got a day job. Only instead of waiting tables or serving drinks behind a bar, he became a drug dealer. As his mentor in the hip-hop industry, Jaz-O, explains, "He chose to quite simply get money, as most of us did in our circle, we just chose to get money and get out of the hood any way we could."[38]

As Jay-Z details in his raps and his old associates attest, he took full advantage of the best market available to him.[39] Looking backwards, Jay-Z rapped that for a while, at least, selling crack came before his artistry.[40] And by all accounts, he was serious about the drug game. He moved from small-time selling in 1988 to turning a kilo of cocaine a week into crack in the early 1990s. But Jay-Z was a different kind of player.

Jay-Z did not floss, at least not much. Though he brags in his raps about owning luxury cars, his compatriots at the time say the reality was different. While everyone else was putting all their money into extravagances, collecting Mercedes Benzes with all the trimmings, he got by with a Lexus. One old friend argues, "To be smart enough to play yourself down to just keep the paper means you're doing business properly. And Jay-Z was always about keeping the paper."[41] Jay-Z was carefully avoiding public scrutiny – he was not on law enforcement's radar – all the while acquiring capital.

Jay-Z, even as he was moving weight in the drug game, kept a hand in the rap scene. But no one in the record industry came calling for him. He was frustrated. According to an old friend, he was thinking, "Why am I so good and these other niggas is getting deals? They're clowns."[42] But he was hesitant to spend his own money promoting his talent – and it took money to record a song that might catch the attention of a record label. By all accounts, Jay-Z was a rational economic actor: he enjoyed rapping, but he was more interested in making money. And at that point the music industry was not cooperating. So he kept selling drugs and he kept accumulating cash.

In 1994, still only twenty-four years old, Jay-Z began to reconsider his situation. He had gotten into a beef and almost was shot. "The longer you go," he told an interviewer, "the higher your odds are that something's gonna happen to you. I knew the first day I stood on the block the clock was going backwards. It was a countdown."[43] Jay-Z decided to get serious about switching careers.

Jay-Z, working with some serious talent, invested part of the money he had earned "grinding G-packs" to put together an album's worth of tracks.[44] Shockingly, in retrospect, he found no music-industry takers for his raps. And here is where Shawn Corey Carter becomes Jay-Z.

Instead of giving up and returning to his primary vocation, Jay-Z partnered up with the well-known Harlem party promoter (and erstwhile crack dealer) Damon Dash, and street savvy Kareem "Biggs" Burke – all of them had made money outside the mainstream – to start up their own label, Rock-A-Fella.[45] Jay-Z, always the word-smith with a gift for the double and triple entendre, was making multiple plays with his label's name.

Jay-Z was the label's original artist and Jay-Z, while no Rayful Edmond or Chambers brothers, had the money to keep the operation afloat. This was no vanity operation or money-laundering front. Jay-Z threw himself into the enterprise, hustling his CD all over the city. He and his partners made T-shirts, stickers, flyers, everything they could think of, to promote the label and Jay-Z's work. According to Jay-Z, he had $900,000 saved up from his illegal enterprise to invest in his legal business. People in the know understood what was happening: "Where that money come from? … It came out of their own pockets. And we know that they didn't work at Target."[46]

As the whole world came to know, Jay-Z pulled it off. Jay-Z, soon enough, became famous and rich the legal way. A 2003 ad for Reebok, promoting the eponymous "S. Carter" sneaker (10,000 pairs were sold within hours of their release) tells the tale of Jay-Z in mythic form. Two stark and beautiful images are shown, side-by-side. On the left, Jay-Z looks straight at the camera, wearing a sharp pin-stripe suit, with his sleeves perfectly shot. The other image shows the arm of a young black man; his bared forearm is covered in rubber bands (back in the day, street dealers wore rubber bands to indicate to crack buyers how much weight they had to sell) in front of a housing project. A caption reads: "I got my MBA from Marcy Projects, Shawn Carter."[47] On both sides of the law, Jay-Z was a disciplined, hard-working, risk-taking entrepreneurial genius. That entrepreneurial zeal, often enough cutthroat – literally in the crack trade and mostly metaphorically in the hip-hop industry – was understood to be a necessity for the young people coming out of poverty who were searching for a way to get paid.

As for Unique and Jay-Z, the hip hop–crack connection was very real. Plenty of artists who came to prominence during the 1980s and 1990s laid claim to it. Raekwon the Chef, from the Wu-Tang Clan, didn't get his name from baking cakes. As a teenager, Snoop Dogg went to prison on crack charges. 50 Cent got caught with ten ounces of crack and served time. The list of such artists is long.

Needless to say, the rapper crack dealer was only a part of the story. Melle Mel, mainstay of the incomparable Grandmaster Flash and the Furious Five, did his best to set the record straight in the 2007 induction speech he gave at the Rock and Roll Hall of Five:

All my life I've been into Hip Hop and it should mean more than just somebody standing on the corner selling dope – I mean that may or may not have its place too because it's there, but I'm just saying – I've never shot nobody, I ain't never stabbed nobody, I'm forty-five years old and I ain't got no criminal record, you know what I mean. The only thing I ever did was be about my music. So, I mean, so, while we're teaching people what it is about life in the ghetto, then we should be teaching people about me trying to grow up and to come out of the ghetto.[48]

Hip hop, in general, and even Gangsta Rap, in particular, in the late 1980s and early 1990s was, of course, neither funded nor populated solely by people intimately – or even casually – connected with the crack trade. Overwhelmingly, mainstream music-industry money laid the foundation for rappers' climb to fame.[49]

Still, crack money did make its way into the scene. How much money crack dealers and cocaine distributors laundered through the hip-hop industry mostly remains a mystery. South Central LA powder cocaine and crack kingpin Michael "Harry O" Harris, besides laundering his money through a limousine service (a common drug-fronted enterprise), a Beverley Hills beauty salon, an electrical contracting business, and other legitimate enterprises claims that he put $1.5 million into the hands of Marion "Suge" Knight to capitalize Death Row records, which became the biggest of the gangsta rap labels, as well as providing James Smith with $200,000 to launch the Houston-based Rap-a-Lot records. The heads of both labels deny Harris's claims. Ruthless Record's president Eric Wright, better known as Eazy-E of N.W.A., stated – bragged – that his relatively modest drug-dealing profits helped fund his label, which released his influential single "Boys-n-the-Hood" (1987) and N.W.A.'s triple-platinum album *Straight Outta Compton* in 1988.[50] Crack kingpins – and even some street-level dealers – had a lot of money to spread.

Likewise, the crack scene yielded a powerful contingent of rappers. Some had been street dealers. Others were compatriots of those who made their living that way. As the socially conscious rapper Nas declared in "Represent," a track from the illustrious *Illmatic* (1994), the work and the hustle of rap and crack were born of the same streets.[51]

The crack dealer turned rapper or hip-hop investor was always more than myth, even as it was mythologized and sometimes exaggerated by the gangsta rappers. Likewise, while the famous beefs between gangsta rappers were sometimes nothing more than cynical acts of self-promotion, too often they really did lead to deadly violence, most famously in the case of Tupac Shakur and the Notorious B.I.G.

Tupac Shakur never sold crack. But he did genuinely embrace the gangsta violent crack culture that did him in. Shakur aligned himself with the LA-based Bloods, some of whom had gotten rich distributing crack. The night of September 7, 1996, Shakur was in Las Vegas. He and Suge Knight of the LA-based Death Row Records had front-row seats for the Mike Tyson championship fight. Mob Piru Bloods sat with them. Both men used the Bloods as bodyguards.

After Tyson knocked out his hapless opponent in the first round, Shakur, Knight, and the Bloods went out to celebrate. Leaving the hotel where the fight had been staged, they spotted a member of the Bloods' rivals, the Crips. This Crip, allegedly a member of the South Side Crips out of Compton, had been involved in an assault on one of Shakur's Bloods bodyguards back in LA. A fight ensued, led by Shakur, which was quickly broken up by security guards.

The Crip, after picking himself up from the floor, gathered with fellow gang members in Las Vegas and they plotted out their revenge. Allegedly with a gun and reward money supplied by the Crips-affiliated Biggie Smalls – who vehemently denied his involvement – who allegedly was also in Las Vegas – which he also vehemently denied – and with whom Shakur had long publicly feuded – that part no one denied – the Crips moved out. In a new white Cadillac they went in search of Shakur, Knight, and the Bloods. They found them. At the front of a five-car caravan, on their way to a nightclub, Knight and Shakur were alone in a black BMW. The Crips opened fire, hitting Shakur four times; a bullet fragment nicked Knight in the head. Shakur died of his wounds six days later.

Days after Shakur's murder, gunfire erupted in Compton, as Bloods sought revenge on the Crips. Three people were killed and twelve were injured, including a ten-year-old girl. Six months later, Biggie Smalls was shot to death while sitting in his Chevrolet Blazer on Wilshire Boulevard in LA.[52]

Such murders, while bemoaned by the mainstream, became part of the Darwinian survival-of-the-fittest plot line that gave the gangsta rapper-crack years both their pathos and their glory in the eyes of legions of young people. The bitter truth of young black men gunned down, despite their wealth and their fame, provided the gangsters and the gangstas the aura of total commitment and authenticity in an era in which the supposed long-standing rules of legitimate financial accumulation and ethical behavior seemed to many to be unmoored from lived experience. Instead, the gangsta/gangster life of predation, violence, and life-threatening and life-taking hustle suggested a darker truth about success in Reagan's America.

In the crack era, white men of good fortune who tripped over the line separating legal and illegal money-making opportunities got in trouble, too, but of a more limited kind; e.g., arbitrager Ivan Boesky and financier Michael Milken spent a couple of years in white-collar prisons and were fined a few hundred million dollars for their shady billion-dollar schemes.[53] Poor black men in the crack industry got killed by their rivals or ended up with prison bids that went on for far longer than a couple of years. As the quotation loosely attributed to the French writer Honoré de Balzac goes, "Behind every great fortune there is a crime."

Crack dealers who could rap at the professional level were a rarity. Likewise, few crack dealers had the opportunity to befriend famous rappers or to invest in the hip-hop industry. Their lives were more circumscribed. Still, like their more renowned colleagues in the crack trade, they, too, often had the need to launder their cash. Most often, they invested locally and without much fanfare.

Thomas Mickens was a Queens kingpin. He was no Rayful Edmond but he made money. He patiently ran a crack crew near Kennedy Airport. At his peak, he had about fifty people working for him. He got his start in the early 1980s, as a teenager, selling powder cocaine and then, while continuing to sell ounces, moved into the crack business as the market shifted. In homage to his success and growing reputation among his hustler peers, he began calling himself "Tony Montana," after the protagonist of the movie *Scarface* (1983), not surprisingly a favorite film among crack dealers and gangsta rappers, alike.

Like many hustlers, Mickens was not a good student; he dropped out of high school. He was not a worldly guy. When he started out, he knew little outside of life in the neighborhood. But, like Rayful Edmond,

Mickens was born into the criminal underworld. His father was an operator in the Queens policy racket or numbers game – the illegal lottery that was popular in black communities around the country in the post–World War II decades. Mickens understood, from an early age, how people got by in the underground economy. His New York City police nemesis, Sgt. Michael McGuiness of the Narcotics Squad, admitted, "Tommy's a smart kid … He probably did the best job of all dealers out here of getting his money into legitimate businesses."[54] Mickens worked hard to launder his money, even while he lived large.

Mickens loved many of the same things as his peers. Mickens had a BMW, a Fleetwood Cadillac, and at one point or another during his four-year run, at least eighteen more cars, including a Rolls Royce for which he paid more than $100,000. Mickens always used cash to buy his cars but he never used his own name in registering them. His sister, his mother, the father of his girlfriend, and even the mother of one of his lieutenants were some of the people who supposedly owned the cars Mickens personally bought and drove. Mickens hid his ownership of his 38-foot Bayliner yacht the same way.

Mickens's more economically sound purchases followed a similar pattern. At a minimum, he bought some twenty pieces of property for upwards of $1.6 million. A *New York Times* front-page exposé on Mickens's financial maneuvers details one of those transactions. He bought a nice building on Grand Central Parkway in Queens for $184,766, with an upfront $69,000 cash payment. The owner agreed to list the official sales price of the property, however, at just $116,000. That way, when Mickens flipped the property, the IRS would not know that he had successfully laundered the original $69,000. Exactly how often Mickens deployed such sleight-of-hand techniques in his real-estate transactions was hard to discern. For sure, he generally paid cash for his properties, breaking down the amounts he paid into checks or money orders of less than $10,000, in a variety of names, to avoid IRS reporting requirements. The *Times* writer was impressed, noting: "Unlike major international traffickers, who have recourse to off-shore corporations, Swiss bank accounts, and other sophisticated schemes, these dealers, sometimes with little education and few contacts outside their neighborhood, find ways –

often with the connivance of legitimate businesses – to hide their assets."[55]

Mickens's real-estate deals were done on the q.t. Several of his other business investments were done more publicly. All around the neighborhood where Mickens's crew sold drugs, Mickens opened up legit businesses. He couldn't help himself; he named all the businesses with the "Montana" brand. He wanted people in his community to know how successful he had become. Mickens's biographer, Ethan Brown, writes, "In the late eighties, the Mickens/Montana brand Montana Dry Cleaners, Montana Sporting Goods, and the Montana Grocery – became as recognizable in southeast Queens as national chains like McDonald's."[56]

As Brown goes on to note, Mickens's decision to call his legit businesses by his street name was not a wise move. It attracted the attention of the police, who knew exactly who "Tony Montana" was. It was also not helpful to Mickens's scheme that some of the employees at his supposedly legitimate, money-cleaning businesses decided to supplement their relatively modest legitimate salaries by selling drugs (not Mickens's!) from behind the counter. This breach in protocol became painfully obvious to both Mickens and law enforcement when an infamous couple of gangsters, known as the "Bonnie and Clyde of the crack era," entered the Montana Dry Cleaners in a failed drug and cash robbery and murdered two of the store's employees.[57]

Mickens's attempts at presenting a legitimate front to interested law-enforcement parties were further hindered by his various forms of conspicuous consumption. How was Mr. Mickens, who reported to the IRS that he was an upholsterer, able to regularly drive around in a Rolls Royce and a Ferrari? Where did he come up with the money to embed several diamonds, a sapphire, and an emerald in his teeth? The authorities arrested Mickens, figured out his various money-laundering ploys, and in 1989 he was sentenced to thirty-five years in prison and fined $1 million. Authorities also seized $2.5 million in assets. "Tony Montana" had not nearly been clever enough in laundering his money.

Thomas Mickens got caught but for a few years, at least, he had almost turned the corner from drug dealer to successful above-board investor and entrepreneur. Crack dealers lower down the food chain rarely even made it that far in turning their illegal profits into a long-term legitimate revenue stream. The urban ethnographer Philippe Bourgois gives an illuminating account of how one unpleasant, dangerous small-time crack operator tried and failed to open a street-corner bodega to launder his drug money and, at least partially, go legit.[58]

The crack dealer, Ray, already had a front business, a small video-game room that advertised Pac-Man arcade machines. The real business of the arcade – the only business – was selling cheap vials of crack. Ray had taken over the place in late 1985 from another crack distributor. Before becoming a crack front, the 250 square foot space had been a candy store, which mostly just sold small bags of marijuana. No one would mistake the Game Room for a legit business. Ray wanted a place to launder his money that could withstand scrutiny.

He decided to open up a bodega. The first step went well. He worked out a good price on taking over the lease from the previous owner, who like many businessmen operating in poor neighborhoods had allowed the small grocery store to be used, alongside its normal operations, for underground activities, as well; gambling in this case. The gambling operators got into a dispute with the legit storekeeper. Arson ensued and the storekeeper decided to retire. Ray knew how to negotiate in this kind of situation. The next step went well, also. Ray had two of his hand-to-hand crack salesmen repair, clean up, and prepare the store, promising them that they could work at the grocery once it opened. Both men were excited about transitioning out of crack sales and into a respectable neighborhood job. One of them, Caesar, told Bourgois, "my career here is going to escalate, because the more money the store makes, the more money I make, 'cause I'm the sandwich man ... Sandwich man! Here! Yo! Take Yours! Ring! Clink! Next!"[59] Caesar was under the influence of synthetic mescaline when he spoke of this dream to his ethnographer friend.

None of it ever happened. Ray could not pull it off. Bourgois argues that Ray's failures "highlight the different 'cultural capitals' needed to operate as a private entrepreneur in the legal economy versus the underground economy." Ray knew how to deal successfully with his crack clientele; he knew how to keep his dealer employees on task; he knew when to resort to violence, which he was most capable of deploying, and when to use persuasion to keep his crack business running smoothly. But he did not know how to work in a civil and effective manner with the middle-class city bureaucrats and food distributors upon whose good will and cooperation he depended to run a legitimate grocery store. It did not help that he was barely literate. Bourgois concludes: "in his forays into the legal economy, Ray's same street skills made him appear to be an incompetent, gruff, illiterate, urban *jíbaro* [an unsophisticated Puerto Rican] to the inspectors, clerks, and petty officials who allocate permits and inventory products, and who supervise licensing in New York City."[60] Ray could not get past the gauntlet of officials who stood between him and his hopes of running a legal business.

The store opened without proper permits for a few days. Business was weak and the supposedly semi-skilled man Ray hired to work on the store's inventory stole from him and fled. The whole thing was just too complicated, too challenging, and too distant from what Ray knew how to do well. Ray closed the store less than two weeks after he had, illegally, opened it. Caesar never became a sandwich man. For the average crack dealer, laundering money was no easy thing.

Most of the people who made a living selling crack did not worry about money laundering. Generally, what they got, they spent. The hand-to-hand sales force and low-level managers were, by and large, just wage earners in an all cash, no benefits business. Due to the criminal nature of their work, few felt comfortable depositing their cash in a bank – the cost of suspicion was too high. And without recourse to the kind of muscle employed by the kingpins to protect their daily or weekly proceeds, the street-level dealers and the corner boys were always at risk of being ripped off by their criminal acquaintances and neighborhood enemies. Then, too, by the late 1980s, most knew that jail or prison was part of the price of pursuing their livelihood. As a result, few thought about long-term financial planning. Instead, the rank-and-file gang bangers and crack crew-members spent their money and they spent a lot of it on self-display.

Street crews put in a lot of time in full public view selling their wares. On their corners and off, too, they had reputations to maintain. To represent the right image to the people they served, to the generation that was coming up behind them, to their foes and their friends, and to the women in the neighborhood, they put effort into displaying their worth through their wealth. The ready cash that lined their pockets was the means by which they backed up those efforts. The documentarians of *Hell up in East Harlem* report: "The soldiers of Wagner Projects became urban fashion trend-setters and East Harlem served as their runway as they sported Marmots, Gore-tex, fitteds [hats] and Nautica sweat-suits."[61] The same could be said in urban neighborhoods all over the country.

Crack crew-members took their looks seriously and they took pride in their gangster reputation. Rather than hide what they were and what they did, many chose instead to fully represent it, often with the overt support of their bosses. For a while, Prince's sales crew with the Supreme Team actually had a uniform. Street corner dealers had to wear a nylon tracksuit or sweatpants with Le Tigre-branded shorts worn over the pants. Corey Pegues recalls that when he first joined Prince's crew, his crew boss took him out shopping and spent $3,000 outfitting him: he picked up five Fila sweat suits, five pairs of Le Tigre shorts, and a varied set of Pumas to go with the outfits. A heavy gold chain completed the look.[62] Supreme Team members were supposed to look good and to visibly demonstrate that they were making money.

In neighborhoods where everyday expenses were by no means guaranteed and most people lived in dilapidated housing and too often faced one kind of tragedy or another born of poverty, personal style was a powerful way to display worth and strength. A New Orleans teenager explained how and why his look mattered to him: "I could get shot tomorrow and my momma coulda been done passin', if I put on them clothes, bam. See what I'm sayin'? Nobody never know what happened cause I'm in a whole different world, I'm coolin' y'all off. I look way better than y'all, I'm too hot to be touched. You can't tell me nuttin', it's just me in my zone and my clothes." Money made that look possible. The same young man: "when you first look at me, I'm 'bout money. Don't think I'm out here grindin' all day, lookin' ashy and stuff … what most thugs is all about, competition, bottom line."[63] Overwhelmingly, the young men on the corner selling crack could not buy a new Mercedes Benz with customized leather upholstery with contrasting piping – though almost all of them might have aspired to it. But they could buy the latest Sergio Tacchini tracksuit, Air Jordans, or a genuine Bulls or

Hawks Starter jacket. Few of their peers not dealing on the street corner could afford to do likewise.

In the late 1980s and early 1990s, drug-dealer-led competition over high-priced fashion-setting clothing items spilled over into violent confrontations in city after city. In Chicago, between late 1989 and early 1990, four young men were murdered for their NFL or NBA team jackets that sold for up to $200. New Air Jordans and similar gym shoes were particularly coveted. A Chicago mother, desperate to keep her son from turning to drug dealing to satisfy his sartorial needs, came up with $175 for a pair of high-status sneakers; he was held up for his shoes within days of their purchase. The boy's mother told a reporter, "These children are out here stealing from one another to be cool ... It's a sad situation. Their parents can't afford to buy the stuff, so they do whatever they can to get it." In Detroit, after a high school student was murdered for his brand new Nikes, the school board there decided to institute a strict dress code that banned a range of the most in-demand expensive items, as well as showy gold chains and other jewelry. The crack dealers and their fellow gangsters had upped the style ante in their neighborhoods and wreaked havoc in their wake.[64]

Clothing and jewelry were not the only high-fashion status items crews popularized in their neighborhoods. A New York writer, who spent weeks talking with teenagers in Harlem reported on another highly coveted consumer item: guns. Along with "gold chains, or a four-finger ring, a fancy 'eight-ball' jacket, a 'dope fresh' pair of sneakers ... a phone beeper clipped to a belt, a pistol sticking from a waistband lets others know the owner is in a crack crew, even if he's not."[65] For real crack dealers, guns were a tool-of-the-trade. But they were more than that, too. Displaying guns was part of the image and displaying ever more powerful and deadly guns demonstrated how serious, how "hard" a player one had become. It wasn't enough to have a pistol, it was better to have an Uzi or a TEC machine gun, or better yet, both. Some of that firepower was a useful signal to street rivals; as President Reagan declared, it was a matter of "peace through strength." Part of it, though, was simply conspicuous consumption of a more death-dealing variety. Photos of crews displaying their weapons became de rigueur in gangster circles.

Like with the high-status, expensive clothes, many young men in the same neighborhoods, even if not drug dealers or gangsters of any kind, followed suit. In part, owning a gun demonstrated toughness. But gun ownership also felt like a necessity to many young men in inner-city neighborhoods. They felt that they had to be ready to defend themselves in the face of nearly omnipresent threats of violence from the gangsters in their midst.

In 1990 in New York City, illegal possession of guns among teenagers was the city's fastest-growing arrest category, rising 400 percent since 1986. The result of the plenitude of guns in such neighborhoods led inexorably to waves of deadly shootings, many of them not related directly to drug-dealing beefs. In New York City in 1988, 40 percent of homicides were drug-related – almost always over control of drug corners or drug rip-offs. In 1990, only 25 percent were. In the middle of the crack years, one in twenty-one black men died from a homicide and the murder rate of young black men was seven times higher than that of whites. Crack-linked violence and threat of violence had helped create a broader culture of gun display and gun murder on some of the hardest city streets in the United States.[66]

Crack dealers were almost always about the business and presentation of intimidation and threat. They wore guns like they wore gold ropes. But their sense of style was always more than that, too. The money they earned in their rough way gave them a freedom to show off their physical vitality, their street style. With everyone's eyes on them, they set the scene. Rappers watched them, borrowing heavily from their swagger and their ostentatious display. With money to burn, they flexed and strained against the everyday; they willed themselves to live large, knowing that prison or death was around the corner. As social bandits and murderous thugs, they grabbed their society's center stage.

CHAPTER 5

Crackdown: The Politics and Laws of Drug Enforcement

BY THE LATE 1980s, CRACK HAD THE NATION IN A PANIC. Murder, death, instant addiction, crack crews, crack kingpins, crackheads, crack whores, crack babies. Crack, the mass media roared, was everywhere. Those stalwart scholars of America's engagement with crack cocaine, Craig Reinarman and Harry G. Levine, argue that "the period from 1986 to 1992 was in many ways the most intense drug scare of the twentieth century." They have a strong case.

The media told quite a few whoppers about crack cocaine during that period, feeding the American public's wildest fears with terrifying, if often untrue or exaggerated, tales of ever-widening drug devastation. America's newsweeklies, especially *Time* and *Newsweek*, helped lead the charge, sometimes into hysteria, and in those pre-Internet days, these newsweeklies had a lot of reach – some 20 million people, most of them middle-class voters, read *Time* at its peak.

Crack coverage took off in 1986. "The rush is so intense and the crash so powerful that it keeps users – even first-time users – focused on nothing but their next hit ... [T]he state of near psychosis that heavy cocaine use produces leads easily to violence ... [A] sixteen-year-old addict confessed to stabbing his mother to death after she caught him smoking crack," *Time* reported in June 1986.[1]

Based on that lurid account readers might well have deduced that individuals high on crack were in a "state of near psychosis" and ever-ready to murder their mothers or anybody else who got in their way ... which just was not true. People high on crack overwhelmingly were too busy being high on crack – and often enough focused on making sexual contact – to kill anybody during their fifteen minutes of head-shattering

Figure 9 Ronald Reagan bill signing: President Ronald Reagan signing the Anti-Drug Abuse Act of 1986. Harlem Congressman Charles Rangel, who pushed hard for the fiercely punitive legislation, stands next to First Lady Nancy Reagan, champion of "Just Say No" to drugs. (Ronald Reagan Presidential Library.)

euphoria. Heavy crack usage carried with it a lot of terrible risks, but becoming a homicidal maniac was not one of them.[2]

The mass media focus on the deadly perils of the crack "epidemic" escalated over the next two years. In the presidential election year of 1988, *Time* put crack on its then-coveted cover, running a long story titled "Kids Who Sell Crack."[3] The powerful story illuminated the lives of young teenagers in America's inner cities caught up in the flash of selling crack. Even decades later there is much to learn from and admire about the story, which drew on the talent and resources of America's most popular newsweekly.

Midway through the story, however, *Time* went off the rails. Wild claims began to be tossed around. "The high is instantaneous, the addiction complete," a DEA agent was quoted as saying. That was not true, but to be fair many contemporary observers of the crack scene feared that it might be. But the article's unsubstantiated claims went much further: "Most of the adolescent crack dealers' clients are children ... Some of the latest abusers are barely out of babyhood."

Figure 10 Inmates at Cook County Jail: As in many other jurisdictions, beginning in the late 1980s, Chicago officials cracked down hard on drug dealers, targeting street corner crack sellers. As a result, poor, young black men were incarcerated in record numbers. (Lloyd Degrane.)

Then the focus zoomed in on some of America's wealthiest communities. White America was put on notice: "it is easy to assume that crack is an exclusively underclass problem. Not so ... There is a terrible symbiosis between the wealthy addicts and the inner-city dealers. Privileged kids who venture into the ghetto to spend hundreds of thousands of dollars on crack are largely responsible for the booming drug business." Rich white suburban teenagers, the article claims, are "largely responsible" for the crack industry in 1988.

This claim seems to be based on the story of one white teenager, "Eric," who grew up in "Los Angeles' posh Brentwood section." Young "Eric," by *Time's* account, definitely spent a lot of money – some $40,000 – buying crack in the "seedy Venice Beach area." Eric, the article, reported, had become a crack addict. But young, wealthy, white Eric was not, in 1988, the average crack customer. Three years earlier, the DEA had concluded that crack was no longer the drug of choice of well-heeled, non-urban cokehead whites (not even then teenagers) but of poor inner-city people. *Time* seemed to be trying to keep white America concerned about the perils of crack cocaine. By arguing that whites were responsible for the crack market, the article made the case that whites were thus responsible for the damage and violent mayhem the drug was inflicting in poor, primarily black, communities. But in so doing, America's influential news magazine also gave its overwhelmingly white readership strong reasons to fear that black "ghetto" crack dealers were targeting their children. Many of those parents wanted something – anything – to be done to stop those dealers from turning their children into drug addicts. The racial – even racist – component of the story is plain to see.

The mass media was by no means solely responsible for white Americans' widely shared fear that crack cocaine was coming for them and their children and that something had to be done to stop it. In the 1980s, illegal drugs were a powerful presence in America, and the new focus on crack simply strengthened Americans' growing sense that illegal drug use had become too common in the United States. There was truth to that concern. In 1980, two out of three high school seniors had tried an illegal drug and one-third of them admitted to regular use.[4] By and large these young people were getting high on marijuana, and by then most people realized that weed was far less risky than a host of other illegal alternatives. Nonetheless, plenty of parents did not want their kids to get stoned on anything. Around the country, parents organized. In Atlanta they formed Families in Action. There was Texans' War on Drugs. And then came the powerful and influential National Federation of Parents for a Drug-Free Youth.

These parents, overwhelmingly white and middle class, had the ear of their congressmen. In January 1980, these parent-based groups secured a Senate hearing on the dangers of marijuana. One of their leaders made her fears, as well as her demands, plain: "I am a mother, not a doctor, not a scientist. I am here to protect my children. I am also here to protect my neighbor's children and the children of this nation."[5] Senators understood the power of this claim and recognized the political fuel it supplied to a "war on drugs."

That hearing in 1980 was narrowly focused on the perils of marijuana. By the mid 1980s, parents' drug fears had only grown. If their kids were attuned to buying and smoking marijuana, what would stop them, parents pondered, from further illegal drug experimentation? What if they bought some crack? Would instant addiction, sexual depravity, and maybe even matricide follow?

People then and later laughed at First Lady Nancy Reagan's heavily publicized campaign to "Just Say No" to drugs. Nonetheless, it was very popular and well received by a majority of the American people when she started it, pre-crack, in 1982. By 1988, people had formed some 12,000 "Just Say No" clubs.[6] In 1989, in the midst of fears over the reach and impact of crack cocaine, even after unprecedentedly fierce anti-drug, anti-crack legislation had been put into federal law, the Gallup polling organization reported that nine out of ten Americans wanted even more punitive measures taken against drug dealers.[7]

Also in 1989, an astonishing 64 percent of those polled for a *New York Times*/CBS survey said that drugs were America's number one problem. People were afraid. Those fears were inflamed by the mass media and politicians' rhetoric. But people were not just pawns of elite manipulation. Between 1985 and 1989, according to the Office of National Drug Control Policy, cocaine use had doubled in the United States. And much of that increase was due to the popularity of crack. Federal authorities estimated that 50 percent of the cocaine smuggled into the United States was cooked into crack, a drug so cheap that anyone, even children, could buy it; a drug so powerful and alluring that many believed it was instantly addictive; a drug intertwined, seemingly, with violence and sexual predation.[8] Yes, people hyped these fears. But as African Americans who lived in poor or economically declining neighborhoods could attest, the hype had a basis in fact. Black community leaders helped lead the demand for a crackdown on crack. Crack scared the hell out of people, and not without reason.

That fear reverberated in American politics. Between 1986 and 1989 Democrats and Republicans engaged in a bidding war over crack policy in the United States. Black and white, liberal and conservative, a bevy of politicians at both the local and the national level fought to prove to the public that they were the most zealous soldiers in the latest iteration of the war on drugs. Step by step, American politicians and law enforcement officials, generally supported by a large majority of the American people, built a complex, often merciless legal apparatus to incarcerate people caught up in the sale and distribution of crack cocaine. Not until 1992 did a coalition of people from diverse backgrounds, led by black elected officials and community activists, begin to seriously challenge this fiercely punitive turn against the ravages of crack cocaine. Even then, their challenge was largely sidelined by the winning politics of the War on Drugs.

* * *

Harlem Congressman Charles Rangel, the "Lion of Lenox Avenue," hated what crack cocaine was doing to his people. He hated the fear it brought to his community. He despaired of the destruction it wrought. Drug addiction and drug-linked criminality were not abstractions for Charlie Rangel. He had seen it before; the pall of narcotics was nothing new for the congressmen or his constituents. Charlie Rangel, who represented America's best-known African American community, was also one of America's fiercest anti-drug crusaders. By the mid 1980s, he made crack dealers his number one enemy.

Rangel came up in Harlem. Fatherless, he dropped out of high school. He got drafted and fought in the Korean war where he earned a purple heart, a bronze star, and then the right, as a veteran, to an education guaranteed by the GI Bill. Gregarious, whip smart, and with a law degree in hand, Rangel turned to New York politics and rose up the ranks fast.

Rangel became Harlem's congressman in 1970. When he took office, New York City was the capital of heroin addiction in the United States and his community was at the epicenter of the scourge. Addicts, in need of cash to feed their habit, prowled Harlem streets. The *Amsterdam News*, Harlem's African American newspaper, reported in 1971: "some sections of the so-called Harlem business section after nightfall [look] like a ghost town. People continue to be afraid to walk the streets at night."[9] The elderly, in particular, felt trapped in their homes, afraid to face the gauntlet of desperate junkies. Break-ins and muggings were commonplace. Harlem business owners were particularly incensed. According to a 1971 survey, they demanded "stricter law enforcement," "more policemen," to "take junkies off the street," and "more severe punishment for criminals."[10]

Illegal narcotics, even more than substandard housing and terrible government services, Rangel's constituents told him, were their number one problem – and thus, should be his number one problem. He later wrote: "Drugs affected every part of every life in my town. Senior citizens were assaulted by addicts, while addicts were fighting and killing one another and had taken over whole streets and neighborhoods. Worse, the corruption was making what was a historically bad relationship between the police and the community a lethal one, as instead of protectors, the police became something of an enabling army for the drug dealers."[11] Rangel took on the whole sad and sordid mess.

In 1971, soon after Rangel took office, he co-founded the Congressional Black Caucus. He helped lead the CBC to focus on fostering economic opportunities for poor people of color. He also challenged his colleagues to take on the illegal drug trade. In 1976, he fought for and became a member of the new House Select Committee on Narcotics Abuse and Control. In 1983 he became its chairman.

Rangel used his chairmanship to hammer away at the Reagan administration's drug policies. President Reagan, he said, did not take the war on drugs seriously. No one, he complained, was in charge of the federal government's anti-drug fight. No one, he argued, made sure that the billions congress appropriated to fight the war on drugs were spent wisely. Rangel wanted the federal government to do much more to stop the flow of drugs into the United States. But Rangel also wanted to make sure that people who sold drugs in the United States – as well as those who simply used them – were punished.

In February 1984, the Select Committee on Narcotics Abuse and Control, under Rangel's control, called for a massive increase in law enforcement's ability to prosecute and incarcerate anyone caught up with illegal drugs. Just before the crack cocaine deluge, Rangel's committee declared: "The odds are overwhelming that an addict or drug abuser who breaks the law will not be arrested. But if arrested, the odds are that the system will not convict or sentence him. There is a need for more prosecutors, more judges, more agents, and more prisons on both the State and Federal level."[12] Chairman Rangel concluded, "Drug trafficking has forced our criminal justice system to be concerned with the quantity of defendants, rather than the quality of justice."[13] Rangel wanted more arrests, more prosecutions, and more jail time for drug traffickers.

Rangel's approach was not purely punitive. He called out, loud and clear, for more and better treatment for drug addicts, and he believed that cutting off narcotics at their source was a critical part of any war on drugs. But Rangel, as he saw it, was siding with the respectable people of his community. Those people, he believed, should not have to countenance drug dealing. They should not be threatened by cutthroat dealers and their junkie customers. Those who sold and abused drugs, Charlie Rangel insisted, belonged in prison.

By the mid 1980s, the lure of heroin had waned in Rangel's Harlem district. Rangel, however, saw a new and overwhelming threat in the form of crack cocaine. Rangel had made his feelings about cocaine, more generally, known in July 1985, when he held a well-publicized hearing on "Cocaine Abuse and the Federal Response." He meant to convince the American people that there was nothing romantic or adventurous about snorting cocaine: "The fact is that cocaine is poison and it kills."[14] He demanded that the Reagan administration do more to stop cocaine distribution in the United States.

In July 1986, Rangel honed in on crack. He co-chaired the first congressional hearing on crack cocaine, joining forces with Congressman George Miller, who chaired the Select Committee on Children, Youth, and Families. Miller (who was white) was one of the most liberal congressmen in the United States, representing the eighth district in the San Francisco Bay area of California. Together, across racial lines, they meant to warn the nation of "the Crack Cocaine Crisis."[15]

Rangel and Miller had brought together a broad spectrum of elected officials to their joint hearing. Rangel opened up the hearing by asking his moderate Republican colleague, Benjamin Gilman, a fellow hardliner on drugs, to make a few comments. The senior Republican on the committee, Gilman echoed Rangel: "We're at an important crossroad in our Nation – the awareness that drug abuse is now epidemic and at the same time that an even deadlier drug is now available for consumption. That drug is crack and it's sweeping across the country like a tidal wave."[16] Gilman's conservative Republican colleague, Congressman Hamilton Fish, spoke up. He congratulated Rangel for holding the hearing and gave much the same message: "Nine months ago, addiction to crack was virtually unheard of, and today it's an epidemic, a plague, that is sweeping the country."[17]

The liberal congressman from Los Angeles, Mel Levine, reported from the frontlines. He explained that in Southern California crack had been sold openly for five years. He offered a few painful anecdotes: crack dealers in his district "were using a stolen stop sign to flag down cars to make additional drug sales." In a different neighborhood, another group of dealers had "set up a trash can slalom course" on a public street "to slow traffic and provide more opportunities for drug sales." The LAPD, under-resourced and without sufficient manpower, Levine told his colleagues, was powerless to stop the wide-open drug trade. Local police needed federal support.[18] Across partisan and ideological divides, congress was in rare agreement: crack was coming for America's youth and it had to be stopped.

The joint hearing convened by congressmen Rangel and Miller had been prompted and powered, at least in part, by a terrible tragedy. On June 19, 1986, University of Maryland basketball superstar Len Bias had died from a cocaine overdose. Just two days before his death, the Boston Celtics had selected Bias as the number two pick in the 1986 NBA draft. Bias, some said, was another Michael Jordan.

The overdose death of this extraordinary athlete had shocked the nation. Michael Weinrub, in a searing article titled, "The Day Innocence Died," memorialized the twenty-two-year-old: "If you were alive then, and you cared at all about sports, or about drugs, you most likely remember it well. It was one of those moments – like JFK, like Martin Luther King Jr., like the space shuttle Challenger earlier that same year – when we, as a society, stopped and stared collectively into the void and declared that human existence was entirely unjust."[19]

The Reverend Jesse Jackson, then America's best-known civil rights leader, gave a eulogy for Bias at the Memorial Chapel at the University of Maryland. He used his time at the pulpit to condemn drug dealers, whom he said preyed on young black people. Referencing the Ku Klux Klan and the horrors of lynching, he said "ropes never killed as many of our young people as the pushers of drugs … Lenny was vulnerable, but all of us are … We must make his death the turning point."[20]

Bias had died from a massive overdose of powder cocaine. He had snorted the drug. He had not smoked crack. But in the aftermath of his death, few noted the difference. Crack cocaine and powder cocaine were conflated. The fact that he was a young black man allowed people to connect his death, however inaccurately, with the sweep of crack through inner-city communities and the massive, often exaggerated attention its usage was receiving in the mass media. Bias's drug overdose gave weight, however misinformed, to the nation's unalloyed drug fears. If the 6'7" Len Bias, a young man in extraordinary physical shape and with the world at his feet, could be destroyed by drugs, it meant that anyone could be.[21]

Politicians felt the public heat and knew that they needed to act. The 1986 mid-term elections loomed, giving both political parties a powerful incentive to move quickly. Speaker of the House Tip O'Neill, an old-school liberal Democrat from Boston, saw drug legislation as a useful tool to take on the Reagan administration, whose best known weapon against illegal drugs was Nancy Reagan's heart-felt but far from tough-minded "Just Say No" slogan.

Officials in the Reagan administration knew they were vulnerable on the drug issue, especially in regard to the well-publicized scourge of crack cocaine. At Charlie Rangel's July hearings, Reagan officials had been forced to admit that they knew little about crack. The head of the Division of Epidemiology and Statistical Analysis at the National Institute on Drug Abuse, under tough questioning, revealed that his scientists had nothing to tell the committee about crack. The ranking Republican member of the committee, Benjamin Gilman, was appalled: "Am I correct, then, that at this point we really don't have any definite knowledge of how extensive the use of crack is in our country with all of our expertise; is that right? ... Here we are at the federal level and we have no idea of how extensive the problem is, let alone what to do about it."[22] In the face of voters' fears over illegal drugs, in general, and the massively hyped perils of crack cocaine, in particular, the Reagan administration was in political trouble, as were Republican incumbents facing the electorate that November.

Both Republicans and Democrats, liberals and conservatives, were aware in 1986 that they actually knew relatively little about the social and epidemiological effects of crack. Likewise, they had "no idea," in

Congressman Gilman's words, "what to do about it." Such gaps in policy-makers' knowledge might have signaled to all parties that they should pause before crafting major legislation, taking the time necessary to learn more about the subject. Congress saw the matter differently. Members of Congress pressed on, knowing that voters were likely to reward action, even if that action was half-cocked.

The Anti-Drug Abuse Act of 1986 was introduced in the House on September 11, 1986. The legislative rush to passage astonished the House Judiciary Committee's principal staffer for drug-enforcement issues. He recalled, "The careful deliberative practices of the Congress were set aside for the drug bill … The development of this bill was the sole instance during more than nine years with the Judiciary Committee that I did not see the usual procedure upon introduced bills followed … [I]t was the fearful image of crack in the public consciousness that drove the legislative package." On the Senate side, the sardonic Kansan Bob Dole, the conservative Republican leader, noted that a few news-paper editorials had wondered if Congress was, perhaps, moving too fast in order to pass anti-drug legislation before the 1986 mid-term election. Dryly, Senator Dole allowed, "[T]hey are probably correct." Dole's liberal Democratic colleague, Senator Lowell Weicker of Connecticut, reminded everyone of the underlying impetus for Congress's rush to legislate: "This is great politics."[23] Almost every politician in Washington cheered on passage of the bill, knowing that it would strengthen his or her re-election chances.

As the House and Senate rushed their respective anti-drug bills to the floor for a vote, there was some debate about how fiercely they should punish crack dealers as compared to powder cocaine dealers. Florida Senator Paula Hawkins, a conservative Republican whose consti-tuents had long been in and around ground zero for both the cocaine-smuggling business and the crack industry, helped start the conversation. She definitely wanted harsher federal prison sentences for cocaine deal-ers. But she had argued for no difference in penalties between dealers of crack and dealers of powder. It was all cocaine, she accurately stated.

Quickly, however, Senator Hawkins realized that public sentiment was not on her side. How about a 20:1 ratio, she opined? The Reagan administration and Senate Republican leadership followed her lead.

This ratio, however, was actually less severe than that offered by the Democratic House leadership, whose initial bid was a 50:1 ratio. After the Reagan administration's made its position clear with its 20:1 ratio, the House Democratic leadership saw political opportunity and went all in. They won the bidding war handily by demanding that crack dealers had to be caught only with 1 percent as much weight as their powder cocaine rivals to earn the same mandatory minimum prison sentences. The Reagan administration and Republican leadership chose not to rebid and the 100:1 ratio between crack cocaine and powder cocaine was written in to the final bill.[24]

Congress singled out relatively small-time crack dealers for extraordinarily punitive prison sentences at the federal level for a few reasons, which, in terms of fairness or equal treatment before the law, did not (and do not) stand up to rational scrutiny. New York Senator Alfonse D'Amato, a hard-nosed, law-and-order Republican, put the best face forward on the matter. On the floor of the Senate, he made two different arguments. First, he argued that crack dealers had developed a method in selling their product that made it difficult to catch them with more than a small amount of drugs in their possession. For proof, he quoted a June 16, 1986 *Newsweek* article: "The crack trade operates like a guerilla insurgency and makes an infuriatingly difficult target for police." Corner dealers, and even crack houses, rarely held more than a few crack vials at a time. Rather than cache and sell their products in the same place, they had created an early version of "just-in-time" inventory control. Dealers sold what they had and then "re-upped" regularly. Quick sales and quick re-supply operations were the name of the game. Police could fairly easily catch the corner dealers but they rarely could knock down the main supply caches and the people who controlled them. So, D'Amato said, law enforcement had to catch the little guys and throw them in prison – it was the only way to shut down crack operations.

D'Amato further justified the long sentences of such small-time dealers by insisting that crack cocaine was more dangerous than powder cocaine. Because, he claimed, crack was a "far more deadly and addictive substance," dealers of crack should be punished far more harshly than those of powder cocaine.[25] In fact, crack was not physiologically more deadly than powder cocaine. And while smoking cocaine (as well as shooting it intravenously) did seem to produce greater drug dependency than did snorting it, crack was certainly not one hundred times more addictive than cocaine's powdered version (even as people who relished the fierce and intense high of crack were more likely to binge dangerously on the drug than people who simply enjoyed the lesser blast that snorting cocaine provided).[26]

D'Amato, at that point, had championed a bill he called "the Crack and Cocaine Meaningful Penalties Act." It was the single harshest measure proposed in this season of maximum ferocity. If D'Amato had his way, a first-time offender caught with 100 grams of powder cocaine or 1 gram of crack cocaine would be given a maximum term of twenty years in jail and a fine of up to $250,000. A second offense would result in a sentence of up to forty years in jail and a fine of $500,000. These were far harsher penalties than were given for second-degree murder or for rape. D'Amato seems to have been the first to demand a 100:1 ratio in terms of how to punish powder cocaine dealers versus crack cocaine dealers (though at one gram, it is hard to label such a person a drug dealer).[27]

D'Amato's explanation – or rationalization – only made sense if the threat of crack cocaine was so extreme that it justified such unequal and patently unfair treatment of small-time criminals. Heroin dealers, after all, were imprisoned longer for possessing smaller amounts of the drug than were dealers of powder cocaine (a 5:1 ratio). The same was true of LSD dealers, although in that case the tiny scale of an effective dose legitimately explains the penalty versus weight ratio. Certainly, belief that crack cocaine was particularly dangerous made possible the 100:1 ratio Congress established for punishing crack cocaine dealers versus powder cocaine dealers.

To say it straightforwardly, Americans' fear of crack was not all in their heads. It was not simply something they had been tricked into believing. Yes, people read mass-media stories that exaggerated the threat of crack, stories that claimed crack was instantly addictive, and that crack addicts, as well as their children, were doomed by the drug's pernicious effects. But there were also people who knew friends or family members who smoked crack and became intransigent users – addicts – who did whatever they could to binge and stay high. People in poor communities watched crack users tear apart their neighborhoods and destroy families.

Crack dealers, themselves, were both pleased and appalled by how many of their customers became desperate to get high, who seemed unable to stay away from the crack pipe. Crack was a threat to the well-being of individuals, families, and communities. But it was in no way so much more destructive than powder cocaine that its sellers deserved to go to jail for so long for being caught with so little.

The Anti-Drug Abuse Act of 1986, as it moved quickly toward passage, became a massive piece of legislation. It gave law enforcement the right to bust into people's homes, without a warrant, and legally use whatever drugs they found therein in criminal prosecutions if they had "a reasonable, good faith belief" that they were acting in accord with Constitutional provisions regarding proper searches. It provided some $6 billion, to be spent over three years, to improve "federal drug eradication, enforcement, interdiction, education, and prevention efforts." It criminalized money laundering. Most critically, the act substantially increased the federal penalties convicted drug dealers faced if found guilty and provided $97 million to build more prisons to house those drug prisoners.

Congress mandated stiff minimum prison sentences for all kinds of drug trafficking. These mandatory prison sentences, especially those that targeted crack dealers, were what gave the bill its political power. Americans wanted to punish drug dealers and their political representatives aimed to please.

In general, these mandatory minimum sentences aimed to imprison drug "kingpins," as well as "middle-level dealers." For example, the bill imposed a ten-year minimum sentence for those found with 1,000 grams of heroin or 5,000 grams of powder cocaine (a little over 11 pounds) or 1,000 kilograms of marijuana (that's 2,200 pounds) or 10 grams of LSD (which is, at least, 40,000 individual doses). Those who possessed 100 grams of heroin or 500 grams of powder cocaine, worth about $7–15 thousand dollars, depending on place and purity, automatically received five-year sentences in a federal penitentiary.[28]

Crack cocaine dealers, however, were treated differently. Crack dealers faced "kingpin" sentences of ten years if they possessed just 50 grams. They faced "middle-level" mandatory sentences of five years if they were caught with 5 grams of crack, as few as 30 vials. A quarter weighs about five grams. The water in a teaspoon weighs five grams. Five grams of crack in 1986 typically retailed for as little as $300, depending on place and quality.[29] Rather than targeting kingpins or even middle-level dealers, the Anti-Drug Abuse Act of 1986 punished street-corner, hand-to-hand crack dealers with mandatory prison terms of five years. Congress was declaring that crack cocaine dealers were, essentially, a hundred times more dangerous or evil than their underworld colleagues who distributed powder cocaine.

The House passed the Anti-Drug Abuse Act of 1986 by a landslide vote, 392–16. Almost all of the members of the Congressional Black Caucus had co-sponsored the bill. When the vote came to the floor of the House, however, the Caucus divided. Several members, including Oakland's Ron Dellums, an original co-sponsor of the bill, voted no. So did Jon Conyers and George Crockett, both of whom represented Detroit. Also opposed was Gus Savage, who represented the Southside of Chicago. And they were joined by a handful of the House's most liberal white members, including Massachusetts's Barney Frank, San Jose's Don Edwards, and Ted Weiss from New York City. No members of the CBC publicly explained their vote, and none of the bill's opponents cited the disparity in punishment for dealers of crack and powder cocaine as reason for their disapproval. Congressman Frank gave the most pointed criticism of the bill, stating: "I am afraid this bill is becoming the legislative equivalent to crack. It is going to give people a short-term high, but it is going to be dangerous in the long run to the system and expensive to boot."[30] Frank believed the bill jeopardized Americans' civil liberties and he recognized that it was going to put a lot of people in prison. He wanted the bill, instead, to emphasize drug treatment, education, and prevention. In the House of Representatives, his was a rare voice.

In the Senate, the bill was equally popular. The Senate did not even hold a roll call vote, passing the measure, instead, by voice. Only one senator spoke out against the disproportionate sentencing provisions of the bill, and only he spoke directly about its racially discriminatory force. New York Senator Patrick Moynihan was, most agreed, a curmudgeon. He was also an independent and often-provocative thinker who had a long history of angering people on all sides of the political spectrum. In 1965, he had incensed a good many black Americans, along with progressives of all kinds, when he argued that the "breakdown" in the black family – the common lack of a bread-winning father in the home – was a major factor in preventing African Americans from moving forward economically.

In 1986, however, he made a very different kind of argument. He insisted that blaming crack and crack dealers for the troubles of poor people, especially poor black people, and then imprisoning small-time crack dealers – overwhelmingly young African American men – was a cynical, public-pleasing ploy by shameless politicians: "If we blame crime on crack, our politicians are off the hook. Forgotten are failed schools, the malign welfare programs, the desolate neighborhoods, the wasted years. Only crack is to blame. One is tempted to think that if crack did not exist, someone somewhere would have received a federal grant to develop it."[31] Moynihan could not have guessed that, in a few years' time, an investigative journalist would make a similar argument that many African Americans came to believe: that the United States government had willfully allowed crack cocaine to invade poor black neighborhoods. Moynihan's arguments, however, drew little support.

With great fanfare, on October 28, President Ronald Reagan signed the Anti-Drug Abuse Act of 1986. At the signing ceremony, a smiling Congressman Charlie Rangel stood next to Nancy Reagan at the president's right side. Reagan read a prepared statement: "The American people want their government to get tough and go on the offensive. And that's exactly what we intend, with more ferocity than ever before."[32]

The New York Times coverage of the signing ceremony highlighted the political nature of the bill. The news account homed in on President Reagan's praise for Florida Senator Paula Hawkins, who stood at the president's left shoulder: "I'd like to single out Senator Paula Hawkins. She took this battle to the public and has been a driving force to rid our society of drug abuse." Hawkins was in the midst of a tough senate re-election campaign (her anti-drug efforts and Reagan's praise were not enough; she ended up losing). Nowhere in the Times's coverage of the new law was any mention made of the grossly disparate, racially based sentencing penalties between dealers of crack cocaine and powder cocaine.[33]

The Drug Abuse Act of 1986 was only the first of many federal laws that massively upped the federal government's war on drugs, in general, and the disproportionately fierce punishment of crack dealers, including low-level street dealers. Just two years later, Congress and President Reagan were back at it. Just before the election of 1988, the same politically inflected legislative process was repeated; this time Congress and President Reagan teamed up to pass the Anti-Drug Abuse Act of 1988.

This time a few elected officials did speak out against what was an even more punitive anti-drug measure. Representative James Scheuer, a white liberal Democrat who represented Queens, specifically called out both Charlie Rangel and the Reagan administration. As the new legislation got off the ground, he blasted the punish-and-imprison premise of the drug hawks. "We badly need a policy debate now and there is none," he stated angrily. "The only debate going on is the debate over who is going to look most like Rambo to the voters in November."[34]

The new legislation originated in the House. It was a bi-partisan bill of the highest order, co-sponsored by the liberal Democratic House Majority leader, Tom Foley of Washington state, and the conservative Republican House Minority Leader, Robert Michel of Illinois. The House voted 346–11 in favor of the bill and, once again, the Senate simply affirmed the bill by voice vote. The new law was uncompromising, making official the belief that more penalties, more punishments, and more prison time were the only way forward. There was no debate about fundamental premises. The bill proudly declared: "[T]he legalization of illegal drugs is an unconscionable surrender in the war on drugs."[35] Just ten years previously the Carter administration had been seriously considering decriminalizing marijuana possession and pondering how to reduce the punishments associated with cocaine use. Those days were long gone.

The bill-signing ceremony took place just days after Vice President George H.W. Bush had been elected president. The lame duck president, Ronald Reagan, made his last speech celebrating the increasingly brutal war on drugs. Though fading mentally, President Reagan rose to the occasion: "This bill helps us close rank on those who continue to provide drugs. Arrests, convictions, and prison sentences of sellers and abusers are rising to record levels ... And now in the eleventh hour of this

Presidency, we give a new sword and shield to those whose daily business it is to eliminate from America's streets and towns the scourge of illicit drugs."[36] The president, in a sentimental moment at the end of his presidency, dedicated this new and even more punishing drug law, one that would sentence even more people to years in prison, to his wife, Nancy Reagan.

Under this law crack, again, was singled out for special treatment. Among the most onerous of new provisions: a person in possession of just one gram of crack, a tiny amount equal to the weight of a small paper clip, would under federal law receive a mandatory minimum jail sentence of five years if that person had already been convicted of two prior possessions of crack. The act also took away, for five years, eligibility for all public benefits, including public housing and student loans, from anyone convicted of any first-time state or federal drug-trafficking offense. Even simple possession resulted in forfeiture of federal benefits (though the penalty could be waived if the person entered a drug rehabilitation program).

Also, to great huzzahs, the act created the "Office of National Drug Control Policy," headed by a director who was soon known by everyone as the nation's "drug czar." Congressmen Charlie Rangel and several other anti-drug "hawks" had long been advocating for a single, powerful official who had the ear of the president and the right to coordinate the massive federal bureaucracy in the war on drugs.

As George H.W. Bush took office, it might seem that the federal government had all the tools and the will it needed to wage war on drugs in general and on crack, in particular. That is not how politicians saw things. The bidding war between political parties was not over. Democratic Senator Joe Biden of Delaware, who had tried and failed to win the Democratic presidential nomination in 1988, was in search of new political fodder. He helped lead the charge.

Six months after President George H.W. Bush took office, Biden went to the National Press Club in Washington, DC and gave a barnburner of a speech. President Bush, he said, had failed his first and most important test of leadership. He had promised a real war on drugs. All he had delivered was "empty promises and hypocrisy."

"Mr. President," he charged, "we've passed 208 new, tough anti-crime laws in the past five years. If you want more, I am sure the Congress will oblige ... You failed to put in your budget the money needed to make these tough laws work." Biden then worked the "war" part of the war on drugs metaphor for all it was worth: "We need another D-Day. Instead you're giving us another Vietnam: a limited war, fought on the cheap, financed on the sly, with no clear objectives, and ultimately destined for stalemate and human tragedy." Biden called for more punishment of drug users and drug dealers. He demanded more federal money to provide for more police, more FBI special agents, more DEA agents, more prosecutors, and more prisons to make sure that drug criminals got the tough treatment Biden believed they deserved. At the Press Club, he sounded a bit like General Jack Ripper in the Cold War classic, *Dr. Strangelove*, he was ready to take the drug war to the enemy – in this case, his fellow Americans – no matter the cost.[37]

Biden was not the only one pressuring President Bush. In late July 1989, Congressman Rangel, never a shrinking violet, also blasted the president's inaction. Rangel, who wanted to maintain a working relationship on drug policy with the new administration, did not make a public statement. Instead he wrote Bush's major domo, James Baker, who was then serving as Secretary of State. In private, Rangel chastised the administration for doing so little, so slowly, "in the struggle for our nation's survival against the international drug barons." He told Baker that Congress wanted action and that members of congress were tired of hearing excuses about the need to give Bush's newly appointed drug czar time to get his footing. "well, let me tell you, that it was never the intention of the Congress to hold up the war, and simply wait for the drug 'coordinator' to come up with a strategy." Bush, Rangel concluded, needed to lead.[38]

Bush got the message, even though it was not one he welcomed. George H.W. Bush had not run for president in hopes of immersing himself in domestic affairs. He had spent his career thinking about and working on issues of national security and international relations. His presidency began as the Soviet empire fell. That was where he wanted to focus his attention – on a momentous, world-historical set of events. But the president understood that America's drug wars could not be ignored.

Polls told him that illegal drugs were the American people's single greatest concern. He had run on that knowledge. He had addressed the issue in his campaign. In his Inaugural Address he had promised to make the war on drugs his priority: "And when that first cocaine was smuggled in on a ship, it may as well have been a deadly bacteria, so much has it hurt the body, the soul of our country. And there is much to be done and to be said, but take my word for it: This scourge will stop!"[39] President Bush had singled out no other domestic policy in his speech.

So, under political pressure, on September 5, 1989, President George H.W. Bush addressed the nation in a speech carried on all the major television networks. In advance of that speech, Bush political advisor Lee Atwater provided talking points to every major Republican leader and constituent group, some 7,700 people or organizations. He urged them to focus the nation's attention on Bush's anti-drug-abuse address. Citing a recent Gallup poll, he reminded them, "It is virtually unprecedented for Americans to rank a social issue as 'the most important problem facing the nation.'"[40]

President Bush spoke from the Oval Office: "All of us agree that the gravest domestic threat facing our nation today is drugs ... Our most serious problem today is cocaine and, in particular, crack." Bush then held up a large bag of crack cocaine.

> This – this is crack cocaine seized a few days ago by Drug Enforcement agents in a park just across the street from the White House ... Let there be no mistake, this stuff is poison. Some used to call drugs harmless recreation. They're not. Drugs are a real and terribly dangerous threat to our neighborhoods, our friends and our families ... When four-year-olds play in playgrounds strewn with discarded hypodermic needles and crack vials – it breaks my heart.

President Bush took command of the war on drugs. He announced a massive increase in federal resources devoted to fighting drugs. He called for more treatment for drug addicts. He promised a greater effort to stop illegal drugs from crossing America's borders. He stressed his support of even more anti-drug education programs in America's schools. But most of all, he told the American people that their government would imprison drug dealers at every level.

Americans have a right to safety in and around their homes. And we won't have safe neighborhoods unless we're tough on drug criminals – much tougher than we are now. Sometimes that means tougher penalties, but more often it just means punishment that is swift and certain. We've all heard stories about drug dealers who are caught and arrested again and again but never punished. Well, here the rules have changed: If you sell drugs, you will be caught. And when you're caught, you will be prosecuted. And once you're convicted, you will do time. Caught – prosecuted – punished.[41]

To bring drug dealers to justice, Bush demanded that Congress double the amount of money the federal government provided to state and local law enforcement. The war on drugs would have the foot soldiers it needed to win. Victory, here, was defined as locking up however many drug dealers it took to stop the flow of narcotics on America's streets. President Bush hoped that the army of drug dealers he meant to stop was more like the Japanese military he had helped defeat during World War II than the Vietnamese insurgents who had more recently fought the United States government to a stalemate, despite taking massive casualties.

President Bush's point man for his amped-up war on drugs was William Bennett, the first "drug czar." Bennett had been Ronald Reagan's Secretary of Education. He had no background in drug enforcement or, for that matter, drug policy. Bennett was, however, a darling of conservative intellectuals. He was an uncompromising advocate for a politics of personal responsibility.

In drug war terms, that meant that Bennett had no patience for the kind of analysis Senator Patrick Moynihan offered as he spoke out against draconian prison sentences for crack offenses. The crack epidemic, in Bennett's mind, had little to nothing to do with racism or poverty or any other sort of sociological explanation. People sold and took drugs like crack because they were bad. Drug abusers had failed the fundamental test of personal responsibility. Thus they deserved severe punishment.[42]

Bennett's views had helped shape the national televised speech President Bush gave on September 5, 1989 – the one where the president held up a big bag of crack that a poor sap of a teenage drug dealer had been lured into selling to federal agents right across from the White House. Bennett made sure that the speech spelled out the personal responsibility message. He quite bluntly told the White House communications shop to rewrite key passages of an early draft. They were emphasizing the wrong thing, he said. The draft focused too much on the dangers of crack cocaine. "The drug itself," Bennett wrote, "is not the enemy." The enemy, he continued, should be defined as "anyone who uses, sells, or looks the other way. Saying that crack is the enemy means that the solution is going after the drugs in bulk – through interdiction – which is exactly what we are in fact deemphasizing." "There is a moral message about behavior implicit in the President's speech," Bennett wrote. People who sell and use crack must be punished.[43]

Bennett, as his critique of the draft speech makes clear, believed that America's drug problem was, fundamentally, a moral problem. In a speech he gave just a couple of months after he became director of the Office of National Drug Control Policy, Bennett laid out his perspective: "Two words sum up my entire approach: consequences and confrontation. Those who use, sell, and traffic in drugs must be confronted, and they must suffer consequences." In near biblical terms, he intoned, "Those who transgress must make amends for their transgressions." He continued, "We must build more prisons. There must be more jails. We must have more judges to hear cases and more prosecutors to bring them to trial. And there must be more federal agents to investigate and solve drug crimes and break networks."[44]

Bill Bennett only lasted twenty-one months as America's drug czar. He resigned, in part, out of frustration. His "czardom," in fact, had little ability to create policy or implement it. Mostly, Bennett had acted as a cheerleader, both within the Bush administration and in public, for a more coherent, hard-nosed, punitive approach to drug abuse in the United States. On that score, and building off of concurrent congressional efforts and presidential inclinations, Bennett had broadly succeeded. Democratic Senator Joe Biden, for one, hailed Bennett, telling reporters that the first drug czar "performed with impressive intellect and success." Representative Charlie Rangel, whom Bennett had called a "gasbag," was less impressed. Rangel was infuriated at Bennett's constant attacks on the supposed moral failings of black families and communities that had, Bennett implied, produced the crack crisis. Bennett's efforts, he said, were a colossal failure.[45]

Bennett's reign as drug czar was relatively brief but his influence on Bush administration policy went deep. The annual National Drug Control Strategy review, released in January 1992, more than a year after Bennett left office, still bore the imprint of his thinking. "Simply put," the official overview of the Bush administration's war on drugs read, "those who chose to use drugs were to be held accountable. Drug use is not caused by poverty ... racism ... or unemployment ... [T]o explain the drug problem by pointing to social conditions is to 'victimize' drug users and deprive them of personal autonomy ... In short, the drug problem reflects bad decisions by individuals with free will."[46] Those individuals, the Bush administration insisted, had to pay the price for their bad decisions.

The combined efforts of Congress and of both the Reagan and Bush administrations led to a massive increase in arrests, prosecutions, and incarcerations of drug abusers at the federal level. The statistics are stark. In 1980, only 4,749 people were in federal prisons for drug offenses; about four out of five of those who were in federal prison were there for non-drug offenses. By 1985, before the crack crackdown had begun and before harsh new drug laws were passed, the number of federal drug offenders had already more than doubled to 9,491. The Reagan administration's crackdown on powder cocaine smuggling and distribution accounts for a good bit of that early increase. But after federal officials waged their war on crack in earnest, the number of people convicted and imprisoned for federal drug crimes exploded.

By 1990, 30,470 out of 56,989 people sentenced to serve time in a federal prison were there on drug offenses. In 1995, the number of drug offenders rose to 52,782 – a figure almost equal to the total number of people in federal prisons for any offense just five years earlier.[47] At the federal level, powder cocaine traffickers (some of whom supplied the crack trade) made up over half of those convicted of drug crimes. In 1993, 32 percent of those convicted powder cocaine dealers were white, 27.4 percent were black, and 39.3 percent were Hispanic, with 1.3 percent other.[48]

At that point, about 20 percent of federal drug offenders were specifically convicted of distributing crack. The racial breakdown for convicted crack dealers was quite different from that of convicted powder cocaine dealers. Of these convicted crack dealers, 88.3 percent were African American, 7.1 percent were Hispanic, and only 4.1 percent were white.[49] Convicted crack dealers, almost all of whom were African American, were more likely than any other drug offenders to go to prison. They received the longest average period of incarceration. Heroin dealers, on average, were sentenced to less than six years. Crack dealers, on average, got over ten years in prison.[50] Young African American men convicted of selling crack or possessing crack with intent to distribute it are, overwhelmingly, the human beings represented by the punishing numbers above.

In 1986, before the federal 100:1 sentencing disparity was enacted, African Americans charged with federal drug offenses already received average sentences 11 percent longer in duration than those given to white drug offenders. But in 1990, after the draconian federal crack sentences went into effect, that difference reached 49 percent. And those long sentences added up. Not only were black Americans arrested much more frequently on drug charges than were white Americans, they were spending far longer in prison once they were sentenced.[51] Black domination of the crack trade – even as whites and Hispanics made up a significant portion of their customer base – pushed black incarceration in federal prisons to levels never seen before in the United States.

Ferocious federal crack cocaine-sentencing politics played a significant role in the mass incarceration of African Americans during the crack years. But federal prisoners of any kind, including those convicted of drug offenses, represent a relatively small percentage of people caught up in the criminal justice system. The state of California, in 1991, had almost 30,000 more prisoners than the entire federal prison system. That same year, when just over 30,000 people were serving federal time for drug offenses, over one million people were arrested for drug offenses at the state and local level.[52]

State drug policies received far less public scrutiny during the crack years – and by scholars in the decades since. But state governments, in typical American fashion, did not all follow the lead of the federal government when it came to prosecuting crack cocaine offenders. A large majority of states – thirty-six in total – did not differentiate between powder cocaine and crack cocaine when it came to sentencing. Not only did they not encode the federal government's 100:1 ratio into their laws, they did not distinguish, in terms of weight, between the two forms of cocaine at all.

Of the fourteen states that did distinguish between crack and powder cocaine, only North Dakota explicitly adopted the 100:1 punishment regime. Virginia offered a different model. Its courts treated small-time dealers of crack and powder cocaine the same, but "drug kingpins" received twenty-year mandatory minimum sentences. A crack kingpin, according to Virginia legislators, was anyone who trafficked in as little as 1.5 kilograms of rock—a lot of weight, but not more than a neighborhood supplier might normally have at hand. For a powder cocaine dealer to be deemed a kingpin, he had to be caught with 500 kilograms, enough to make him a major supplier in the entire state. The ratio there, in terms of weight, was a cruel 333:1.

California, among those states, was more typical. It simply and deliberately sentenced crack dealers to longer prison terms than powder dealers, basically adding an additional year of imprisonment.

State legislators and local authorities, overall, were nowhere near as unjust as the federal government when it came to disparities in sentencing, even when they distinguished between the forms of cocaine.[53] Still, that relative lack of sentencing discrimination hides as much as it reveals.

Illinois serves as an example. The state did not distinguish between crack and powder cocaine; the two were treated the same. Nonetheless crack dealers (who were overwhelmingly African American) were sentenced to prison in massive and massively disproportionate numbers compared to powder cocaine dealers (who were more likely to be white or Hispanic). The growing population of young black men in Illinois prisons during the crack years did not stem from changes in the state's legal code. That population grew because authorities in Cook County – Illinois's most populous county, which is dominated by the city of Chicago – devised a kind of juridical assembly line that incentivized local police, prosecutors, public defenders, and judges to lock up hordes of young black street-corner crack dealers. These were young men who were often making little more than $150 a week as hand-to-hand men. For that crime, these black Chicagoans, if repeat offenders, could spend years in jail or prison and be branded for the rest of their lives as felons, making future legitimate employment much more difficult.

No one who was paying attention would argue that Chicago did not have a serious problem with crack in the late 1980s and early 1990s. When former Florida governor Bob Martinez, who had replaced Bob Bennett as national drug czar, visited Chicago in September 1991, he heard first-hand from residents of some of the hardest-hit crack neighborhoods about the devastation the drug was causing. The prior month, 121 people had been murdered, almost all of them African American and many of them caught up in the city's crack trade.[54] That was the highest monthly number of murders in the city's history. Chicago had a deserved reputation for criminal violence, including the infamous 1929 Valentine's Day Massacre, but the city had never seen anything like what was happening in the early 1990s; 928 people were murdered in 1991, the highest per capita ever (until the next year). Of the dead, almost 30 percent were under the age of twenty-one and about 80 percent, overall, were African American.[55]

Martinez's visit to some of Chicago's poorest public-housing projects had been a publicity stunt but it was not just a made-for-TV moment. Martinez liked to get out of Washington and see the gritty reality of the drug war he oversaw. Local residents had given him an earful.

Back in Washington he told reporters that public-housing residents in Chicago insisted that he act against the crack dealers who were endangering their families: "They do not ask me to study the root causes of poverty – they want the sheriff, and if the sheriff can't do the job, they want the cavalry. They told me they deserve safety for their children just as much as the people who live on the [wealthy, overwhelmingly white suburbs of the] North Shore."[56] What America needed to rein in illegal drug use, Martinez insisted, was the "sheriff" and the "cavalry": the punitive arm of the state.

Martinez was not the only one who saw it that way. Black Chicagoans lived with the devastation. In the spring and summer of 1989, as crack dealers began selling openly in the city's massive public housing projects and on street corners throughout black neighborhoods on the south and west sides, the city's venerable African American newspaper, the *Chicago Defender*, demanded action. In August, the paper ran a stern editorial, "Don't Let Crack Paralyze Chicago." The black community, the *Defender* stated, needed to be protected from the scourge.[57]

The white politicians who ran Chicago in the late 1980s and early 1990s did not take their orders from the *Chicago Defender*. And the man who had become Chicago mayor in April of 1989, Richard M. Daley, son of the legendary Chicago Mayor Richard J. Daley, had been elected without the benefit of many black votes. Still, Daley understood that the violence and the open drug dealing in the city did no one any favors. Politically, he needed law and order. Economically, the city needed law and order. In hopes of gaining black support, in order to appease business interests, and in order to keep his white constituents loyal, the new mayor wanted something to be done about the runaway violence and the drug gangs that were terrorizing south and west side neighborhoods and giving the city a black eye. He just wasn't sure what.

Law enforcement was not standing by while the city's violent crime rate soared. The Chicago police were arresting a lot of people. However, small-time drug dealers were far from the head of the queue when it came to arrests, prosecutions, or convictions. Violent criminals headed those categories. Brutal muggings, rape, assaults, shootings, and murders were all up in the city, way up. These crimes often had nothing to do with the drug trade. The police and prosecutors worked these violent crimes the hardest. Even with this kind of juridical triage in effect, so many people were being arrested in Chicago and in the larger Cook County jurisdiction on felony charges by the late 1980s, even before crack dealing was perceived as a major problem, that the criminal court system was reeling.

When it came to finding an answer to the overcrowding, gridlock, and chaos in the courts, Thomas R. Fitzgerald, the Presiding Judge of the criminal division of the Cook County court system, was in the hot seat. Fitzgerald was born and raised for that job; he was a second-generation, politically connected member of the Democratic Party political machine; his father had been a judge before him. Fitzgerald had graduated from the John Marshall Law School, practically a required educational experience for Chicago pols of his generation. Following the well-trod path of politically ambitious Chicagoans, he had then become a prosecutor in the Cook County State's Attorney's Office. Soon thereafter, he was elected to a Cook County Judgeship, the youngest man to so serve. In 1987, Fitzgerald had won near-universal praise for cleaning up Chicago's notoriously corrupt Traffic Court. In 1989, when he took over leadership of the Cook County courts criminal division, he was known as a smart, savvy man of integrity and substance, "a judge's judge."[58]

Fitzgerald knew that he had the support of Mayor Daley to come up with some kind of fix, to do something to keep the wheels of justice turning. The criminal courts focused on defendants accused of the most violent crimes; these cases took almost all of the system's resources. As a result, defendants accused of less violent felonies were shunted through the system, waiting for longer and longer periods of time for their charges to be adjudicated. Judge Fitzgerald also knew that Chicago police, aware of the clogged court system, often did not arrest people for what they perceived to be petty crimes, including small-time drug transactions. The police did not simply ignore these kinds of infractions; they instead resorted to "street justice." In other words, police officers seized the small timers' drugs and their guns, occasionally administered a beat down, and then let the "mopes" go.

When Fitzgerald took charge, the numbers facing the Cook County court system were astounding. In 1975 about 6,000 felony cases were filed in Cook County. In 1987, the number topped 28,000. About half of those defendants were charged with one or more felony drug counts.[59] These were the defendants who almost never received swift adjudication. They also, in the main, avoided prison. (On the other hand, those charged with the most serious drug offenses might spend months in jail awaiting trial.) Chicago was not alone in this regard. In New York City in 1987, a person arrested for a drug-related felony faced only a 15 percent chance of serving time in prison.[60]

Both Chicago's police and its court system felt institutionally overwhelmed by the drug problem. They simply did not have, they believed, either the administrative capacity or law-enforcement support to manage the explosive growth in drug felony cases. At this point Chicago authorities, led by Judge Fitzgerald, decided to try something different. They devised an efficient, scaled-up criminal justice system that was capable of arresting, arraigning, and prosecuting the tens of thousands of people charged with narcotics felonies.

Under the direction of Judge Fitzgerald – and with no legislative changes, with no open public debate – Chicago launched a high-speed incarceration machine. This was the fall of 1989, just as crack sales were beginning to explode in Chicago. Those authorities planned the reform – and this is key – even before the crack cocaine trade took off in Chicago. They built their machine to better process the huge number of drug dealers already in the criminal justice system, but also in anticipation of the increasing numbers likely to come.

Crack dealers would provide those numbers. The crack trade business model, with its open-air markets, 24/7 service, and reliance on a constant flow of steady, frequent, repeat customers made it easy to spot and catch the street dealers. Such small-time crack dealers might well have escaped the over-stressed criminal justice system in previous years. Now, however, Cook County's system allowed interconnected law-enforcement authorities to sweep up legions of the easy-to-catch hand-to-hand crack dealers, prosecute them, and imprison them.

Under Fitzgerald's lead, Cook County crafted a new court system. In October 1989, the country opened a suite of five dedicated night narcotics courts with their own dedicated judges, assistant district attorneys, public defenders, and administrators. In March 1991, three more night narcotics courts were added. These nighttime courts would be a kind of second shift for the entire judicial system; their primary purpose was to imprison lots of small-time drug dealers, especially those who were caught in "possession with intent to distribute."[61] The court's supervisors believed that this expanded two-shift system would allow both violent felons and drug felons to be moved much more efficiently through the courts. They were right.

During the day, Cook County criminal courts focused almost exclusively on non-drug felonies. Felony defendants who pled not guilty could choose to have their cases heard either by a jury or simply by a judge in a bench trial. Then, starting at 4 p.m. and continuing until sometime between 9:30 p.m. and midnight, the new night narcotics courts focused in turn on drug felony charges. All cases heard at night court were bench trials. If a defendant wanted a jury trial, he had to begin the process in the evening and then insist that his case be continued during the day. Because assistant district attorneys and the defendants' lawyers, almost always public defenders, would be forced to work such day drug cases on top of their night work for no additional pay, neither legal team had much incentive to insist on a daytime jury trial or, in the case of the public defender, to urge their client to seek such a remedy. In general, PDs discouraged such requests, making clear that requesting a jury would delay the trial and almost certainly leave the defendant waiting in jail for his day in court.[62]

Beginning in October 1989, this targeted judicial system rippled through all levels of the legal system in Chicago, as well as the broader jurisdiction of Cook County. Chicago police responded to the beefed-up administrative capacity of the dedicated night narcotics courts by arresting thousands of small-time dealers. These petty dealers, as well as some of their customers, were swept up and charged with felonies; many of them ultimately served prison time.

Once crack use and sales took off in Chicago, the night narcotics court system provided authorities with a spectacularly useful tool in taking on the new, highly visible illegal industry. Federal officials, who were beating the bushes for new ways to capture, process, and punish drug offenders, especially crack dealers, enthusiastically embraced the Cook County narcotics court experiment. The Bush administration publicized Cook County's model, urged other jurisdictions to emulate it, and in late 1990, provided large-scale grants that allowed Cook County to open three additional night drug courts in the spring of 1991.

These courts – and dedicated drug courts, in general – offered far greater judicial capacity. Cook County's night courts allowed local authorities to arrest, process, and prosecute a much greater number of people. In 1992, a veteran Chicago public defender commented in a *Chicago Tribune* story on the changes the drug courts had wrought in law enforcement and in the judicial system: "During the 1970s and 1980s, it was not uncommon for police to approach youths to confiscate their weapons and drugs but then leave the youths on the street ... [Now] the police arrest almost everyone caught with drugs." The result, he believed, was that "drug dealers are angry" and far more likely to resist arrest or even to attack police violently.

One of the night court judges, in the same *Tribune* story, put a different spin on the change: "Before the message was, 'we don't consider these cases important.' Now the message is, 'All that stuff is a crime, and you do have to worry about it.'" The *Chicago Tribune* journalist reporting on the courts noted that while first-time offenders arrested with small amounts of drugs were unlikely to go to prison, they did receive a felony conviction, which meant that the second time they were arrested – and a great many were arrested more than once – they almost always were sentenced to prison.[63] Drug courts were one of the means by which drug offenders, in general, and crack dealers, in specific, were quickly channeled into the criminal justice system and into a lifetime of state-sanctioned punishment. While the booming carceral state of the 1980s and 1990s was engineered in part by federal authorities and presidential administrations, it was overwhelmingly built on the practical and institutional efforts of local decision-makers such as those in Chicago.

As Chicago, between 1989 and 2000, fought its local war on drugs, a group of public defenders, county prosecutors, private lawyers, police, court personnel, and judges found themselves working a night shift to increase the productivity of the drug war. Tens of thousands of defendants followed in their wake. To the satisfaction of many, the narcotics night court system did what its founders intended. According to an Office of National Drug Control Policy (ONDCP) report, during its first twenty-six months, the Cook County program cut "average disposition time for criminal cases" by about 25 percent, from 142 to 108 days, and cut the criminal courts' backlog by 22 percent.[64] In 1991 alone, the courts disposed of nearly 13,000 felony drug cases. The average such case took just a few minutes to clear, and public defenders typically spent five minutes or so preparing for each. Surprisingly, however, fewer night court defendants pled guilty to charges – about 60 percent – than was true nationally, where the rate was around 90 percent.[65]

That surprising rate is because, in Chicago's night court, public defenders frequently contested drug charges. Cary Gold was one of those PDs. Assigned to night court fresh out of law school, she had grown up in the city and lived just a few blocks from one of Chicago's most notorious public housing projects, Cabrini-Green. Though just over five feet tall, she had a no-nonsense attitude that kept her clients more-or-less in line and willing to trust her. She bristled with energy and intelligence.

Almost from the start, Gold observed a pattern that offered a way to defend her clients, most of whom were charged with possession of crack cocaine with intent to distribute. Harried police were rounding up so many petty drug dealers that their paperwork was often sloppy and disorganized, as was the resulting court testimony. That made it easy for them to misremember things – "to go off paper" – and make mistakes when challenged by defendant lawyers.[66] Gold got many more clients off, or at least got their charges reduced, than the five minutes she had to prepare for each case would have suggested.

The need for speed, both in arrests and in prosecutions, did not actually produce a greater conviction rate. It did, however, mean that far greater numbers of people were charged with drug felonies. Understand, too, that because many people arrested were too poor to afford bail money, even those who were eventually found not guilty almost always had spent at least three months in the Cook County jail, awaiting the disposition of their charges.

Existentially, at least for some of those who participated in this fast-speed, nighttime system of justice, the experience came to resemble the proverbial Kafka-esque nightmare. Gold, who worked the night courts for about eighteen months in 1991 and 1992 when the police were doing massive roundups of Chicago's street-corner crack dealers, can only say, "Once the sweeps started, it was out of control behavior. It was a world, this bizarre bubble that we were all supposed to be happy about being in. We were all supposed to play our part and it was supposed to be acceptable ... They would bring [outside] groups in [to observe the courts] and you could look at their faces: 'They think this is good?' And nobody really did. It was a weird way to serve people."[67] Chicago's political leaders had created an efficient incarceration machine that devoured the lives of the city's petty drug dealers. At the height of the crack years, these were, overwhelmingly, young black men.

Chicago's Cook County judicial system was among the first jurisdictions to create a dedicated drug court, but forty-two such courts were created in the United States during the five years between 1989 and 1994.

Four years later, the number had almost quadrupled. These drug courts received extensive federal funding. A 1997 GAO report reported $85 million in direct federal funding. The Office of National Drug Policy, however, claimed that the federal government had provided $2.2 billion in drug-related funding for courts, prosecutors, and corrections in the 1992 fiscal year alone, up from $1.3 billion in 1989, and that some of that new federal money had been funneled by local authorities into the drug courts.[68]

Chicago's night narcotics court, along with the other drug courts that sprang up around the nation to manage the mass arrests of crack dealers, were just one of many state, county, or municipal approaches to the crack trade. In New York City (as discussed earlier) the NYPD went from largely ignoring street-corner crack dealers to raining hell down on them, arresting thousands of hand-to-hand men in coordinated sweeps, after the murder of a policeman by drug dealers in Queens. Police officers worked with prosecutors to take those dealers off the street and lock them up in jail or in prison.

The LAPD went even more full throttle. The *Los Angeles Times* reported that, as violence associated with the crack trade expanded, LA police officers took the "war on drugs" literally: "Officers in South L.A. had adopted paramilitary tactics, crashing through the walls of suspects' homes and wearing balaclava hoods during raids." As a result, according to the *Times*, "Racial animosity and two-way distrust between residents and the police, which would boil over in the 1992 riots, was palpable and meant little cooperation from the community during law enforcement investigations."[69]

Historian Donna Murch demonstrates the connection between the LAPD's militarized war on drugs and the concomitant efforts of California politicians to punish drug dealers (or even those presumed to be involved with illegal drug distribution). The California legislature, alone, passed some eighty measures that gave local law enforcement new authority and resources to crack down on street gangs, which many blamed – often with good reason – for playing integral roles in drug dealing, in general, and crack distribution, in particular. Murch persuasively argues: "Defining the war on drugs as a war on gangs justified the criminalization of everyday life in black and brown Los Angeles. Modes of dress, movement, color of shoelaces, hand gestures, and mere association became defined as prosecutable offenses."[70] California authorities even passed legislation in 1988 that allowed prosecutors to "enhance" the sentences of gang members convicted of a crime – often drug dealing – with additional time of one to five years in prison.

In 1977 the California Department of Corrections imprisoned 19,623 people. Just over two decades later, gang sweeps, enhanced sentencing, and a massive, militarized crackdown on crack and other drug dealers had increased those numbers more than eightfold: some 162,000 people were imprisoned in the year 2000; 64 percent of those prisoners were black or Hispanic. Partly responsible was the passage of Proposition 184 in 1994. This proposition, supported by 72 percent of California voters, further codified a nearly identical effort passed by the state legislature. Often referred to as a "three-strikes" law, this measure doubled the prison sentence for a two-time convicted felon and gave a mandatory minimum sentence of at least twenty-five years' imprisonment for a person convicted of a felony for the third time. In other words, after 1994, if a twenty-year-old small-time drug dealer was caught and convicted three times for selling a few crack vials, he would not be released from prison until he was at least forty-five years old.[71]

Local situations mattered, and Southern California was at the epicenter of cocaine distribution and crack sales in the 1980s and early 1990s. A great many of the citizens of California, in accord with law-enforcement personnel and the state's politicians, responded with nearly unmatched punitive ferocity to this massive illegal industry and the violence that often accompanied it. Their punitive efforts were matched in kind, if not in extent, throughout the United States. Pressured by their fearful and angry constituents, politicians at the state and local level poured on the gasoline, creating an incarceration bonfire that consumed the lives of hundreds of thousands of young people, overwhelmingly young black men, many of whom dreamed only of stacking cash in the crack trade.

CHAPTER 6

Crack's Retreat: A Nation's Slow, Painful, and Partial Recovery

T HE CRACK MARKET BEGAN TO BREAK IN THE MID 1990S. Dealers noticed that fewer new customers were showing up at the drug corners. In New York City, business started to slow as early as mid 1991.

Willie T., a Harlem dealer, worried about the downturn. He had started as a small-scale crack operator in 1988 with two partners and $200 in cash. Almost immediately, he was netting a solid $1,000 a week. He was able to take weekends off and could keep a low profile. But by May 1991 his profits had dropped to as little as $300 a week. He told a *New York Times* reporter, "It's real slow now ... instead of ten buyers, there might be three." The good news, from his perspective, was that his old customers still bought as much crack as they could afford. But new customers were hard to come by.

To keep his business going, he had started moving around, taking more risks by selling to whites in Greenwich Village twice a week, and even chancing an occasional trip to New Jersey. People there told him they were looking for a new high and asked him if he sold Angel Dust (an animal tranquillizer, also known as PCP, that had first become popular in the mid 1970s). He found a source and started selling it to make up for his diminishing crack sales. Like so many in the crack business, he pondered getting out of drug dealing altogether before he took a long prison bid (he had already served time for a variety of non-drug offenses). "But not just yet," he told the reporter, who added that "Willie ... [is] tottering on the edge of what for him is the great unknown of the straight world, a place where he has no reputation, no standing and no clear sense of how to proceed." A convicted felon with no regular job experience, Willie T. knew full well that the odds of him landing any kind of

Figure 11 "Drugs is Hell": This mural appeared in Harlem in the early 1990s. Note the crack vials in the Grim Reaper's hand. Young people, in particular, began to turn away from crack in the mid 1990s. (Camilo J. Vergara.)

legitimate wage labor position were poor. So he kept on doing what he knew best.[1]

All over the country, though at different times in the decade, crack sales had begun to slip. Sudhir Alladi Venkatesh, the premier ethnographer of the underground economy of that era, writes that crack cocaine had become "a faltering economic sector" in Chicago by 1995. Gangs such as the Gangster Disciples, which had done so well organizing crack distributorships, were forced to search out new hustles.[2]

The Office of National Drug Control Policy was seeing the same thing in the multiple surveys they used to measure drug use and attitudes towards drugs. As early as 1992, the ONDCP was noting a strong decline in teenagers' positive attitudes towards drug use, in general, and towards cocaine (in all forms), in specific. According to their research, 1988 was the highpoint for cocaine use. Between 1988 and 1992, the number of high school seniors who disapproved of any kind of cocaine use had increased 47 percent. Cocaine, in general, was losing its allure. Crack was ever more perceived as a drug for life's losers.[3]

Too many people had watched what crack could do to you. Drug historian Jill Jonnes records young people's disdain for habitual crack users. A young black man describes his neighbors: "They're crackheads. They live on my block and they rob all the time; they rob off their best friends, their families. They're like fiends." Another young man added: "I don't want to be like some people out there … They lose their homes because they're on it. I don't want to get involved with that."[4]

In 1997, the Department of Justice celebrated the good news. Young people, the DOJ reported, were fast turning away from crack. They regularly used the pejorative phrase "crackhead." Young people in poor neighborhoods, DOJ officials were pleased to note, "even took to abusing crackheads." In typical bureaucratese, the DOJ argued that "such a change in attitude among youths heralded the beginning of the decline phase of the crack epidemic."[5] The DOJ had numbers to back up their findings.

In major American cities, the DOJ explained, people who were arrested underwent mandatory drug testing. Those tests showed a precipitous decline in the use of "cocaine/crack" (and while the test didn't distinguish between the two, the DOJ concluded that "most of the arrestees whose urine contained cocaine metabolites had smoked crack").[6] In Los Angeles, for example, 65 percent of people born in 1964 who were arrested in 1988 tested positive for "cocaine/crack"; by 1996 the percentage had dropped to 49 percent. Those who were thirteen years younger, born in 1977, were much less likely to use crack/cocaine: only 15 percent of those born in 1977 tested positive. Sharp declines, by age cohort, were also reported in Chicago, Philadelphia, Houston, New Orleans, Miami, Detroit, and Kansas City. There were exceptions – Phoenix and Atlanta, for example – where arrestee drug records showed crack use at a plateau in 1996.[7]

It was becoming clear that even people on the wrong side of the law who had come of age during the crack crisis wanted nothing to do with crack and the personal devastation that seemed to follow in its wake. As even career criminals rejected crack, the crack market moved even further downscale. New customers, in most places, were in short supply. And while older steady customers remained, their numbers were dwindling, too. Crack was hard on the body and the soul. Customers were lost to arrests, to death, to illness, destitution, detoxification, and simply to age. By 1996 the DOJ, at least, was confident that crack was an "epidemic" in decline.

For the men who made money in the crack trade, or who had dreamed of the stacks of cash they had seen others earn, the decline in business was tough. Gang leaders knew their rank and file had to get paid if they were going to stay loyal and remain in the thug life. Chicago gang ethnographer Sudhir Alladi Venkatesh reported that, on the South Side of Chicago, the gang he had come to know intimately was "in trouble." Gangbangers, he wrote, "expected gang membership to deliver the benefits of a corporate position: namely, a steady income and a mobility path to greater fortune down the road."[8]

Without the high returns of the crack trade, gang leaders had to become entrepreneurial. Some returned with a vengeance to older trades, especially extortion. They leaned hard on neighborhood storeowners and especially on people who ran semi-legit or underground activities, whether shade-tree mechanics, unlicensed hair and nails salons, or dice games. They got deeper into the sex trade, running prostitutes. And of course they kept selling drugs. Even as crack sales declined they did not, by any means, come to a stop. There were still heroin addicts to serve, as well as people looking for other means to get high. Drug dealing was still a viable business but employment was down and the crazy, visible wealth the crack trade had provided to inner-city teenagers was on a steep decline.

Of course, not everybody just folded their tents. Some of the kingpins who had gotten their start during the crack years and managed to avoid the hawk eye of law enforcement just went with the market flow. The Black Mafia Family, for example, which began in Detroit in the late 1980s but was soon thereafter headquartered in Atlanta, found ways to take leadership in the powder cocaine business. Even though powder coke sales were also down in the late 1990s, there was still plenty of demand. The BMF, run by the brothers Terry and Demetrious Flenory, had national distribution and a Mexican connect that could supply whatever the brothers' massive operation could move. Up until they went to prison in 2007 – along with some 150 other members of the drug-trafficking organization – the BMF partied in public, waving their bottles of Cristal or Perrier-Jouët. They drove Bentleys and they consorted with major hip-hop stars like it was 1991.[9] The flossing and the general carrying on continued for a few years, but by the mid-to-late 1990s the crack cocaine business was a stagnating industry.

The organic intellectuals of the inner city, hip-hop artists, watched the decline of the crack trade with mixed emotions. Their scene and the crack scene went epic at roughly the same time and the young black men who led the way felt the passing. Some showcased the wild wonder of the era; others paid heed to the destruction. A few rhymed about the social and political conditions that made the illegal millions a way of life, a way of temptation, and a likely path to incarceration.

Maybe nobody has recalled those times in rhymes better than Dennis Coles, better known as Ghostface Killah, original member of the Wu-Tang Clan. In his 2006 epic, *Fishscale* (the title comes from the slang term for uncut, sparkly, straight from-the-kilo, highest-grade cocaine), Ghostface Killah neither romanticizes the era nor condemns it. He's a storyteller, passing along the highs and lows, speaking far less about million dollar pay days and thick gold ropes and more to the often harsh, everyday routines of an underground business.[10]

In "Crackspot," he starts with a cook; is anybody watching the pot on the stove? Next verse down, a "basehead" dies from a too-strong hit, rocks dropping out of his pipe. Then comes fear of busts and wired informants, free crack stems for good customers, and sad sacks turning over their Play Station 3s and X-Boxes for a handful of vials. In Ghostface Killah's "Crackspot" track, selling crack is a good business, but it comes attached to a lot of aggravation and fearful consequences.

In "Kilo," another track from *Fishscale*, Ghostface Killah is more light-hearted. He speaks to the dream of dealing in weight, moving past hand-to-hand sales and on to wealth. In that sublime realm, women are easy (down with their "panties"!). "Kilo" celebrates the possibilities of actually making it, of reaching upward past street sales to the magic land of wholesale distribution. No more working for others, shouting out the colors of your boss's vials (colors chanted on the track by Wu-Tang Clan member Raekwon). In this story, the "kid" has his kilo. In a joyful refrain, Ghostface Killah kindly reminds his listeners that a kilo is a thousand grams. That's enough weight to make a new life, but only if you're not taken down by your rivals or the police. Even in semi-mythic celebration, Ghostface Killah is a realist.

A less well-known but lyrically adept rapper, Kaseem Ryan, known as Ka, recalls the crack years in a far less lighthearted way. In 2016, he told a *Rolling Stones* interviewer, "Everybody in my family was on crack. I felt like my youth was just stolen from me. A lot of my music is me trying to come to grips with that and make sense of it all. Why did I have to live through that?"[11] Ka was a boy and a teenager in the East Brooklyn neighborhood of Brownsville when crack hit.

In Ka's masterpiece, "Up Against Goliath," he tells the story of crack from the angle of a young man – a boy, really – caught in a desperate place and time. This young man has a gun. But he has it to protect his mother and himself. He gets involved in the crack trade, but as the title of the track states, he's just a David, slinging rock on a street corner because he's "Up Against Goliath." Picture that Goliath, as you will, from the perspective of a young black man living in one of the poorest, angriest, most desperate places in Ronald Reagan's America. To paraphrase Ka's lyrics, this boy does not march in small-town parades led by drum majors and girls twirling batons. This boy watches his peers squeeze off shots. This boy sells crack to his neighbors, knowing it's wrong. In this boy's community, people who sell crack just to get by hope not to be killed by a rival crew. They know that when they are caught by the police, arrested, and tried, they will receive no mercy from a judge who doesn't even see them as people.[12] Ka wonders why he had to grow up as he did. The crack years were a scourge that he in no way wishes to glorify.

Most academic scholars of the crack years agree with Ka: the crack years were a nadir for the nation. They, however, do not emphasize the deadly nature of the crack business model or the personal and community devastation of habitual crack use. Instead, they examine how the American polity declared open season on economically disadvantaged young men of color. In their cogent accounts, "Goliath" is the carceral state and "David" is the young black man imprisoned in it. Michelle Alexander, among the first and the foremost of these scholars, has famously labeled the mass incarceration of young black and brown men "The New Jim Crow."[13]

Alexander does not blame the mass incarceration of young men of color solely on the crackdown on crack. The whole war on drugs, she states, going back to the 1970s, targeted black men. That broader war always hit people of color hardest.

In Alexander's telling, the War on Drugs, in general, and the crackdown on crack, in particular, were simply the latest tools of a racist society that had used any means necessary – from enslavement to Jim Crow laws to the War on Drugs – to create a "system of racialized social control."[14] Federal legislation that condemned crack sellers – disproportionately black men – to sentences of great length for possessing even 5 grams of crack, showed just how racially unjust that war had become by 1986. Such federal legislation, along with the various forms crack laws took at the state and the local level, put young black men into jails and prisons in numbers that crushed families and whole communities. Given the mass roundup and imprisonment of young black men, she argues, crack laws and the implementation of those laws were blatantly racist; they produced a new racial caste system.

Alexander does not really explain why presidents, Congress, the courts, state legislatures, local law enforcement, and most every other element of government chose to enact and enforce racist laws. She offers as a warrant an assumption that the white majority, for reasons of collective and personal self-interest, wants a racial caste system and supports whatever efforts are needed to maintain it. Whites, she writes, insist on "their racial privilege ... it [is] an aspect of human nature ... to cling tightly to one's advantages and privileges and to rationalize the suffering and exclusion of others."[15] The war on crack, in this telling, is a war on black people.

Others have complicated that story without fully dismissing it. James Forman, Jr., son of the iconic civil rights leader of the same name, begins his powerful 2017 book, *Locking up Our Own*, with a true story. It's 1995. Forman is in a Washington DC courtroom defending a fifteen-year-old African American boy charged with illegal possession of a handgun. Forman pleads the boy guilty; he asks the judge for mercy. Instead, the judge gave the teenager, a first-time offender, a six-month sentence.

Forman, in his telling, was furious. He knew that young black men were being locked up in record numbers, often for non-violent crimes.

Nearly half of people behind bars in the mid 1990s were African American. His client had just become another tragic statistic. It was, Forman felt, racial injustice at work.

Then, Forman had a discomforting thought: "It wasn't only Brandon [the convicted teenager] and the other young men in the cellblock who were black. So was everybody in the courtroom – not just the judge, but the court reporter, the bailiff, and the juvenile prosecutor. So was the police officer who had arrested Brandon, not to mention the police chief and the mayor."[16] The very courtroom building in which Brandon had been tried was named after a black man and the gun and drug laws of the District of Columbia had been written by a city council that was largely African American. If the juridical system in Washington DC was racist, then it was of a very strange kind. Forman ended this story with a troubling, if unexpected statistic: in 2014, after decades in which African Americans had been locked up in record numbers, 64 percent of black Americans told pollsters that the legal system treated criminals "not harshly enough."[17]

Forman explains black Americans' responses to people they perceived as criminals in a way Congressman Charlie Rangel would have had no problem understanding. Black people were, disproportionately and historically, the victims of crime. Law-abiding black Americans had long been scared by the violence in their neighborhoods and angry that the police were either unwilling or unable to bring law and order to their communities. President George H.W. Bush's first drug czar, Bill Bennett, rarely received warm applause from black audiences when he spoke before them. But in 1989 he received a strong reception at the Houston area Urban League. In his speech, the one-time chair of the National Endowment for the Humanities riffed off of African American novelist Ralph Ellison's *Invisible Man* (1952). He told the audience: "the new 'invisible man' is the black inner city citizen who doesn't do drugs ... the point that needs to be made – the point that needs to be driven home – is that most blacks in our inner cities are law abiding citizens who lead decent lives and disdain drugs. Most black Americans are victims, not perpetrators, of drug crimes, and America needs to see that."[18]

Along those lines, James Forman notes, in the 1980s and 1990s Washington DC council members were inundated with complaints from their constituents: "we feel like prisoners in our homes, strangers on our streets," they protested.[19] These black residents of Washington DC sought more police protection against the criminals that lived amongst them. Despite the fearsome statistics, not all black people saw the punishing hand of the carceral state. There was a divide within the black community, both in perception and experience. The incarceration rate for young black men (ages twenty to thirty-nine) who had attended college, even if briefly, *declined slightly* between 1972 and 2010; for those who dropped out of high school, their incarceration rate *increased sevenfold*.[20]

Despite such caveats, Forman does not shy away from the significant role of racism in the making of the carceral state. He argues persuasively that systemic poverty and housing segregation and bad schools and the ways that police and the courts operate – all the myriad avenues that are supposed to provide equal opportunity or guarantee equal protection before the law in the United States – had never been successfully divested of racism. Too many African Americans, thus, had been steered by a series of racially inflected pathways to lives that made criminality a strong possibility and in which incarceration, rather than a "second chance," was a likely outcome. Forman finds racism buried in the accretions of America's hard shell.

In that hard racist shell, crack cocaine was a siren call for too many poor black Americans who had had too few choices. Making that illegal money off of "white gold" was hard to resist, even with its attendant risks, which most definitely included imprisonment. Still, unlike Alexander, Forman emphasizes his sympathy for the victims of crime, as well as for the victims of racism – some of whom, of course, are the same people.

Legal scholars further complicate the hows and whys of racially disparate incarceration rates during the crack years. David Sklansky, author of the definitive law article on the passage of the 1986 Anti-Drug Abuse Act, argues, "The federal crack penalties provide a paradigmatic case of unconscious racism." Here is a term – "unconscious racism" – that will take several forms over the decades that have followed.

Public records, Sklansky demonstrates, reveal not a single racist comment made by a single member of Congress in discussing passage of the 1986 Anti-Drug Abuse Act. Yet, Sklansky reasonably insists, Congress "would have shown more restraint in fashioning the crack penalties, or more interest in amending them ... [if they] did not apply almost exclusively to blacks." He goes on to quote a criminal defense attorney: "Maybe I'm cynical, but I think that if you saw a lot of young white males getting five- and 10-year minimums for dealing powder cocaine, you'd have a lot more reaction."[21] That commonsense observation is hard to ignore. Congress knew that their bill would not result in the arrest of hundreds of thousands of young white weed dealers, whose trade took place in the unpoliced precincts of suburban basements or on the quiet, unlit cul-de-sacs of exurban sub-developments.

Nicole Gonzalez Van Cleve, in her ethnography of the Cook County Criminal Court, says much the same thing. She accuses the mass incarceration machinery of that court system of practicing "colorblind racism." The professionals who run the court system, like Congress, do not make avowedly racist statements. They do not practice overt racism. Instead, they ignore everything that led so many young black and brown men to end up before them: "the intensification of surveillance and policing that impact the lives of the poor and people of color." These are the practices embraced by so many big city police forces – with the LAPD leading the way and the federal government providing a good deal of the money – that swept the nation during the crack years.

These tools of the carceral state, Van Cleve argues, produce "a culture of racism." This culture proceeds, even as it pervades the workaday lives of the men and women who process the long lines of black and brown criminal defendants that come before them. In Chicago, the decision of lawmakers to speed up the criminal justice system in the late 1980s created a feedback loop. The racialized nature of arrest and prosecution and punishment became naturalized. Even as that court system in Cook County increasingly became run by black professionals, the inherited "culture of racism" that, in Van Cleve's words, "existed long before they arrived at the courthouse," continued to operate. Such naturalized, "colorblind racism" is hard to uproot, as it is built into the mechanics of the system.[22]

These concerns about the racist aspects of mass incarceration, in general, and the war on crack, in particular, are far from merely an academic debate. Policymakers, too, have wrestled with such racial outcomes. The infamous 100:1 crack cocaine versus powder cocaine ratio mandated by the 1986 Anti-Drug Abuse Act especially stuck in the craw of some lawmakers and social-justice activists.

The first major national break with the merciless war on crack came in 1992 and was led by Detroit congressman John Conyers. His district had been hit hard by crack and his constituents wanted protection from its ravages. Conyers had, at first, accepted the police sweeps and the locking-up of dealers. But he had never been happy about it. Drug use and drug sales had harmed his district. But the war on drugs, as it was being fought, did likewise; it was destroying the lives of too many of the people he was supposed to represent. By 1992 he'd had enough.

In the spring of 1992, Congressman Conyers began to speak out. Conyers, a founding member of the Congressional Black Caucus, served as chair of the Government Operations Committee, a leadership position that gave him the authority to investigate how, exactly, the war on drugs was being fought. He discovered that, of the billions spent, almost none went into researching how to prevent addiction and how to wean people off of drugs. Conyers wanted a radical rethinking of American drug policy: public health solutions, he believed, not incarceration, were the answer to America's drug problems, in general, and to the crack crisis, in specific.[23]

Conyers broke completely with the Bush administration and with conventional wisdom on drug policy in June 1992. The time had come, he announced to the national press corps, to develop an "alternate drug strategy to change [the] emphasis on law enforcement with prevention." He released a document: "The War on Drugs – Failure and Fantasy – What Has the $35 Billion Investment Brought?" He called for a reversal of current spending priorities. Instead of spending 70 percent of federal drug money on law enforcement and 30 percent on education, treatment, prevention, job training, and everything else, he proposed to flip the budget 180 degrees. The War on Drugs had failed the American people, Conyers claimed, and it had most certainly done little to help the people of Detroit who he represented.[24]

Conyers was not alone. The statement he released to the press on June 4, 1992 was produced with fifty-eight national organizations. Conyers, a long-time labor-union champion, had worked closely with the AFL-CIO and AFSCME. Medical groups, including the American Hospital Association, had signed on. Not surprisingly, so did a raft of groups involved with treating drug addiction.[25] The call for a national debate on drug policy that specifically addressed the crack cocaine crisis, demanded by Congressman James Sheuer in 1988, had finally begun in earnest.

Over the next few months, more and more people spoke out against the war on drugs. Drug experts reported: "enforcement has had little effect on the supply or use of drugs." St. Louis Police Chief Clarence Harmon wanted to put fewer people in prison and more into treatment centers: "With more treatment and job training and other alternatives we could see a dramatic lowering of the crime rates."

Congressman John Conyers was hopeful. But he understood the political problem. President Bush, along with every other politician running for re-election, faced a wary electorate. Conyers observed, "Drug education and treatment have gained a name as a wimp activity. If you favor these things, you're a softy." Even as the scientific and medical community, as well as an increasing number of law-enforcement personnel, had begun to seriously rethink drug policy, voters remained afraid.[26]

Democratic presidential nominee Bill Clinton, his political antennae finely attuned to every vibration of the electorate, felt that political pressure to be tough on drugs. His concern was heightened by the Bush campaign's efforts to attack Clinton on that very issue. As the election loomed, President Bush's drug czar, Bob Martinez, ripped into Clinton's position on the drug war. When it came to fighting against vicious drug dealers, Martinez told reporters, "You are comparing an elephant to an ant." He argued that while President Bush made sure that the dealers were locked up and the public was protected, Arkansas Governor Bill Clinton had made sure that drug offenders served "minimal sentences" and were soon back on the streets peddling their poisons.[27]

Clinton, ever worried about "culture war" issues, including drug policy, fought back. His campaign issued statements declaring: "the fact is, Bill Clinton has increased penalties for repeat offenders, drug dealers, and violent criminals."[28] Clinton, whatever his actual feelings on drug policy, believed that he had to campaign as a drug-war hardliner.

Republicans had held the presidency for twenty of the prior twenty-four years, and running as champions of law and order and "family values" had helped them win election after election. Clinton believed he could not be soft on crime; he could not risk taking on the war on drugs.

Clinton's cautious policy prescriptions and his extraordinary campaign skills won him the presidency. In office, he continued to be a drug hardliner. His hardline approach came to a head in 1995 when he signed into law harsh new drug penalties. He chose to side with the Republicans who ruled both the House and the Senate. He rejected the pleas of the Congressional Black Caucus and white Democratic liberals, as well as the legal advice of the congressionally authorized US Sentencing Commission, to end the objectively racist crack cocaine versus powder cocaine sentencing disparities.[29] Clinton's Democratic Party had taken a beating during the 1994 congressional mid-term elections and he believed that the only way he could be re-elected to the presidency in 1996 was by moving to the right. He believed he had to win back some of the conservative whites who had voted Republican in the mid-terms. It was, he believed, not the right time to put racial justice ahead of political necessity.

Clinton chose not to speak directly to the American people about his decision. Instead, in late October 1995, he issued a written statement glorifying his tough-on-crime policies. He rejected any reduction in crack cocaine sentencing. Crack, he said, "has had a devastating impact" on inner-city communities and "I am not going to let anyone who peddles drugs get the idea that the cost of doing business is going down."[30] Rather than reduce the penalties for selling crack cocaine, he suggested instead that Congress should increase the prison terms of people caught selling powder cocaine. The decision by both the Republican-controlled Congress and President Clinton to totally reject the strong recommendation of the US Sentencing Commission to bring crack cocaine prison sentences in line with powder cocaine prison sentences was the first time ever that advice of the non-partisan, expert Commission had been ignored.

Civil rights leader Jesse Jackson spoke for many in the black community in 1995 when he condemned Clinton's politically motivated decision. It was, he said, "a moral disgrace." Jackson, like many other black leaders, had come to see how badly the tough anti-drug measures he himself had supported in the mid 1980s had backfired. The policy of incarcerating so many petty crack dealers for so long was devastating a generation of poor young black men; the punishment did not fit the crime. Jackson accused Clinton of being "willing to sacrifice young black youth for white fear." Both Clinton and Attorney General Janet Reno, Jackson charged, understood that "crack is code for black."[31]

Congressman Melvin Watt, who had tried hard to convince his congressional colleagues to accept the US Sentencing Commission's recommendations to end the crack versus powder cocaine sentencing disparities, was sad and angry. He spoke a simple truth: "If somebody is convicted of selling $225 worth of crack cocaine, they get the same penalty as somebody who sells $50,000 worth of powder cocaine ... Poor young kids who can afford only crack go to jail. Rich young kids who can afford powder go home and sleep in their own beds."[32]

Extraordinarily, at the federal level, the draconian crack laws stayed in effect until the presidency of Barack Obama. Not until 2010 did Congress and the president agree to reduce the 100:1 crack versus powder sentencing disparity. Even then, the "Fair Sentencing Act" maintained an 18:1 ratio. Not everyone signed on. The Republican ranking member of the House Judiciary Committee, Lamar Smith of Texas, insisted: "Reducing the penalties for crack cocaine could expose our neighborhoods to the same violence and addiction that caused Congress to act in the first place." But he was in a decided minority. Championed by the Congressional Black Caucus, the bill even gained the support of arch-conservatives such as Alabama Senator Jeff Sessions (later to serve as Attorney General under Donald Trump) and South Carolina Senator Lindsey Graham.

States, too, began sentencing reform. In 2009, under the leadership of New York's first black governor, David Patterson, the merciless 1973 mandatory-minimum drug sentencing law championed by presidential want-to-be Nelson Rockefeller was finally rolled back. Hip-hop giants such as Russell Simmons, Shawn Carter, and Sean Combs had helped organize and fund the coalition that won the political battle. A movement, pushed from below and accepted by some of those in power, had taken root in the United States.

Passage of the 2010 Fair Sentencing Act was a victory for equality before the law but the damage caused by the 1986 federal Anti-Drug Abuse Act was enormous. The 1986 law had widened the sentencing gulf between blacks and whites. African American men convicted of drug dealing saw their sentences increase in length by some 60 percent, while white drug dealers saw only a small increase in their prison time. Black convicts served about the same time in prison for drug offenses as whites did for violent offenses.[33] Fiercely punitive laws aimed at crack dealers did not put much of a dent, if any, into the sales of crack, but they did result in the long-term imprisonment of legions of economically disadvantaged young black men. Upwards of 80 percent of all federal crack defendants were African American.[34]

Black Americans, during the height of the crack years, divided over what to do about the scourge of crack. But in the mid 1990s, many found a plausible explanation for the rise of crack and, in it, found a common enemy: the CIA. Their understandings stemmed from the work of an investigative journalist named Gary Webb, who in 1996 wrote a series of articles, titled "Dark Alliance," for the *San Jose Mercury*. Webb built his reports on a series of rumors that had been floating around for more than a decade.

The CIA, the story went, had worked with Nicaraguans to smuggle cocaine into the United States. In so doing, the CIA was supporting the Contra rebels in Nicaragua; the Contras were championed by the Reagan administration in their war against leftists in Central America. The money these Nicaraguan smugglers earned from the cocaine trade helped support the Contra's guerrilla war against the leftist Sandinista Nicaraguan government. These CIA backed Nicaraguans, Webb argued, had supplied much of the cocaine that flowed into Los Angeles in the early 1980s, and that cocaine had directly supplied the crack market in black communities. Ergo: the CIA was responsible for crack cocaine and the destruction of hundreds of thousands of black lives.[35]

Soon after Webb's story broke, African Americans demanded answers. Some 2,000 people marched in Los Angeles, angrily denouncing the CIA and the US government. Congresswoman Maxine Water, representing South-Central LA, which had been hit so hard by the crack scourge, was furious: "I cannot exaggerate my feelings of dismay that my own government may have played a part in the origins and history of the problem."[36] The Congressional Black Caucus, joined by other members of Congress, demanded an explanation from the CIA and commenced a series of hearings. Jesse Jackson jumped into the fracas. Black talk radio shows thundered with well-known African Americans angrily denouncing the CIA and the government.

To cut to the chase, Webb's story is almost completely wrong ... almost, but not completely. As early as 1989, Senator John Kerry had denounced the CIA for ignoring Nicaraguan drug smuggling in order to keep up its ties with the Contras, who included amidst their ranks a slew of low-lifers and criminals. And there is no doubt that Nicaraguan smugglers did supply some of the cocaine that drug kingpin Ricky Donnell "Freeway Rick" Ross distributed in LA and that a good deal of that coke was cooked into crack. And those Nicaraguan connects did, for at least a short period of time, have a relationship with the Reagan-supported Contras (though no clear relationship with the CIA has been proved). However and most importantly, as a series of contemporary investigative accounts by journalists reported, these Nicaraguans were relatively small-time. Many others, most especially Colombian and Mexican cartels, were responsible for the vast flow of cocaine pouring into California and the rest of the United States.[37] The CIA may well have looked the other way at cocaine smuggling in Nicaragua, but Rickey Ross's Nicaraguan connects played little if any role in the funding of the Contras and, more broadly, Nicaraguan-supplied cocaine was peripheral to the spread of crack in the United States. Drug expert Michael Massing unequivocally condemns Webb's CIA-Nicaraguan crack cocaine conspiracy theory: "As a look at how crack emerged in the United States, it is ludicrous ... It was not Managua, but Medellín and Cali, that controlled the flow of cocaine into the United States."[38]

The *New York Times*, the *Washington Post*, the *Los Angeles Times*, and others poured resources into investigating Webb's allegations. They unanimously reported that Webb had greatly exaggerated the story. Webb did not understand the wholesale cocaine market in the United States. Webb's own newspaper, the *Mercury News*, reviewed Webb's work and repudiated it: "We oversimplified the complex issue of how the crack epidemic in America grew."[39] Webb resigned from the newspaper and, tragically, committed suicide in 2004.

While Webb's reporting has been widely dismissed – and condemned – by the mainstream press and other experts, it has not been forgotten by a critical audience. Hip-hop artists have kept Webb's reporting alive. In dozens of raps, Ronald Reagan and his CIA are denounced as the head of a vast drug-trafficking ring that brought crack to America's black communities.[40] Jay-Z, in his 2007 track, "Blue Magic," calls out Reagan, Oliver North (Reagan's point man in Nicaragua), and the entire Iran–Contra scandal for the spread of crack. In "Blue Magic," Jay-Z declaims that it's President Reagan who turned young black men into crack-dealing "monster[s]."[41] The inestimable Kanye West goes further. In his 2005 track, "Crack Music," he argues in rhyme that Ronald Reagan (personally?) cooked up crack to destroy black radical political activism. Tupac Shakur, in "Changes," makes much the same charge.

The rapper who best makes the case for the relationship between Ronald Reagan and the spread of crack sales in poor black America takes a different, far more telling take. The Atlanta rapper Michael Santiago Render, aka Killer Mike, does charge in his track, "Reagan," that the Reagan administration brought the cocaine that started the mess, but that's not his main point. Reaganomics, he says, is where it all began. It was Reaganomics that looked to profits first and people last. Reaganomics, he insists, was a system tailor-made for the rich and one that loathed the poor. Reaganomics left poor people defenseless before the predations of the rich. Reaganomics turned prisons into just another profit center and the police into an occupying force. And according to Killer Mike, the rappers who ignore all of that in order to glorify the flossing and the showboating, the "balling" and the "dancing," have a lot to answer for, as well.[42]

This book began with a story about a man who, fresh out of prison, observed the crack game in its earliest formation. Fortified by his prison-found religion, he resisted temptation. He understood, however, the lure of selling the "white gold."

In the Reagan years, and in the neo-liberal, free-market-obsessed era that followed, selling crack made cold, hard sense. With old-school industrial jobs fast disappearing, with labor unions in free fall, with all kinds of steady, traditionally male jobs moving far from inner-city neighborhoods, young men had to make choices. Their choices, in the 1980s and 1990s, were driven by the same hopes and dreams of many of their better-off peers.

Ivan Boesky's infamous 1986 University of California, Berkeley, business school commencement speech in defense of greed was not an accidental byproduct of the era. His speech, and the response it got from his audience of young plutocrat hopefuls, spoke volumes about the times. "Greed is all right," he told his student audience. "Greed is healthy," he assured. "You can be greedy and still feel good about yourself." His young audience, as one, erupted in applause.[43] Boesky, of course, soon thereafter went to prison. But those business school students went to work.

Predation and corruption were part of the business model for some of the men and the occasional woman who made the eighties and the nineties go-go. The capitalist virtue of destructive creation was in high gear. Monetizing anything that gave off the glimmer of profit, no matter the short-term human cost, was par for the course.

Selling crack was a cruel business but it was, at least short-term, a profitable one. When Norman Tillman, the young man who helped elevate the crack trade in Chicago, was asked in 2015 how he justified what he had done, he said the obvious: "Hell, we were like 20 years old … All we saw was the money, the fancy cars, the trips, the $20,000 Rolex watches. We were just kids caught up in the power it gave us. We didn't see what was happening until it hit home."[44] For him, "hitting home" was the shooting death of his drug-dealing brother by a rival crew. Tillman then got out of the game. He did so with his life, but not much else. Even after so much money flowed through his hands, in the end he had little to show for it but a heavy heart.

The crack years were cruel years; the world of crack often diabolical. Many can and should be blamed for its misery and violence, including those who chose to seek profit in ways that destroyed lives. Nonetheless, we must recognize that most of those who sought financial success in the crack trade operated within the parameters of their worlds, parameters largely set by the various elites who controlled the mainstream economy, law enforcement, schools, public policy, and all those other chutes and ladders that create and deny opportunity in America. Those same elites, for too many years, treated people in the crack trade – whether sellers or buyers – with disdain. They degraded them, lied about them, and humiliated them. They locked them up. They made their hard lives worse.

Nobody, not even the most romanticizing gangsta rapper, has said it in Boesky's terms: "Crack is all right, Crack is healthy. You can sell crack and feel good about yourself." But for a short while between the early 1980s and the mid 1990s, crack was the main chance for tens of thousands of unemployed, undercapitalized young men who dreamed of a world where they were rich and respected and admired.

The crack sellers and the crack bingers invented a consumer marketplace with the tools they had on hand and within the possibilities they could imagine. Within their economic and cultural realm, in a broader culture of entrepreneurial greed, what they did made sense.

Acknowledgments

I first began thinking about writing this book in 2006. At the time, I lived at the run-down edge of Center City Philadelphia on the second floor of an old shoe factory. Just below my living-room window, across the alleyway officially known as "Pearl Street," a group of men operated a small crack cocaine business. Their clients were mainly the homeless men who bedded down nightly in the Sunday Breakfast Rescue Mission, a shelter at the alley's 13th Street intersection. Several times a day the crack crew would take a break to smoke a blunt or two, and they usually began talking loudly after they had each taken a few hits. At that point, I would go down the fire stairs of my building and politely ask the men to keep their voices down. Soon enough I became acquainted with the head of the operation. He would apologize for disturbing me, and then we would talk for a few minutes in a neighborly fashion.

He was a man I guessed to be in his mid-forties. He was always sharply dressed in creased pants, a snappy silk shirt or tasteful sweater, alligator shoes, and, when the weather required it, a mid-length black leather coat. He seemed to like to chat with me and often complimented me on my own less elegant sartorial choices. He had an eye for good shoes. After a few visits, I came to believe that he had recently been released from prison. He implied that his brother in New York City was helping him to get back on his feet by setting him up in business. He also suggested that in his younger days, before being incarcerated, he had enjoyed a good deal of success and a lavish lifestyle. In manner and style, he was a hustler – but he was good company.

I had lived in New York City, on 106th Street just off West End Avenue, during the height of the crack years, so I was well acquainted with people who binged on crack cocaine – our building had an open vestibule that was a perfect spot for "hitting the pipe." And until my wife and I discovered it, our seven-year-old son had gathered together an impressive collection of crack vials with their different colored caps. But I had not, until moving to Philadelphia years later, ever talked with someone who made a living in the crack trade. My conversations with my civil and clearly capable crack-dealing acquaintance planted a seed that I have now, a number of years later, brought to fruit. So, my belated thanks to the crack crew that operated on Pearl Street between 12th and 13th Street in Philadelphia. While I don't know specifically what brought those men to the crack trade, I now think I understand a good deal more about why men like them decided to become crack dealers, especially at the tail end of the twentieth century.

Others have contributed to this book in more conventional ways. My editor, Deborah Gershenowitz, heard out my book pitch and has been cheering me on ever since. She has been a delightful fellow traveler on this project's journey from idea to book. My earnest thanks, as well, to the entire team at Cambridge who have been so dedicated and helpful. Ashley Neale took time from her own rich scholarship to craft the book's index. My thanks to the University of Kansas for making me the Roy A. Roberts Distinguished Professor; funds associated with the professorship supported my research.

As always, a host of my fellow historians have counseled me and supported me throughout the researching and writing of this book. I am much obliged to my fellow historians Peter Pihos, Elaine Carey, and Will Cooley, who read sections of this manuscript in various forms. Their combined historical knowledge of Chicago gangs, drugs, policing, and the racial-justice struggle strengthened this book and steered me towards a better, more accurate portrait of the history I have tried to write. Peter's incisive analysis rethinking the relationship between criminality, crime victims, and the carceral state was a critical intervention. Will helped set me straight on the Chicago scene and Elaine generously offered up her encyclopedic knowledge of the Mexican drug trade; her extraordinary, hard-won research is inspiring. Thanks, as well, to the eminent drug historian David Courtwright for his thoughtful comments on a paper I presented on the Cook County night drug courts at the Policy History

Conference. Bush 41 biographer Jeff Engel, graciously, helped smooth my way at the George H.W. Bush Presidential Library. At the library, archivist Chris Pembleton was an excellent guide. Melanie Newport, a scholar of the carceral state, pointed me to some rich visual sources. My special gratitude goes to Alex Elkins, whose encyclopedic knowledge of the history of policing and criminal justice in the United States, as well as his deep sensitivity to issues of racial justice, contributed so much to this book. His careful reading of draft chapters was greatly appreciated.

A shout out, as well, to a few scholars who I don't know personally but whose work made this book possible. My work draws heavily from the work of three extraordinary ethnographers: Elijah Anderson, Philippe Bourgois, and Sudhir Alladi Venkatesh. These scholars are all academic superstars and I am just one of the many writers working on issues of racial justice and urban life indebted to them. Read their work. I am grateful for the amazing work of Chicago gang historian Zach Jones, whose site, Chicagoganghistory.com is the best source for a detailed, sure-handed historical overview of Chicago's gangs, gang territory, and gang culture. I am also indebted to the extraordinary work of the prolific Seth Ferranti, whose writing on crack kingpins, based in part on the interviews he did with his fellow prison inmates, is an indispensable take on the American criminal underworld. Mr. Ferranti was finally released from prison in 2015 after having been sentenced to twenty-five years for distributing LSD.

Dan Frank, my lifelong friend and a superb writer, read over the manuscript and offered sage advice. An extraordinary educator and public intellectual, he has worked on issues of equity, social justice, diversity, and inclusiveness for decades; his friendship is a rock I have leaned on since I was a boy.

Suzin and Marc Kadish brought a depth of knowledge and experience to this project and shared it generously. Suzin's tales helped inspire this book. She has lived aspects of the history I have tried to recount and she brought those times to life for me. Her matter-of-fact storytelling was worth a thousand newspaper articles. I could not have written this book without her. Likewise, Marc's storied life as a criminal attorney figures throughout this book. His lifelong commitment to racial justice is inspirational and helped guide this project.

Thanks, too, to Marc, for introducing me to Clifford Bey. Mr. Bey generously shared his insights into the world I needed to understand in order to write this book. While Mr. Bey made it crystal clear that he would not be able to tell me anything about any criminal matters of any kind, he was willing to tell me about his own life and the world as he saw it. I spoke to two other men while researching this book who asked that I not identify them in any way. Their insights were nonetheless critical.

Beth Bailey, my dearest darling, read every word of every draft of this manuscript. She is still, more than thirty-five years later, teaching me how to write. I wrote part of this book in Penestanan, part in Wirksworth, and most of it in Lawrence. Most of the time, Beth was never more than a few feet away and in Penestanan we wrote every morning seated across from each other at a small table, sipping coffee after a breakfast of mangoes, papaya, starfruit, and bananas. Writing the first chapter of this story in Indonesia helped give me the intellectual distance I needed to explore the heavy emotions of this American tragedy.

My final thanks go to my son, Max. When I first started thinking about this book, I knew I could not research it without Max's help. He understood things I did not. He knew hip hop; he had friends and acquaintances who had experiences in the world I was researching; and he had an intellectual knowledge of the cross currents of urban youth cultures far superior to my own. In very concrete ways, he worked with me on bridging the gaps I needed to cross to write this book. Max was involved with this project from the beginning and his help, influence, and support can be felt throughout it. He read the draft manuscript and helped me make it better and more authentic. With all my love, this book is dedicated to my son, Max.

Notes

CHOOSING CRACK: AN INTRODUCTION

1. Clifford Bey, interview with author, Chicago, September, 2018. Mr. Bey's story will be told in more detail in Chapter 3.
2. William Julius Wilson, *The Declining Significance of Race: Blacks and Changing American Institutions* (University of Chicago Press, 1978).
3. Philippe Bourgois, *In Search of Respect: Selling Crack in El Barrio* (New York: Cambridge University Press, 1995).

1 FIRST COMES COCAINE, THEN COMES CRACK: ORIGIN STORIES

1. This chapter would not have been possible to write without the pioneering work on the history of cocaine by Paul Gootenberg, especially his landmark book, *Andean Cocaine: Global Drug* (Chapel Hill: University of North Carolina Press, 2008). His influence and published research is felt directly throughout this chapter.
2. For the early history of cocaine in the United States, especially in regard to the move towards prohibition and criminalization, I am indebted to and reliant throughout this section on the pathbreaking work of Joseph F. Spillane, *Cocaine: From Medical Marvel to Modern Menace in the United States, 1884–1920* (Baltimore: Johns Hopkins University Press, 2000). I am also indebted to Gootenberg, *Andean Cocaine*, Chapter 5.
3. Spillane, *Cocaine*, p. 33.
4. Quoted in Gerald T. McLaughlin, "Cocaine: the History and Regulation of a Dangerous Drug," *Cornell Law Review* 58:3, p. 540.
5. The definition comes from Archie Hobson, *The Oxford Dictionary of Difficult Words* (New York: Oxford University Press, 2004), p. 16.
6. Gootenberg, *Andean Cocaine*, chapters 2 and 3.
7. See Catherine Carstairs, "'The Most Dangerous Drug': Images of African-Americans and Cocaine Use in the Progressive Era," *Left History* 7:1, p. 49.
8. Paul Gootenberg, "Between Coca and Cocaine, A Century or More of US–Peruvian Drug Paradoxes, 1860–1980," Working Papers of the Latin American Program, the Woodrow Wilson International Center for Scholars, Washington DC, 2001, p. 11.

9. Spillane, *Cocaine*, p. 53.

10. Gootenberg, *Andean Cocaine*, p. 119.

11. Charles A. Bunting, *Hope for the Victims of Alcohol, Opium, Morphine, Cocaine, and Other Vices* (New York: Pusey and Co., 1888), p. 71. I came across this source in Spillane and he quotes from this passage, as well.

12. "Deadly Dope," *Cincinnati Enquirer*, December 31, 1910, p. 1, Newspapers.com, www.newspapers.com/image/33336952/?terms=cocaine.

13. "Beware of Cocaine in Catarrh Remedies," *The Evening Republican*, December 31, 1910, p. 6, Newspapers.com, www.newspapers.com/image/302699014/?terms=cocaine.

14. Both quotes are from Carstairs, "'The Most Dangerous Drug'"; the first appears on p. 51 and the second on p. 53.

15. I am relying on the evidence and account provided by David J. Courtwright, "The Hidden Epidemic: Opiate Addiction and Cocaine Use in the South, 1860–1920," *Journal of Southern History*, 49:1, p. 68.

16. *Ibid.*

17. Courtwright, "The Hidden Epidemic," p. 68. See also, William Ivy Hair, *Carnival of Fury, Robert Charles and the New Orleans Race Riot of 1900* (Baton Rouge: Louisiana State University Press, 1976), pp. 76–78

18. Quoted in Hair, *Carnival of Fury*, p. 77. The entire paragraph is based on Hair, pp. 76–78.

19. For Hollywood and cocaine see Timothy Dean Lefler, *Mabel Normand* (Jefferson: McFarland and Company, 2016), p. 105. David Courtwright makes the case for the cross-racial cultural transmission of cocaine use but also for the more general use of cocaine by the demi-monde and the underworld in note 81 of his important work *Dark Paradise: A History of Opiate Addiction in America* (Cambridge: Harvard University Press, 1981), p. 227.

20. Fred V. Williams, *The Hop-Heads* (San Francisco: W.N. Brunt, 1920), p. 17; the material first appeared in the *San Francisco Daily News*.

21. Alan A. Block, "The Snowman Cometh – Coke in Progressive New York," *Criminology* 75, p. 79.

22. "Murder at the Metropole," May 31, 2016, Infamous New York, https://infamousnewyork.com/2016/05/31/murder-at-the-metropole-charles-becker-herman-rosenthal-case-147-west-43rd-street/. Full disclosure: Mr. Rosenthal is likely a distant relative of the author.

23. Block, "The Snowman Cometh," p. 90.

24. For a recent, comprehensive history of Prohibition see Lisa McGirr, *The War on Alcohol* (New York: Norton, 2015).

25. *Narcotic Drugs Import and Export Act*, 67th Congress, May 26, 1922, Sess. II, CHS. 201, 202, 1922, p. 596.

26. Spillane, *Cocaine*, Chapter 8.

27. Both the quote and the number come from Spillane, *Cocaine*, p. 155.

28. "Pool Room Man Before Court in 'Drug Deal,'" *San Francisco Chronicle*, November 11, 1920, p. 1, newspapers.com, www.newspapers.com/image/27409193/?fcfToken=662

b74454c4e63762b6d474b65484562486f7641304e726d4779345668386d4461363369
6b6941576378506d713175373070684c72724e6234387a676e6b4f47.

29. "Denies Smuggling Cocaine," *Washington Post,* November 7, 1920, p. 7, newspapers.com, www.newspapers.com/image/28847621/?fcfToken=66444862733670466a734e6f55494 b4d5a65696b59674675474266766c6d2b496f4b685a535469464b717158676357584b433 175656a7453705779345641624f.

30. "Young Girls are Found Victims of 'Drug' Ring," *The Oregon Journal,* August 1, 1920, p. 4, newspapers.com, www.newspapers.com/image/77195725/?fcfToken=43437578 6d523562424e5871795832645947484b55336d3432355470627065564f795155474f6 b5948794e4f4664313837363658702b2b527442734a6856796e.

31. "Drug Under Dead Man's Bunk," *The Baltimore Sun,* November 10, 1920, p. 2, newspapers.com, www.newspapers.com/image/214664171/?fcfToken=64772b6f6e685978 50554a54304d524f2f4d656d42784b54595259685a56735741537331633872425979 6e6355477a513632426173766d62736a567074426c6e2b6a6a4d585230393936424d3d.

32. That number comes from a search done on newspapers.com for the entire United States. The number probably includes the same story printed in several papers, though I found very few examples for 1920 of such repetition since most stories were local in nature.

33. Block, "The Snowman Cometh."

34. This account draws, in whole, on Block, "The Snowman Cometh."

35. This trade has received relatively little attention and even such a respected and well-informed cocaine scholar as Paul Gootenberg has argued that in the United States "cocaine rapidly receded in the 1920s ... no major underworld figures pursued possibilities" and that there were only "tiny seizures" of cocaine in the 1920s; Gootenberg, *Andean Cocaine,* pp. 249–250.

36. David Pietrusza, *Rothstein* (New York: Carroll and Graf, 2003). For a compelling portrait of Rothstein, see Nick Tosches, "A Jazz Age Autopsy," *Vanity Fair,* May 2005, pp. 174–191.

37. According to the Dutch drug historian Marcel de Kort, cocaine was smuggled from the Netherlands to the United States but despite the massive amounts of cocaine legally produced in the Netherlands in the 1920s, the illicit coke was produced in Germany and then illegally smuggled from Rotterdam to the United States. See Marcel de Kort, "Doctors, Diplomats, and Businessmen," Paul Gootenberg, ed., *Cocaine: Global Histories,* (New York: Routledge, 1999), p. 129.

38. Pietrusza, *Rothstein,* p. 328 and Jill Jonnes, *Hep-Cats, Narcs, and Pipe Dreams* (Baltimore: Johns Hopkins University Press, 1999), pp. 83–84.

39. Jill Jonnes, "One Man Invented the Modern Narcotics Industry," *American Heritage* 44:1, p. 48. In addition, Jonnes has an excellent chapter on Rothstein and the drug trade in *Hep-Cats,* pp. 72–86. Also useful is the account of Rothstein's drug business in Pietrusza's *Rothstein,* pp. 316–329. Additional information was found in Wilbur E. Rogers, "4 Arrests Bare Rothstein as the Backer of Biggest International Drug Ring," *Brooklyn Daily Eagle,* December 9, 1928, pp. 1, 3, newspapers.com, www.newspapers.com/ image/59886951/?fcfToken=3161574a37727438443739442f4d4c4c38696a6976534

f782b694c6752633158625 8684b456378624d6179753843545338575a6
d356e503952724d38712f3255.

40. Quoted in an Associated Press story that was distributed nationally; "Four Seized in Rothstein, Drug Inquiry," *Star Tribune*, December 9, 1928, p. 4, newspapers.com, www.newspapers.com/image/182431595/?fcfToken=4c366d2f714b67302f5666487 3682f75303449345a304859465667705562496e6a6b54447836336e47706f535563696a 67737779674a734e427333527356484d2f6e655a504834495936733d.

41. The quote is from an Associated Press story that was distributed nationally: "Ton of Narcotics Seized at Pier by Federal Agents," *The Sedalia Democrat*, December 19, 1928, p. 3, newspapers.com, www.newspapers.com/image/74288711/?fcfToken=567a7048365 66a45614b434363514c41794f705164 6e454a6c4a5976667054797a70724b377a4a5a4d5 270644536373951422b51744c3955746d7a5631702f66. Other details are taken from Pietrusza, *Rothstein*, pp. 326–7. Drugs continued to be found linked to Rothstein's ring up to a year and half later; see the AP story, "Drug Seizure Linked to Rothstein," *Cincinnati Inquirer*, June 29, 1930, p. 1, newspapers.com, www.newspapers.com/image/ 103007711/?fcfToken=6e6d33564f565a3838572b3978464a7a54752f2f3059464a70733 95831374c6a716c736131697335374b75616a7a687a5847706658756464634f6569434e7 172735144446c7539514647633d.

42. Nicolas Rasmussen, "America's First Amphetamine Epidemic 1929–1971," *American Journal of Public Health* 98:6, pp. 974–985.

43. "Dope Raid Sets Record," *Los Angeles Times*, April 21, 1935, p. 25, newspapers.com, www .newspapers.com/image/159504596/?terms=cocaine

44. "Trade in Opium Is on Increase, Anslinger Says," *The Greenville News*, November 23, 1935, p. 7, newspapers.com, www.newspapers.com/image/188262617/?terms=cocaine.

45. Gootenberg, *Andean Cocaine*, p. 251.

46. "$30,000 Dope Seized in S.F.," *Oakland Tribune*, July 21, 1940 p. 7, newspapers.c om, www.newspapers.com/image/136084574/?terms=cocaine. The quote is from an AP story: "Japanese Plot to Flood US with Dope is Charged," *Lincoln Star*, July 22, 1940, p. 10, newspapers.com, www.newspapers.com/image/74557385/? terms=cocaine.

47 Ira Gitler, *Swing to Bop* (New York: Oxford University Press, 1985), p 174.

48. I was alerted to this story in *Andean Cocaine*. Gootenberg mentions the arrests briefly on p. 263. The arrests were reported on by UPI and the story was printed in papers around the United States. For the details on the ring members and the arrests, see: "Mothers Lured by $25,000,000 Narcotics Ring," *St. Louis Post-Dispatch*, December 13, 1964, Newspapers.com, www.newspapers.com/image/142228211/?terms=%22sybil%2BHo rowitz%22; "Indict Dope Smugglers," January 1, 1965, *The Troy Record* (New York), Newspapers.com, www.newspapers.com/image/10886163/?terms=%22sybil%2BHor owitz%22; and David Anderson, "US Reports $25 Million Cocaine Smuggling Ring," December 12, 1964, *New York Times*, www.nytimes.com/1964/12/12/us-reports-25-mil lion-cocaine-smuggling-ring.html?_r=0. "'Con's Case is First on List of Jury Trials," *Lincoln Journal Star*, April 24, 1953, Newspapers.com, www.newspapers.com/image/6 6158418/?terms=%22sybil%2BHorowitz%22; Marjorie Marlette, "New Yorkers Believe

Lincoln Now Safe from 'Con Games,'" *Lincoln Journal Star*, May 5, 1953, Newspapers. com, www.newspapers.com/image/46656717/?terms=%22sybil%2BHorowitz%22; "Grand Larceny Charge Dropped," *The Courier-News*, December 19, 1959, newspapers. com, www.newspapers.com/image/221815412/?terms=%22sybil%2BHorowitz%22.

49. Coda: Horowitz and Bradbie got two years in prison. Ralph Santana, the ringleader, received a fifteen-year sentence. While in prison he met other big-time narcotics operators with a range of international connections, and from his prison cell, with his new associates, he organized an international heroin- and cocaine-smuggling business. The ring, which used Canadian cocktail waitresses among others to smuggle in the drugs, got busted and Santana had to serve a few extra years in prison. Released in the 1980s, he was able to buy a place in Fort Lauderdale and took up his old trade. He went into business with a planning commissioner in the Poconos and brought in massive loads of both heroin and cocaine which were brought up to the Poconos and distributed from there. In 1987 he and his partner were caught. Santana ended his days in prison. Arnold Lubaschinov, "$65-Million Street Value Estimated – Plot Began in Atlanta Penitentiary," *New York Times*, November 10, 1973, www.nytimes.com/197 3/11/10/archives/65million-street-value-estimatedplot-began-in-atlanta-peniten tiary.html; and Tyra Braden, "Santana Pleads Guilty To Trafficking Federal Prosecutor Will Seek Life In Pocono Drug Ring Case," *The Morning Call*, October 13, 1989, http://articles.mcall.com/1989-10-13/news/2721583_1_heroin-and-cocai ne-drug-ring-import-heroin.

50. Anderson, "US Reports."

51. David Farber, *The Age of Great Dreams* (New York: Hill and Wang, 1994), p. 173.

52. By the mid 1970s, it was common to see weed dealers operating openly in the parking lots of big manufacturing plants, selling to shift workers both entering and exiting factories. Student weed dealers operated in high schools and even middle schools – author's observations from back in the day.

53. Martin Torgoff, *Can't Find My Way Home* (New York: Simon and Schuster, 2004), p. 265. A great insider, celebrity-oriented, book on illegal drugs in late twentieth-century America.

54. Torgoff, *Can't Find*, p. 265.

55. Torgoff makes this point, *Can't Find*, pp. 263–267.

56. Torgoff, *Can't Find*, p. 265.

57. Ann Crittenden and Michael Ruby, "Cocaine: The Champagne of Drugs," *New York Times Magazine*, September 1, 1974, p. 14.

58. Jonnes, *Hep-Cats*, p. 308. Jonnes pointed me, as well, to the *NYT* story.

59. Useful charts on cocaine use are provided in the critically important overview of crack cocaine, Reinarman and Levine, *Crack in America*, pp. 30–31.

60. Guy Gugliotta and Jeff Leen, *Kings of Cocaine*, New York: Simon and Schuster, 1989, p. 12.

61. I am following the account given by Gugliotta and Leen, *Kings of Cocaine*, Chapter 2.

62. Gugliotta and Leen, *Kings of Cocaine*, chapters 2–4.

63. In the Kindle edition of Gugliotta and Leen, *Kings of Cocaine*, location 800 of 7109.

64. Art Harris, The Drug Game," *Washington Post*, March 11, 1984, www.washingtonpost
.com/archive/lifestyle/1984/03/11/the-drug-game-undercover-in-miami/79d11c78-
755c-4888-912f-aeb02bfbd055/?utm_term=.4c6af344b1d3.
65. "Price of Cocaine has Risen," *New York Times*, September 2, 1984, p. 2.
66. Quoted in Harris, "The Drug Game."

2 CRACK THE MARKET: COMMODIFICATION AND COMMERCIALIZATION

1. Seth Ferranti, "LA's Original Gangster – Tootie Reese," Gorilla Convict, April 22, 2015,
www.gorillaconvict.com/2015/04/las-original-gangster-tootie-reese/.
2. Jesse Katz, "Tracking the Genesis of the Crack Trade," *Los Angeles Times*, October 20,
1996, http://articles.latimes.com/1996-10-20/news/mn-59169_1_crack-cocaine.
3. For important overviews of the origins of crack cocaine see: Gordon Witkin, "The Men
Who Created Crack," *US News and World Report*, 111:8, p. 44; Michael Agar, "The Story of
Crack: Towards a Theory of Illicit Drug Trends," *Addiction Research and Theory* 11:1, pp.
3–29; Katz, "Tracking the Genesis of the Crack Trade"; Michael Massing, "Crack's
Destructive Sprint Across America," *New York Times Magazine*, October 1, 1989, www
.google.com/search?client=safari&rls=en&q=%E2%80%9CCrack%E2%80%99s+Dest
ructive+Sprint+Across+America,%E2%80%9D&ie=UTF-8&oe=UTF-8; and Jonnes,
Hep-Cats, Chapter 17.
4. Katz, "Tracking the Genesis of the Crack Trade."
5. "Richard Pryor's Tragic Accident Spotlights a Dangerous Drug Craze: Freebasing,"
People, June 30, 1980, https://people.com/archive/richard-pryors-tragic-accident-spot
lights-a-dangerous-drug-craze-freebasing-vol-13-no-26/.
6. Katz, "Tracking the Genesis of the Crack Trade."
7. Peter Katel, "The Many Conspiracies of Crack Cocaine: Supply-Siders Lacked the
Whole Story," *Christian Science Monitor*, November 18, 1996, www.csmonitor.com/199
6/1118/111896.opin.opin.1.html.
8. Massing, "Crack's Destructive Sprint Across America."
9. The story and quote are from Witkin, "The Men Who Created Crack," Chapter 3
10. For a compelling account of crack's American origins, see also the DEA's official
history: Drug Enforcement Administration (DEA), "DEA History, 1885–1990," pp.
58–59, www.dea.gov/about/history/1985-1990%20p%2058-67.pdf.
11. Both quotes are from Selwyn Raab, "Brutal Drug Gangs Wage War of Terror in Upper
Manhattan," *New York Times*, March 15, 1988, p. B1.
12. This portrait comes from the memoir by Corey Pegues, *Once a Cop: The Street, the Law,
Two Worlds, One Man* (New York: Simon and Schuster, 2016).
13. Pegues, *Once a Cop*, pp. 22 and 23–24.
14. Katz, "Tracking the Genesis of Crack."
15. Bourgois, *In Search of Respect*, pp. 146 and 141.
16. Pegues, *Once a Cop*, pp. 27–28.
17. Pegues, *Once a Cop*, pp. 31, 32.
18. Pegues, *Once a Cop*, p. 58.

19. My section on the Supreme Team is derived from many sources. The best account of the Team and the Queens scene in which they operated is given by Ethan Brown, *Queens Reigns Supreme: Fat Cat, 50 Cent, and the Rise of the Hip Hop Hustler* (New York: Anchor Books, 2005). Especially valuable, too, is the rich account provided by Seth Ferranti, *The Supreme Team* (St. Peters, Missouri: Gorilla Convict Publications, 2012). Ferranti is a prolific author who wrote *The Supreme Team* while serving a 304-month federal sentence for distributing LSD. Ferranti's work is based on many sources, including interviews with his fellow prisoners. Ferranti bases some of his material on Brown's book. Also important: Peter Blauner, "Fat Cat and the Crack Wars," *New York Magazine*, September 7, 1987, pp. 46–54; the profile written by Tiffany Chiles and Soulman Seth [Ferranti], "Supreme Team," *Don Diva* Issue 0023, pp. 28–38; and the online material collected to promote the forthcoming memoir of Supreme Team stalwart Ronald "Tuck" Tucker https://manumitpublishing.wordpress.com/tag/truths-of-a-southside-ambassador/. Also useful are a detailed press release put out by the Justice Department, "Kenneth 'Supreme' McGriff and 8 Leaders, Members and Associates of McGriff's Enterprise Charged with Racketeering, Homicide and Drug Distribution," January 26, 2005, www .justice.gov/archive/usao/nye/pr/2005/2005jan26.html; *United States of America, Appellee, v. Gerald Miller, Ronald Tucker, Roy Hale, Waverly Coleman, Harry Hunt, Shannon Jimenez, Raymond Robinson, Aka "ace" Wilfredo Arroyo, Aka "c-justice," Aka "c.j.," David Robinson, Aka "bing," Defendants-appellants*, 116 F.3d 641 (2d Cir. 1997), US Court of Appeals for the Second Circuit – 116 F.3d 641 (2d Cir. 1997), Argued Dec. 16, 1996. Decided June 20, 1997, https://law.justia.com/cases/federal/appellate-courts/F3/11 6/641/612012/; Ran Britt, "The Infamous Kenneth 'Supreme' McGriff and the Supreme Team," September 27, 2015, Die Young, http://theranreport.blogspot.co m/2015/09/the-infamouskenneth-supreme-mcgriff-and.html; "Bimmy Former 'Supreme Team Drug Gang' Drug Boss," DJ Cisco Radio Network LLC, published September 21, 2016; and, finally, the Supreme Team is memorialized by 50 Cent, "Ghetto Qu'ran," produced by Trackmasters, 2000.

20. Ferranti, *The Supreme Team*, p. 57.

21. Pegues, *Once a Cop*, p. 59.

22. Brilliantly explored in the work of Sudhir Alladi Venkatesh, especially in *Off the Books* (Cambridge: Harvard University Press, 2006).

23. Ferranti, *The Supreme Team*, p. 36.

24. Drawn from the telling portrait of Supreme written by Seth Ferranti, *Street Legends*, volume I (NP: Gorilla Convict Publications, 2008), pp. 19–22.

25. The Supreme Team's use of codes is mentioned in Chiles and Ferranti, "Supreme Team," p. 29.

26. The Notorious B.I.G., "Ten Crack Commandments," 1997.

27. Ferranti, *The Supreme Team*, p. 81.

28. Ferranti, *Street Legends*, p. 27.

29. Chiles and Ferranti, "Supreme Team."

30. The use of color-coded caps was common, at least in New York City. In the early 1990s, my son picked up the colorful caps – yellow, red, and purple – that littered the sidewalks

near our apartment on 106th Street. When his mother and I discovered his collection, he had over fifty caps. Crack was sold openly on both Amsterdam Avenue at 105th and Columbus Avenue at 107th and crack users got high all over the neighborhood, including in the unlocked vestibule of our small apartment building.

31. This biographical material is drawn mostly from the thirty-eight-minute interview Bimmy did with DJ Cisco in 2016 that is available on YouTube. While Bimmy skirts around issues of violence, he is open about his life in the drug game, drawing the ire of many commentators who state that drug dealers should keep quiet about their work lest law-enforcement officials use their words to hurt others. This historian is thankful for Bimmy's willingness to discuss his past. A small point: Bimmy corrects DJ Cisco when he says, as others have, that Bimmy's crew sold "blue"-capped vials. Bimmy insists that they were green, except for a short time when he ran out of the green and briefly used "rainbow"-colored caps he bought in Harlem, which created a beef with Prince.

32. Ferranti, *Street Legends*, p. 29.

33. *United States of America, Appellee, v. Gerald Miller et al.*

34. Brown, *Queens Reigns Supreme*, pp. 25–26.

35. Chiles and Ferranti, "Supreme Team," p. 34.

36. Brown, *Queen Reigns Supreme*, p. 32.

37. "The Suarez-Perlaza Murders," in *United States of America, Appellee, v. Gerald Miller.*

38. 50 Cent, "Ghetto Qu'ran."

39. Tom Hayes, "Drug Kingpin Guilty of Murdering Rapper," *Washington Post*, February 1, 2007, www.washingtonpost.com/wp-dyn/content/article/2007/02/01/AR2007020101022.html.

40. Serranti, *The Supreme Team*, p. 95.

41. Blauner, "Fat Cat and the Crack Wars," p. 52.

42. DEA, "History," p. 59.

43. Leonard Buder, "Dealer Guilty of Ordering Officer Killed," *New York Times*, December 12, 1989, pp. B1–2.

44. George James, "Drug Crackdown is Expanded to East Harlem," *New York Times*, November 16, 1988, p. 1.

45. All of the above, including quotations, is drawn from *United States of America, Appellee, v. Gerald Miller.*

46. *Goons of New York – The YTC Story*, Infominds, published January 2, 2018 on YouTube. This powerful video features Chango, who ran the YTC, detailing his years as a crack crew leader. He is extraordinarily frank in detailing what he did and why he did it – he served time for all the criminal events he recounts. Puerto Rican crack dealers played a major role in East Harlem from the mid 1980s on through the crack years, as well as on the Upper West Side/Manhattan Valley a few blocks south and east of Columbia University. For an extraordinary account of a relatively small but lucrative Puerto Rican crack operation in East Harlem see Bourgois, *In Search of Respect.*

47. Randy Kennedy, "Major Bust But Drug Sales Go On," *New York Times*, July 3, 1994, p. 5.

48. James C. McKinley, Jr., "US Agents Seize 17 in Raids to Dismantle Jamaican Drug Ring," *New York Times*, December 8, 1990, p. 1.

49. Drawn from perhaps the best book yet written on a major crack gang by the extraordinary author, Jonathan Green, *Sex Money Murder: A Story of Crack, Blood and Betrayal* (New York: Norton, 2018).

50. The info on crack being sold in the Robert Taylor Homes in 1985 "or so" comes from Sudhir Alladi Venkatesh, *American Project* (Cambridge: Harvard University Press, 2000), p. 135. For sure in 1987, an independent cocaine and heroin ring – possibly associated with the El Rukns – led by Mario Claiborne was selling crack around 44th and Greenwood, in the neighborhood east of some of Chicago's biggest public housing projects – but they did not sell in the projects, which were controlled by major Chicago gangs. See the statement by convicted crack dealer Mario Claiborne, *United States v. Claiborne*, October 19, 1992, United States of America, Plaintiff, Mario Claiborne, also known as Chuck, Defendant. Claiborne would eventually be arrested in 1991 and sentenced to life in prison.

51. "A Different Kind of War on Crack," *Chicago Defender*, February 21, 1989, p. 11.

52. Robert Blau, "Crack Breaks the Chicago Barrier," *Chicago Tribune*, August 27, 1989, http://articles.chicagotribune.com/1989-08-27/news/8901080131_1_crack-chicago-police-highly-addictive-drug/2.

53. Robert Blau, "City Police Report Slight Increase in Crack Seizures," *Chicago Tribune*, November 15, 1989.

54. Natalie Y. Moore and Lance Williams, *The Almighty Black P Stone Nation* (Chicago: Lawrence Hill Books, 2011), p. 249. Ironically, the authors had already provided contrary evidence to this thesis on p. 175. Nonetheless, this remarkable, insider history is a thorough and compelling study and I rely on it throughout my discussion of the P. Stone Nation. For background on the Stones during their early years, see James Allen McPherson, "Chicago's Blackstone Nation," *The Atlantic*, May 1969. McPherson briefly explores the Stone's anti-heroin efforts and the murder of a dealer. He provides evidence based on testimony presented at the murder trial of Stone's president Eugene "Bull" Hairston that the dealers were shot not to keep heroin out of the community but to eliminate a rival narcotics operation; the Stones, he suggests, were already selling narcotics by 1967. Will Cooley also provides excellent historical background on black street gangs in Chicago with a focus on the Blackstone Rangers in the 1960s and 1970s and their commitment, not to social activism during that period, as some have suggested, but to criminal activities: Will Cooley, "Stones Run It: Taking Back Control of Organized Crime in Chicago 1940–1975," *Journal of Urban History* 37:6, 2011, pp. 911–932.

55. Moore and Williams, *The Almighty Black P Stone Nation*, p. 175.

56. My thanks to historian Elaine Carey for sharing her expertise with me on the Mexican drug trade, in general, and on the Herrera family, in specific. She notes that the Herrera family worked with multiple producers and suppliers across western Mexico and members of these various drug rings intermarried to assure trust and cooperation. See the important book by Elaine Carey, *Women Drug Traffickers: Mules, Bosses, and Organized Crime* (Albuquerque: University of New Mexico Press, 2014).

57. For a useful overview of the Herrera family and the Chicago illegal drug market more generally, see: Gad Bensinger, Thomas Lemmer, and Arthur Lurigo, "The War on Drugs in Chicago: Thinking Locally, Acting Globally," May 2006, www.researchgate .net/publication/313038349_THE_WAR_ON_DRUGS_IN_CHICAGO_THINKING_ LOCALLY_ACTING_GLOBALLY.

58. Larry Green and Wendy Leopold, "120 Arrested in Raids on Major Drug Ring," *Los Angeles Times*, July 24, 1985, http://articles.latimes.com/1985-07-24/news/mn-4736_1 _federal-agents and Maurice Possley, "15 Sentencings Cripple Drug-Smuggling Family," *Chicago Tribune*, February 7, 1987, http://articles.chicagotribune.com/1987- 02-07/news/8701100346_1_biggest-drug-bust-drug-dealing-mexican-drug-suppliers.

59. George Papajohn, "'King' Wheat's Killing Mirrors Change in Gangs," *Chicago Tribune*, August 19, 1994, http://articles.chicagotribune.com/1994-08-19/news/9408190365_ 1_four-corners-vice-lords-gang.

60. An attorney who defended leaders of the P. Stone Nation/El Rukns in the 1970s and 1980s, suggests that part of the reason Jeff Fort embraced Moorish Science while in prison and urged other gang members to convert, as well, was so that they could all meet privately in prison both to worship and to take care of business. The attorney does not suggest that this was the only reason for the conversion – Fort had long been interested in ideas and practices that resonated with his views on community solidarity and the myriad forms through which racism operated in the United States; the teachings of Moorish Science spoke to those concerns.

61. "Gang Chief Guilty in Rival's Slaying," *New York Times*, October 20, 1988, p. 25

62. Mark Konkol, "Freeway Boy Who Brought Crack to Chicago," October 28, 2014, DNA Info, www.dnainfo.com/chicago/20141028/englewood/freeway-boy-who-brought-cra ck-chicago-regrets-damage-done-hometown.

63. Moore and Williams, *Almighty Black P Stone Nation*, pp. 250–251.

64. To be clear, the story that follows is based on the account given by Moore and Williams in *Almighty Black P Stone Nation*, pp. 249–255. Williams worked closely with the young men who were part of the 8-Tray Stones from the 1980s to the present. He later became a professor and assistant director of Northeastern Illinois University's Carruthers Center for Inner City Studies.

65. Moore and Williams, *Almighty Black P Stone Nation*, pp. 249–250.

66. Moore and Williams, *Almighty Black P Stone Nation*, p. 251.

67. Moore and Williams, *Almighty Black P Stone Nation*, p. 252.

68. Anthony Burke Boylan, "1.3 Million Awarded to Family of Man Slain by Cop," *Chicago Tribune*, August 8, 1999, http://articles.chicagotribune.com/1999-08-08/news/99080 80225_1_keys-home-police-officials-shooting The article title says it all regarding the death of Mr. Keys.

69. Judy Pasternak, "US Moves to Crack Powerful Chicago Gang," *Los Angeles Times*, September 1, 1995, http://articles.latimes.com/1995-09-01/news/mn-41129_1_chi cago-s-gangster-disciples.

70. This figure and a general outline of the Gangster Disciples' operations are given in: *United States of America, Plaintiff-Appellee v. Sonia Irwin, Defendant-Appellant*, 149 F.3d 565,

No. 97–3105, United States Court of Appeals, Seventh Circuit, Argued Jan. 21, 1998. Decided July 1, 1998. For an outstanding overview of the Gangster Disciples' history and Larry Hoover's early years, I have relied on Zach Jones' extraordinary website, Chicago Gang History, https://chicagoganghistory.com/about/, especially his long, thoroughly researched essay, "Gangster Disciples." Also very useful is the history and material gathered by George W. Knox, "The Impact of the Federal Prosecution of the Gangster Disciples," National Gang Crime Research Center, Chicago, 2008, which includes many extraordinary primary sources on Hoover's leadership and efforts to manipulate Chicago politicians. In addition, I have drawn on chapters 3 and 4 of the ethnographic study of the Robert Taylor Homes in the 1990s by Sudhir Alladi Vankatesh, *American Project: The Rise and Fall of a Modern Ghetto* (Cambridge: Harvard University Press, 2002). These chapters explore the role of the Gangster Disciples (called by the pseudonym, the "Black Kings") in the public housing project. Given my interests in the GDs' business model, I tended to depend more on those accounts that focused on their drug business and on Larry Hoover's role in organizing operations.

71. George Papajohn and William Recktenwald, "Living in a War Zone Called Taylor Homes," *Chicago Tribune*, March 10, 1993, http://articles.chicagotribune.com/1993-0 3-10/news/9303190679_1_gang-war-gangster-disciples-gang-members.

72. I draw on personal observation. My sister lived a few blocks away from Cabrini-Green during these years and a legendary wine store, Sam's, somewhat remarkably, operated across the street from the border of Cabrini-Green, giving me ample opportunity to observe the scene. The neighborhood has been completely transformed since Cabrini-Green was knocked down, a process that began at the end of the 1990s.

73. Jones, "Gangster Disciples."

74. Edward McClelland, "White Flight, By the Numbers," NBC Chicago, May 6, 2013, www .nbcchicago.com/blogs/ward-room/White-Flight-By-The-Numbers-206302551.html.

75. Jones, "Gangster Disciples." In this section, I generally follow Jones's cogent history of the GDs and Hoover. In doing my research, I talked with people who know Larry Hoover; they all stated that he was a talented, charismatic man who, generally, did right by his community. No one I spoke with said they had any direct knowledge of his involvement in the crack industry.

76. Many of Hoover's communiqués are reproduced, in whole, in Knox, "The Impact of the Federal Prosecution of the Gangster Disciples."

77. This material and the quotation come from *United States of America v. Sonia Irwin*.

78. Alderman Virgil Jones to James Williams, June 17, 1993; the document appears in Knox, "The Impact of the Federal Prosecution of the Gangster Disciples."

79. Pasternak, "US Moves to Crack Powerful Chicago Gang"; and John O'Brien, Matt O'Conner, and George Papajohn, "U.S. Goes Behind Bars to Indict 39 Gang Leaders," *Chicago Tribune*, September 1, 1995, http://articles.chicagotribune.com/19 95-09-01/news/9509010253_1_indictments-gang-leaders-gang-members.

80. Katz, "Tracking the Genesis of the Crack Trade."

81. Michael Isikoff and Nancy Lewis, "Making a D.C. Link to the Colombian Source," *Washington Post*, September 3, 1989, www.washingtonpost.com/archive/politics/1989 /09/03/making-a-dc-link-to-the-colombian-source/3d9e8b72-8097-43d5 88aa-02d29 e8a7c3b/?noredirect=on&utm_term=.705fae666a46.

3 CRACK UP: THE COST OF HARD-CORE CONSUMPTION

1. Quoted in the essential sociological study of inner-city life in Philadelphia during the crack era, Elijah Anderson, *Streetwise: Race, Class, and Change in an Urban Community* (University of Chicago Press, 1992), p. 88. Chapter 3, "The Impact of Drugs," is a powerful account of what crack usage did to the community. City-by-city comparisons of overall crack impact are found in Table 1 of the major study done by Roland G. Freyer, Jr., Paul S. Heaton, Steven D. Leavitt, and Kevin Murphy, "Measuring Crack Cocaine and Its Impact," April 2006, p. 33, https://scholar.harvard.edu/files/fryer/files/fhlm_crac k_cocaine_0.pdf.
2. The statistic is drawn from NIDA, *National Household Survey on Drug Abuse: Population Estimates 1991* (Rockville, MD: National Institute on Drug Abuse, 1991).
3. Based on the work of Craig Reinarman, Dan Waldorf, Sheigla B. Murphy, and Harry G. Levine, "The Contingent Call of the Pipe," in *Crack in America*, Craig Reinarman and Harry G. Levine (eds.) (Berkeley: University of California Press, 1997), pp. 77–112.
4. This claim, which I find convincing, appears throughout the literature on crack. For a good summary see Craig Reinarman and Harry G. Levine, "Crack in Context," in *Crack in America*, Reinarman and Levine (eds.), pp. 2–3. See also, Philippe Bourgois, "Crack and the Political Economy of Social Suffering," *Addiction Research and Theory* 11:1, 2003, p. 32 and Carol Anne Acker, "How Crack Found a Niche in the American Ghetto," *BioSocieties* 5:1, 2010, pp. 70–88.
5. DEA, "History," pp. 58–59.
6. Numbers on crack and powder cocaine usage are tricky. The half a million number comes from the NIDA National Household Survey for 1990 as reported in the US General Accounting Office Fact Sheet for the Chairman, Select Committee on Narcotics Abuse and Control, House of Representatives, "Drug Abuse: The Crack Cocaine Epidemic: Health Consequences and Treatment," January 1991, p. 12; the statistics on powder cocaine usage decline come on p. 2. When this report was being given to the House Select Committee, a senior administrator at HHS, working on anti-drug measures, wrote a colleague arguing that the data on powder and crack cocaine use underreported the problem due to the small and misleading sample used in the NIDA surveys; he argued that they needed to develop "a much larger sample size that will provide better precision"; see Mark Barnes to John Schall, "Comments on January 8, 1991 Draft of Strategy III," January 12, 1991, 03776-010, Paul Korfonta Files (PK), George H.W. Bush Presidential Library (GB). The GAO report that uses the half a million number makes a similar disclaimer right in the text on p. 2, stating that the NIDA survey "underestimates the actual extent of the cocaine problem . . . Because the survey does not include certain populations, namely patients at drug treatment centers,

the homeless, and arrestees who have a higher incidence of drug use, the actual extent of the problem could be much higher." It was also admitted that 18 percent of households selected for the survey refused to participate. A personal note: my Chicago high school class in spring 1974 was selected to fill out a precursor (a pilot survey by the University of Michigan, I believe) to the NIDA National High School Survey (which actually began in 1975); several of us, being annoying adolescents, reported that we used heroin and LSD every day.

7. Based on conversations with users. For a useful, dependable overview see: Erowid, "Cocaine Effects," The Vaults of Erowid, www.erowid.org/chemicals/cocaine/cocai ne_effects.shtml.

8. Jefferson Morley, "This Journalist Smoked Crack So He Could Write This Article," *New Republic*, October 2, 1989, https://newrepublic.com/article/120143/what-crack-cocai ne-really.

9. Claire E. Stark, *Fast Lives: Women Who Use Crack Cocaine* (Philadelphia: Temple University Press, 1999), pp. 40 and 41.

10. Quoted in Sheigla B. Murphy and Marsha Rosenbaum, "Two Women Who Used Cocaine Too Much," in *Crack in America*, Reinarman and Levine (eds.), p. 104.

11. Quoted in Bourgois, *In Search of Respect*, p. 80.

12. Reinarman and Levine, "The Crack Attack," in *Crack in America*, Reinarman and Levine (eds.), p. 34.

13. Pegues, *Once a Cop*, p. 74.

14. Quoted in Tanya Telfair Sharpe, *Behind the Eight Ball: Sex for Crack Cocaine Exchange and Poor Black Women* (New York: Routledge, 2005), p. 99.

15. DEA, "History," pp. 58–59.

16. *Crack in America*, Reinarman and Levine (eds.), p. 173.

17. Bourgois, "Crack and the Political Economy of Social Suffering," p. 32.

18. Eric C. Schneider, *Smack: Heroin and the American City* (Philadelphia: University of Pennsylvania Press), 2008, p. ix.

19. *Ibid.*, p. x.

20. Reinarman, Waldorf, Murphy, and Levine, "The Contingent Call of the Pipe," in *Crack in America*, Reinarman and Levine (eds.), p. 90.

21. *Ibid.*, p. 92.

22. For an incisive look at the famous campaign commercial, Michael Beschloss, "The Ad That Helped Reagan Sell Good Times to an Uncertain Nation," *New York Times*, May 7, 2016, www.nytimes.com/2016/05/08/business/the-ad-that-helped-reagan-sell-good-ti mes-to-an-uncertain-nation.html.

23. "Reagan Quotes King Speech in Opposing Minority Quotas," *New York Times*, January 19, 1986, p. 20.

24. See Sudhir Alladi Venkatesh, *American Project* (Cambridge: Harvard University Press, 2000), p. 116.

25. "Opposing Minority Quotas," *New York Times*, January 19, 1986, p. 20.

26. Anderson, *Streetwise*, pp. 58–59. Northton is the fictional name Anderson uses for the poor, nearly all-African-American West Side Philadelphia neighborhood near the University of Pennsylvania.
27. Anderson, *Streetwise*, p. 66.
28. William Julius Wilson, *The Declining Significance of Race: Blacks and Changing American Institutions* (University of Chicago Press, 1978).
29. "Interview: William Julius Wilson," Frontline, PBS.org, Spring 1997, www.pbs.org/wgbh/pages/frontline/shows/race/interviews/wilson.html.
30. Venkatesh, *American Project*, p. 114. Residents in such projects faced work disincentives; their low-cost housing could be lost if they became wage earners.
31. Interview, William Julius Wilson.
32. Bourgois, *In Search of Respect*.
33. Ken Auletta, *The Underclass* (New York: Random House, 1982).
34. For example, Lawrence M. Mead, *Beyond Entitlement* (New York: Free Press, 1985).
35. Elijah Anderson, *Code of the Street* (New York: Norton, 2000), pp. 110–111.
36. Pegues, *Once a Cop*, pp. 75 and 76.
37. Quoted in Paul Adler's brilliant account of the Chambers brothers and the crack trade in Detroit, *Land of Opportunity*, p. 141.
38. *Ibid.*, p. 141.
39. Based on personal observation and discussion with NYC neighbors at the time.
40. Bourgois, *In Search of Respect*, p. 79.
41. Anderson, *Streetwise*, p. 79.
42. Anderson, *Code of the Street*, p. 60.
43. Sharpe, *Behind the Eight Ball*, pp. 109–110.
44. *Ibid.*, p. 134.
45. Scott Gold and Andrew Blankstein, "'It was a terrifying time,' More than 100 women died during a 10-year period that serial killers roamed South L.A.," *Los Angeles Times*, August 4, 2010, http://articles.latimes.com/2010/aug/04/local/la-me-serial-killers-20100804.
46. *Ibid.*
47. Freyer, et al., "Measuring Crack Cocaine and Its Impact," Figure 2, p. 40
48. *Ibid.*
49. Statement of Jane L. Ross, *Parental Substance Abuse: Testimony Before the Subcommittee on Human Resources, Committee on Ways and Means*, House of Representatives, October 28, 1997, United States General Accounting Office, p. 4, www.gao.gov/archive/1998/he98040t.pdf.
50. Sharpe, *Behind the Eight Ball*, p. 24. The "crack baby" phenomenon will be discussed at greater length in Chapter 5.
51. Anderson, *Streetwise*, pp. 95–96.
52. Anderson, *Code of the Street*, p. 228.
53. Clifford Bey, interview with author, August 7, 2018, Chicago. The story and quotes that follow are all taken from this interview.

54. Jenni Gainsborough and Marc Mauer, "Crime and Incarceration in the 1990s," September 2000, The Sentencing Project, p. 18, www.prisonpolicy.org/scans/sp/Dim Ret.pdf.

55. Caroline Wolf Harlow, "Drugs and Jail Inmates," August 1991, Bureau of Justice Statistics, p. 1, www.ncjrs.gov/pdffiles1/Digitization/130836NCJRS.pdf; and US Department of Justice, Office of Justice Programs, and Bureau of Justice Statistics, *Drugs and Crime Facts, 1992* (Rockville, MD: Drugs and Crime Data Center and Clearinghouse, March 1993), p. 4.

56. Anderson, *Streetwise*, p. 85.

57. Quoted in Adler, *Land of Opportunity*, p. 142.

58. Personal observation; I often heard the boss and his crew discussing such matters as they smoked weed outside my living-room window. I also chatted many times with the head of the crew, usually when he and his men were taking their weed breaks and had grown boisterous; I tried to impress upon him that, like them, I was working and needed them to be less raucous. In using this material I am cheating chronologically, as I observed his crew operating from late 2004 to 2005. The police, eventually, forced them to find a new location.

59. Adler, *Land of Opportunity*, pp. 140–141.

60. Sharpe, *Behind the Eight Ball*, p. 103.

61. Sharpe makes this analytic point in *Behind the Eight Ball*, p. 114.

62. All quotes are from the documentary film by Anthony Gonzales and Zair Jones, *Hell up in East Harlem* (Street Certified Studios, 2001).

4 CRACK MONEY: MANHOOD IN THE AGE OF GREED

1. Ms. Tee, *Harlem Heroine* (New York: Royal-T Publishing, 2015), p. 9 (Kindle).

2. William M. Adler, *Land of Opportunity* (New York: Atlantic Monthly Press, 1995), p. 3. This account is based completely on Adler's work.

3. Adler, *Land of Opportunity*, pp. 3–4.

4. Ms. Tee, *Harlem Heroine*, p. 73.

5. Juan Williams, "The Mind of Rayful Edmond," *Washington Post*, June 24, 1990, www .washingtonpost.com/archive/lifestyle/magazine/1990/06/24/the-mind-of-rayful-ed mond/bcca1e79-d0da-496b-a326-75bd276f96c8/?utm_term=.9abd7739a0d6.

6. Ms. Tee, *Harlem Heroine*, p. 94.

7. Anderson, *Code of the Street*, pp. 123–124.

8. "Transcript: Donald Trump's Taped Comments About Women," *New York Times*, October 8, 2016, www.nytimes.com/2016/10/08/us/donald-trump-tape-transcript .html.

9. Ms. Tee, *Harlem Heroine*, p. 94.

10. Much of what follows is based on two strong pieces by Seth Ferranti, "When Crack was King," Gorilla Convict, October 24, 2011, www.gorillaconvict.com/2011/10/when-cra ck-was-king-2/ and "The Thug of Enforcement of the Rayful Edmond Crew," Gorilla

Convict, January 13, 2013, www.gorillaconvict.com/2013/01/the-thug-of-enforce
ment-the-story-of-the-rayful-edmond-crew/; Williams, "The Mind of Rayful Edmond";
and Mark Jones, "1989: Bringing Down DC's Drug King," November 14, 2014,
Boundary Stones: WETA's Local History Blog, WETA, https://blogs.weta.org/boun
darystones/2014/11/14/1989-bringing-down-dcs-drug-king. For the murderous dark
side of Edmond's operation see: *United States v. Edmond*, 730 F. Supp. 1144 (D.D.C
1990), February 5, 1990, https://law.justia.com/cases/federal/district-courts/FSupp/
730/1144/1985064/. As the notes that follow attest, the *Washington Post* ran many
stories on Edmond.

11. Elsa Walsh, "Edmond Convicted on All Counts in Drug Conspiracy Case," *The
Washington Post,* December 7, 1989, p. A1.

12. Tracy Thompson, "Ex-Clothier in Georgetown Convicted of Money Laundering,"
Washington Post, October 16, 1991, www.washingtonpost.com/archive/local/1991/10
/16/ex-clothier-in-georgetown-convicted-of-money-laundering/90252f59-1029-4d39-8
aa3-edfe07b185c6/?utm_term=.bc0528360be7.

13. Both quotes are from Ferranti, "The Thug of Enforcement."

14. Ferranti, "When Crack was King."

15. Ferranti, "When Crack was King."

16. Ferranti, "The Thug of Enforcement."

17. *Ibid.*

18. Both quotes are from Bill Brubaker, "Courting Rayful Edmond," *Washington Post,*
November 2, 1989, www.washingtonpost.com/archive/politics/1989/11/02/court
ing-rayful-edmond/759cb0e3-44ad-4237-82a8-87e2385da714/?utm_term=.14770d
2e0539.

19. Brubaker, "Courting Rayful Edmond."

20. Ferranti, "The Thug of Enforcement."

21. This story and the supporting details come from Brubaker, "Courting Rayful Edmond."

22. Michael Weinrub, "The Day Innocence Died," ESPN.com, www.espn.com/espn/etick
et/story?page=bias.

23. Nancy Lewis and Sari Horowitz, "Hundreds Flee Fatal Shootout Near SE Club,"
Washington Post, October 28, 1988, www.washingtonpost.com/archive/politics/1988/
10/28/hundreds-flee-fatal shootout-near-se-club/f39e436f-32b1-4eb1-904c-db0
f57919049/?utm_term=.244317da8dcf.

24. Gonzales and Jones, *Hell up in East Harlem.*

25. Ross Scarano, "The Oral History of the Tunnel," Complex, August 21, 2012, www.co
mplex.com/pop-culture/2012/08/the-oral-history-of-the-tunnel.

26. Scarano, "The Oral History of the Tunnel."

27. *Ibid.*

28. Combs was raised in the suburbs, but his father had been a mid-level drug dealer who
had been killed after being arrested. Combs attended Howard University before moving full-time into the music industry; Dan Charnas, *The Big Payback* (New York: New
American Library, 2011), pp. 459–461.

29. Shaheem Reid, "Puff Daddy Clarifies Infamous 1995 Source Awards Speech on 'Drink Champs' Revolt," November 25, 2016, Revolt, https://revolt.tv/stories/2016/11/25/ puff-daddy-clarifies-infamous-1995-source-awards-speech-drink-champs-0700ec0ef9.

30. Scarano, "The Oral History of the Tunnel."

31. Gonzales and Jones, *Hell up in East Harlem*.

32. Gatien was charged in 1996 with selling drugs at his clubs – primarily Ecstasy – but was found not guilty. In 1999 he was found guilty of massive tax evasion, paid a large fine, served a short time in prison, and was deported to his native Canada.

33. Ms. Tee, *Harlem Heroine*, p. 43. In addition to drawing on Ms. Tee's account of Unique (she was one of his lovers), I also draw upon Jeff Hooten, "Drug Kingpin Gets Life Without Parole," *Daily Press* [Norfolk VA], September 15, 1994, www.dailypress.com/ news/dp-xpm-19940916-1994-09-16-9409160096-story.html#; Jennifer Kingston Bloom, "Neighborhood Report: Washington Heights; Lawyer Continues Battle for New Nightspot at Site of Old Club 2000," *New York Times*, March 26, 1995, p. 13; Ryan K. Smith, "Who is Unique Hall?," Don Diva Global Media, https://dondivamag.com/ who-is-unique-hall/; and United States Court of Appeals, Fourth Circuit. *United States of America, Plaintiff-Appellee, v. Wainsworth Marcellus Hall, Defendant-Appellant*, No. 94–5739. Decided: August 19, 1996.

34. Ms. Tee, *Harlem Heroine*, p. 43. For eleven years I lived across the street from a completely legitimate business, High End Stereo in Philadelphia, that drug dealers and other underground figures frequented. The skilled technicians at High End tricked out an amazing assortment of super luxury vehicles with insane sound systems but also attention-grabbing lighting systems, rims, and wheels, and a slew of other fantastical accouterments.

35. Bloom, "Neighborhood Report."

36. Ms. Tee, *Harlem Heroine*, p. 44.

37. Jordon Bonfante and James Willwerth, "Entrepreneurs of Crack," *Time* 145:8, February 27, 1995, p. 22; and Jesse Katz, "Tracking the Genesis of the Crack Trade."

38. Zack O'Malley Greenburg, *Empire State of Mind* (New York: Penguin, 2012), p. 22. A lot has been written about Jay-Z; this book is particularly useful for my purposes because Greenburg focuses in on Jay-Z as a businessman and entrepreneur. Particularly insightful, too, is the long piece by Touré, "The Book of Jay," *Rolling Stone*, December 15, 2005, www.rollingstone.com/music/music-news/the-book-of-jay-2-103299/.

39. For an amazing autobiography of Jay-Z as told solely through his lyrics see "Jay Z's Life Story (In Lyrics)," Genius, June 6, 2016, https://genius.com/a/jay-z-s-life-story-in-lyrics. Not every lyric reflects the absolute empirical reality of Jay-Z's life but his raps powerfully represent his life course.

40. Jay Z, "December 4th," (2003).

41. Greenburg, *Empire State of Mind*, p. 24.

42. Quoted in Touré, "The Book of Jay."

43. Quoted in Touré, "The Book of Jay."

44. The quote comes from the seminal work by Dimitri Bogazianos, *5 Grams: Crack Cocaine, Rap Music, and the War on Drugs* (New York: NYU Press, 2011), p. 54.

45. For a pithy, well-reported account of the origins of Rock-A-Fella see Charnas, *The Big Payback*, pp. 562–571.
46. Greenburg, *Empire State of Mind*, p. 34; Jay-Z, "U Don't Know" (2001).
47. The Reebok ad and a story about its significance can be found in a pithy piece by Matt Welty, "Jay-Z's Reebok Deal Changed the Sneaker Industry Forever," Complex, December 4, 2016, www.complex.com/sneakers/2016/12/jay-z-reebok-influence. I was alerted to the ad by Bogazianos, *5 Grams*, p. 53.
48. Quoted in the acclaimed work by Tricia Rose, *The Hip Hop Wars* (New York: Basic Books, 2008), p. 1.
49. As is richly told by Charnas, *The Big Payback*.
50. Eithne Quinn, *Nuthin' but a 'G' Thang* (New York: Columbia University Press, 2005), pp. 56–58.
51. A point well developed by Bogazianos, *5 Grams*, especially in Chapter 3, "Rap Puts Crack to Work."
52. Chuck Philip, "Who Killed Tupac Shakur?" *Los Angeles Times*, September 6, 2002, http://articles.latimes.com/2002/sep/06/business/fi tupac6. Shakur's murder remains officially unsolved and the *LA Times* reporting, while compelling, is not definitive.
53. Milken's schemes, for sure, were overwhelmingly legal ones and his marketing of "junk bonds" often produced capitalization campaigns that led to market efficiencies. Milken was operating in fast-moving capital markets where legal and illegal were often blurry; Boesky not so much.
54. Steven A. Holmes, "A Drug Dealer Finds Many Eager to Launder his Drug Money," *New York Times*, January 24, 1990, p. 1. This article, as well as the detailed account of Mickens given by Brown, *Queens Reigns Supreme*, provide the material for this section.
55. Holmes, "A Drug Dealer Finds Many Eager to Launder his Drug Money," p. 1.
56. Brown, *Queens Reigns Supreme*, p. 32.
57. Brown, *Queens Reigns Supreme*, pp. 61–62.
58. This account, in its entirety, is taken from Bourgois, *In Search of Respect*.
59. Bourgois, *In Search of Respect*, p. 134.
60. Both quotes are from Bourgois, *In Search of Respect*, p. 135.
61. Gonzalez and Jones, *Hell up in East Harlem*.
62. Pegues, *Once a Cop*, p. 55. One more personal note: Le Tigre was a brand introduced by the Campus Sweater and Sportswear Company in the late 1970s aimed at inner-city youth to compete with Lacoste and its alligator emblem which was, at the time, wildly popular with white upper-middle-class youths and preppies of all ages. My father represented Le Tigre in Chicago for Campus until the mid 1980s.
63. Vern Kenneth Baxtera and Peter Marina, "Cultural Meaning and Hip-Hop Fashion in the African-American Male Youth Subculture of New Orleans," *Journal of Youth Studies* 11:2, April 2008, p. 109.
64. William Schmidt, "A Growing Urban Fear: Thieves Who Kill for 'Cool' Clothing," *New York Times*, February 6, 1990, p. 20.
65. Eric Pooley, "Kids with Guns," *New York Magazine*, August 5, 1991, p. 24.
66. Pooley, "Kids with Guns," pp. 20–29.

5 CRACKDOWN: THE POLITICS AND LAWS OF DRUG ENFORCEMENT

1. Jacob V. Lamar, Jr., Michael Riley, and Raji Samghabadi, "'Crack' A Cheap and Deadly Cocaine is a Fast-Spreading Menace," *Time* 127:16, June 2, 1986, p. 3.
2. A sober look at the issue is provided in: Paul J. Goldstein, Henry H. Brownstein, Patrick J. Ryan, and Patricia A. Bellucci, "Crack and Homicide in New York City," in *Crack in America*, pp. 113–130.
3. Jacob V. Lamar, Jonathan Beatty, Russell B. Leavitt, and Janice C. Simpson, "Kids Who Sell Crack," *Time* 131:19, May 9, 1988, pp. 20–27. All quotes that follow are from this cover story.
4. Jonnes, *Hep Cats*, pp. 390–392.
5. Michael Massing, *The Fix* (New York: Simon and Schuster, 1998), p. 153. This section on parental response to drugs is drawn from Massing's account.
6. "Just Say No," Her Causes, Ronald Reagan Presidential Foundation and Institute, www.reaganfoundation.org/ronald-reagan/nancy-reagan/her-causes/. For a critical look at "Just Say No," see Massing, *The Fix*, pp. 174–175.
7. Michael Wines, "Poll Finds Public Favors Tougher Laws Against Drug Sale and Use," *New York Times*, August 15, 1989, p. 16.
8. *National Drug Control Strategy*, September 1989, Office of National Drug Control Policy (ONDCP), Box 2, Daniel Casse Files (DC), George H.W. Bush Presidential Library GB) and "Information Brief – What America's Users Spend on Illegal Drugs," n.d. (12/90?), Box 2, DC, GB.
9. Michael Javin Fortner, *Black Silent Majority* (Cambridge: Harvard University Press, 2015), p. 141. This section on Harlem and the heroin epidemic in the late 1960s and early 1970s is drawn from Fortner's work.
10. Fortner, *Black Silent Majority*, p. 142.
11. Charles Rangel and Leon Wynter, *And I Haven't Had a Bad Day Since* (Thomas Dunne Books: New York, 2007), p. 189.
12. *Annual Report for the Year 1983 of the Select Committee on Narcotics Abuse and Control*, Ninety-Eighth Congress, First Session (Washington: US Government Printing Office, 1984), p. 39.
13. *Annual Report for the Year 1983*, p. 95.
14. Opening Statement of the Honorable Charles B. Rangel, *Cocaine Abuse and the Federal Response, Hearing Before the Select Committee on Narcotics Abuse and Control, House of Representatives, July 16, 1985* (Washington: GPO, 1986), p. 63.
15. "The Crack Cocaine Crisis," *Joint Hearing Before the Select Committee on Narcotics Abuse and Control and the Select Committee on Children, Youth, and Families, House of Representatives, Ninety-Ninth Congress, Second Session, July 15, 1986* (Washington: GPO, 1987).
16. "The Crack Cocaine Crisis," p. 2.
17. "The Crack Cocaine Crisis," p. 3.
18. "The Crack Cocaine Crisis," p. 7.
19. Michael Weinrub, "The Day Innocence Died," espn.com, www.espn.com/espn/eticket/story?page=bias.

20. Roy S. Johnson, "At Services for Bias, Tributes and Warnings are Offered," *New York Times*, June 24, 1986, p. 5.

21. When Don Rogers, a defensive back for the Cleveland Browns, died from a cocaine overdose just eight days after Bias the public was even more distraught and fearful.

22. "The Crack Cocaine Crisis," p. 43. This section draws on analysis by Massing, *The Fix*, pp. 182–183. Massing quotes Gilman, as well.

23. These quotes are all drawn from the essential source on the 1986 Anti-Drug Abuse Act: David Sklansky, "Cocaine, Race, and Equal Protection," *Stanford Law Review* 47, 1994, pp. 1283–1322. The quoted passages appear in note 55, p. 1294.

24. Sklansky, "Cocaine, Race, and Equal Protection," p. 1296. In 1995, the United States Sentencing Commission was set up by Congress to look at the 100:1 ratio and concluded in solemn bureaucratese: "Taken as a whole, the abbreviated, somewhat murky legislative history simply does not provide a single, consistently cited rationale for the crack-powder cocaine penalty structure." See United States Sentencing Commission, *Cocaine and Federal Sentencing Policy*, Washington DC, August 1995, p. 121.

25. Senator Alfonse D'Amato, *Congressional Record – Senate*, 132, Part 11, p. 14822.

26. The toxicity and addictive qualities of crack versus powder cocaine is not a completely sorted out matter; see John P. Morgan and Lynn Zimmer, "The Social Pharmacology of Smokeable Cocaine," in Reinarman and Levine (eds.), *Crack in America*, pp. 131–170.

27. D'Amato, *Congressional Record*, p. 14822.

28. For a comprehensive look at the penalties associated with the act and on how it was to be implemented, see US Department of Justice, Criminal Division, *Handbook on the Anti-Drug Abuse Act of 1986* (Washington: GPO, March 1987).

29. For a complicated look at the price of crack in the mid 1980s, see Jonathan P. Caulkins, "Is Crack Cheaper than (Powder) Cocaine?" *Addiction* 92:11, 1997, pp. 1437–1443.

30. Quoted in Doris Marie Provine, *Unequal Under the Law: Race in the War on Drugs* (University of Chicago Press, 2007), p. 112.

31. Provine, *Unequal under the Law*, p. 111.

32. Gerald M. Boyd, "Reagan Signs Anti-Drug Measure: Hopes for a 'Drug-Free Generation,'" *New York Times*, October 28, 1986, p. 19.

33. *Ibid.*

34. Clifford D. May, "Washington Talk: Drug Enforcement; Once-Lonely Voice Finds an Audience," *New York Times*, June 6, 1988, p. 16.

35. H.R. 5210 – *Anti-Drug Abuse Act of 1988*, 100th Congress (1987–1988), Summary, Congress.gov, www.congress.gov/bill/100th-congress/house-bill/05210. The description of the bill that follows comes from this lengthy, official summary.

36. "Remarks on Signing the Anti-Drug Abuse Act of 1988," November 18, 1988, https://www.reaganlibrary.gov/research/speeches/111888c.

37. Joe Biden, Speech at National Press Club, Washington, DC, July 31, 1989, 04148-022, Stephanie Dance Collection (SD), George H.W. Bush Presidential Library, College Station, TX (GB).

38. Charles Rangel to James Baker, July 21, 1989, 04148-022, SD, GB.

39. George Bush, Inaugural Address, January 20, 1989, www.presidency.ucsb.edu/ws/ind ex.php?pid=16610.
40. Lee Atwater, chairman RNC to Republican Leaders September 5, 1989, 02301-006, Michael Jackson (MJ), GB.
41. George Bush, "Address to the Nation on National Drug Control Strategy," September 5, 1989, https://www.c-span.org/video/?8921-1/president-bush-address-national-drug-policy.
42. For a near contemporary look at Bennett's background, see Edward Fiske, "Reagan's Man for Education," *New York Times*, December 22, 1985, p. 30.
43. Bill Bennett to David Demarest (Director of Communications), September 1, 1989, 02301-005, Michael Jackson (MJ), GB. Bennett was a hardliner but he also was a stickler about accuracy. He told the speechwriters that the anecdote they had included about a little boy and crack was made up and should be cut from the speech – it wasn't. He also told the speechwriters that the notion of addicted "crack babies" that they had included in the speech was also inaccurate and carefully explained the most up-to-date science on the issue – his correction was noted.
44. William Bennett, "Drugs: Consequences and Confrontations," Washington Hebrew Congregation, May 3, 1989, 02183-001, Steve Danzansky Files (SDy), GB.
45. David G. Savage, "Bennett, First US Drug Czar, Quits," November 9, 1990, *Los Angeles Times*, http://articles.latimes.com/1990-11-09/news/mn-4120_1_drug-policy.
46. *National Drug Control Strategy*, p. 1, January 1992, 07130-012, Box 1, Daniel Casse files (DC), GB.
47. The Sentencing Project, "Trends in US Corrections," p. 3, https://sentencingproject .org/wp-content/uploads/2016/01/Trends-in-US-Corrections.pdf.
48. United States Sentencing Commission (USSC), *Cocaine and Federal Sentencing Policy*, February 1995, p. xi.
49. *Ibid.*
50. USSC, *Cocaine and Federal Sentencing Policy*, p. 150.
51. The Sentencing Project, "Trends in US Corrections," p. ii.
52. Bureau of Justice Statistics, *Sourcebook of Criminal Justice Statistics –1992* (Washington, DC: GPO, 1993), p. 422.
53. USSC, *Cocaine and Federal Sentencing Policy*, pp. 129–134.
54. John Kass and William Recktenwald, "More Jails Called Cure to Killings," *Chicago Tribune*, September 5, 1991, Section 2, p. 1.
55. "1991 Chicago homicides second-highest ever," June 2, 1991, NWI.com. More people were murdered in 1974, but the city had many more residents. The 1992 numbers were 262 below the age of twenty-one out of 928 murders. 1993 was actually worse, with 943 murders. A good statistical overview of this grim subject is: Chicago Police Department, Research and Development Division, *Chicago Murder Analysis*, 2011.
56. Bob Martinez, National Press Club, September 5, 1991.
57. "Don't Let Crack Paralyze Chicago," August 31, 1989, *Chicago Defender, Chicago Defender Digest.*

58. Joan Ginagrasse Kates, "Thomas Fitzgerald, Former Illinois Supreme Court Chief Justice, Dies at 74," *Chicago Tribune*, November 3, 2015, www.chicagotribune.com/ne ws/ct-ct-thomas-fitzgerald-illinois-chief-justice-20151103-story.html.

59. "Lights Out Soon for Night Drug Court," December 11, 2000, *New York Times*, www .nwitimes.com/uncategorized/lights-out-soon-for-night-drug-court/article_590d89f8-3f 90-53cf-a7cd-4d8fc484c437.html.

60. "Criminal Justice Recommendations," July 20, 1989, p. 5, 04148-022, Stephanie Dance File (SD), GW.

61. This account is primarily based on an interview I did in Chicago in October 2017, with a person who required anonymity. The name used in the chapter is a pseudonym.

62. Interview, Chicago, October 2017.

63. Terry Wilson, "Night Courts Bursting at Seams," July 21, 1992, *Chicago Tribune*, http:// articles.chicagotribune.com/1992-07-21/news/9203050663_1_night-court-drug-cases-judges.

64. *National Drug Control Strategy*, p. 121.

65. "Lights Out Soon for Night Drug Court."

66. Interview, Chicago, October 2017.

67. Interview, Chicago, October 2017.

68. General Accounting Office, "Drug Courts," July 1997; and *National Drug Control Strategy*, January 1992, pp. 121–122.

69. Gold and Blankstein, "'It was a terrifying time.'"

70. Donna Murch, "Crack in Los Angeles: Crisis, Militarization, and Black Response to the Late Twentieth-Century War on Drugs," *Journal of American History*, 102:1, p. 167.

71. I rely throughout this section on Murch's work in "Crack in Los Angeles."

6 CRACK'S RETREAT: A NATION'S SLOW, PAINFUL, AND PARTIAL RECOVERY

1. Joseph B. Treaster, "Crack Dealer Feeds a Family and Habits of Fewer Addicts," *New York Times*, May 16, 1991, p. 1. I tracked down this article after seeing it cited by Jonnes, *Hep-Cats*, p. 409.

2. Venkatesh, *Off the Books*, p. 291.

3. *1992 National Drug Control Strategy* – many charts and statistics are provided to demonstrate this change over time.

4. Jonnes, *Hep-Cats*, p. 410.

5. National Institute of Justice (NIJ), "Crack's Decline: Some Surprises Across US Cities," US Department of Justice, July 1997, p. 3.

6. NIJ, "Crack's Decline," p. 2.

7. NIJ, "Crack's Decline," pp. 4–11.

8. Venkatesh, *Off the Books*, p. 291.

9. For a remarkable account of the BMF see Mara Shalhoup, *BMF: The Rise and Fall of Big Meech and the Black Mafia Family* (New York: St. Martin's Press, 2010).

10. Ghostface Killah, *Fishscale*, Def Jam, 2006.

11. Elias Leight, "Ka: How New York MC Makes Understated Rap Minimalism," *Rolling Stone*, August 31, 2016, www.rollingstone.com/music/music-news/ka-how-new-york-mc-makes-understated-rap-minimalism-249331/.
12. Ka, "Up Against Goliath," 2012. To order the album, *Grief Pedigree*, and more on Ka, go to Brownville Ka, https://brownsvilleka.com.
13. Michele Alexander, *The New Jim Crow: Mass Incarceration in the Age of Colorblindness* (New York: The New Press, 2010).
14. Alexander, *The New Jim Crow*, p. 4.
15. Alexander, *The New Jim Crow*, pp. 257–258.
16. James Forman, Jr., *Locking up Our Own: Crime and Punishment in Black America* (New York: Farrar, Straus, and Giroux, 2017), pp. 8–9.
17. Forman, *Locking up Our Own*, p. 9.
18. William Bennett "America's New 'Invisible Man,'" Houston Area Urban League, July 18, 1989, 02301–010, Michael P. Jackson Files, GB.
19. Forman, *Locking up Our Own*, p. 10.
20. *The Growth of Incarceration in the United States: Exploring Causes and Consequences*, Jeremy Travis, Bruce Western, and Steve Redburn (eds.) (Washington, DC: The National Academies Press, 2014), pp. 64–65, esp. figs. 2–15. My thanks to Peter Pihos for this citation.
21. Sklansky, "Cocaine, Race, and Equal Protection," p. 1308.
22. Nicole Gonzalez Van Cleve, *Crook County: Racism and Injustice in America's Largest Criminal Court* (Stanford University Press, 2016), pp. 6–7.
23. William Raspberry, "A Common-Sense Approach to Drug Addiction," *Chicago Tribune*, April 6, 1992, p. 17.
24. Congressman John Conyers, press release, June 4, 1992, 07132–011, box 1, Daniel Casse (DC), GB.
25. Conyers, press release.
26. Joseph B. Treaster, "The 1992 Campaign," *New York Times*, July 28, 1992, p. 1.
27. Clipping, *Newark Star-Ledger*, October 15, 1992, 07132–011, Box 1, DC, GB.
28. Clipping, *Newark Star-Ledger*.
29. US Sentencing Commission, "Cocaine and Federal Sentencing Policy," February 1995.
30. Ann Devroy, "Clinton Retains Tough Law on Crack Cocaine," *Washington Post*, October 31, 1995, p. 1.
31. Devroy, "Clinton Retains Tough Law on Crack Cocaine."
32. Devroy, "Clinton Retains Tough Law on Crack Cocaine."
33. The Sentencing Project, "Federal Crack Cocaine Sentencing," p. 5, www.sentencingproject.org/wp-content/uploads/2016/01/Federal-Crack-Cocaine-Sentencing.pdf.
34. ACLU, "Cracks in the System: 20 Years of the Unjust Federal Crack Cocaine Law," www.aclu.org/other/cracks-system-20-years-unjust-federal-crack-cocaine-law.
35. For a comprehensive version of the charge and Webb's story of both his findings and how his investigation impacted his life, see Gary Webb, *Dark Alliance: The CIA, the Contras, and the Crack Cocaine Explosion* (New York: Seven Stories Press, 1998). In 2014, a movie version of the story, *Kill the Messenger*, was released.

36. Roberto Suro and Walter Pincus, "The CIA and Crack: Evidence is Lacking of Alleged Plot," *Washington Post*, October 4, 1996, www.washingtonpost.com/archive/politics/1 996/10/04/the-cia-and-crack-evidence-is-lacking-of-alleged-plot/5b026731-c5dc-4234-b3bd-9e0fd2e21225/?utm_term=.4a98cf444485.

37. Jeff Leen, "Gary Webb was No Journalism Hero, Despite what 'Kill the Messenger' Says," *Washington Post*, October 17, 2014, www.washingtonpost.com/opinions/gary-we bb-was-no-journalism-hero-despite-what-kill-the-messenger-says/2014/10/17/026b75 60-53c9-11e4-809b-8cc0a295c773_story.html?utm_term=.859922d4db3c. Leen was an investigative reporter who covered the drug trade in Miami during the 1980s and 1990s and an expert on the activities of the Medellin Cartel before he joined the *Washington Post*.

38. Massing, *The Fix*, pp. 177–178.

39. Leen, "Gary Webb was No Journalism Hero."

40. A valuable overview is provided by Matthew Pulver, "Ronald Reagan's Hip-hop Nightmare: How An Ugly Cocaine Controversy Reignited 30 Years Later," Salon.com, November 17, 2014, www.salon.com/2014/11/17/ronald_reagans_hip_hop_night mare_cocaine_controversy_reignites_30_years_later/. The artists and tracks I discuss below are referenced in Pulver's account.

41. Jay-Z, "Blue Magic," *American Gangster* (2007).

42. Killer Mike, "Reagan," *R.A.P. Music* (2012).

43. Taken from Robert Collins, *Transforming America* (New York: Columbia University Press, 2007), p. 96.

44. Jack Fisher, "'Freeway': Crack in the System," Euroweb, February 25, 2010, www.eur web.com/2015/02/freeway-crack-in-the-system-must-see-exploration-into-rebuilding-t he-human-condition/.

Index